CW00763239

LEARNING FIELDS
Volume 2

LEARNING FIELDS
Volume 1
Educational Histories of European Social Anthropology
Edited by Dorle Dracklé, Iain R. Edgar and Thomas K. Schippers

LEARNING FIELDS
Volume 2
Current Policies and Practices in European Social Anthropology Education
Edited by Dorle Dracklé and Iain R. Edgar

LEARNING FIELDS

Volume 2

Current Policies and Practices in European Social Anthropology Education

Edited by

Dorle Dracklé and Iain R. Edgar

Berghahn Books
New York • Oxford

First published in 2004 by

Berghahn Books

www.berghahnbooks.com

© 2004 Dorle Dracklé and Iain R. Edgar

All rights reserved.
No part of this publication may be reproduced in any form or by any
means without the written permission of Berghahn Books.

Library of Congress Cataloging-in-Publication Data

Current policies and practices in European social anthropology education /
edited by Dorle Dracklé and Iain R. Edgar
    p. cm.
    Includes bibliographical references and index.
    ISBN 1–57181–564–3 (alk. paper)
    1. Educational anthropology--Europe. 2. Anthropology--Study and
teaching (Higher)--Europe. I. Dracklé, Dorle. II. Edgar, Iain R.

LB45.C88 2003
306.43--dc21   2002043681

British Library Cataloguing in Publication Data

A catalogue record for this book is available from the British Library.

ISBN 1–57181–564–3 hardback

Printed in United Kingdom by Biddles / IBT Global

Contents

List of Figures

Foreword

The essays collected here present serious issues concerning the state of anthropological teaching practice in some European contexts. This is something with which we are constantly concerned in our daily teaching duties. More often than not, we practise what we preach. As teachers, we often fall back on our set patterns and methods of delivery and lecturing, patterns that have become largely unavoidable after years of teaching and offering the same courses. As anthropologists living in both the classroom and in public, we present our public persona and do not consciously reflect on the ways in which we communicate, how we gesture, and how we express ourselves with others. These are not easy issues to deal with. Similarly, anthropologists working in Europe have avoided asking questions about whether or not anthropology should be taught similarly to other disciplines. Neither have we asked whether our subject deserves special consideration: if anthropology differs from the other social science fields, as I believe it does, then how is this difference translated in the classroom and in teaching/learning settings. These are serious problems and should in no way be avoided. The pioneering volume, *Learning Fields Volume 1: Educational Histories of European Social Anthropology,* deals with the little known, and much less understood, aspects of teaching and learning processes within the field of social and cultural anthropology. The editors, Dorle Dracklé, Iain Edgar, and Thomas K. Schippers deserve high acclaim for their efforts and painstaking task of assembling such a broad perspective on teaching and learning anthropology.

Anybody reading the two volumes published by Berghahn and team-edited by members of the Teaching Anthropology Network of the European Association of Social Anthropologists (EASA), should be aware that these books have a short, but very telling history. How did this concern with teaching practices arise? What is the significance of publishing such endeavours? First of all it must be stated that, unlike educators in general, anthropologists have been rather diffident about their classroom activities (though see the introduction for an historical résumé of anthropological writing about the educational context). For a long time they have even appeared almost ashamed of their actual fieldwork practices; but the postmodernist trend of the 1980s and, increasingly, the 1990s changed all that. There is really no good reason for this lack of attention paid to their 'home-grown' (teaching) practices, especially in view of the fact that anthropologists are so used to dealing with human diversity and cultural complexities in both time and space. That is why it is important to provide a brief account of the beginnings of the present volume. It was at the biennial meeting of EASA in Barcelona in 1996 that Ulf Hannerz sounded the anthropological alarm-bell by stating that while we know a lot about what we do in the field, we know practically nothing about our own scholarship inside the classroom. Hannerz proposed to form a network – an informal anthropological think-tank – aimed at exchanging views on what it is we do. His call did not fall on deaf ears. Under the umbrella of the Teaching Anthropology Network, a group of scholars began to meet regularly at annual international gatherings: first in Barcelona in 1996, then in Stockholm in the same year; in 1997 in Piran (Slovenia); in 1998 in Frankfurt am Main; in 1999 in Göttingen; in 2000 in Krakow; and in 2001 in Lisbon. At every meeting increasing numbers of interested scholars came forward to inform us of their special and varied activities. In one way or another, these network meetings all concerned the way we practise and teach anthropology, the difficulties that arise in the process, and, not least of all, the most novel and up-to-date methods of transmitting knowledge and enhancing students' performance in the anthropological classroom.

It is, however, important to realise what this volume offers and what it cannot do. It obviously presents a somewhat incomplete overview of a few areas of teaching practices. Underlying this concern is the following assumption: if it is true that the main goal of general education is to promote a society's and country's economic development, then it must also hold true that anthropological education should contribute to cultural advancement. This should also allow for the possible development of critical voices, and of universal as well as culture-specific values and interests. These concerns have often been voiced in general educational discussions. Anthropological education, on the other hand, appears to be much more controversial and far less well understood. Even though there exists a whole range of views as to what anthropology should offer to students, amongst scholars and the general public alike, most contributors take it for granted that anthropology has much to offer besides just exciting and exotic materials intended to widen the general interests of students. Nevertheless, there is disagreement among practising academics as to whether anthropology properly contributes to the general development of the intellect. There are those of us who strongly believe that it does; there are others who are less convinced. Needless to say, anthropology cannot be expected to do the job on its own. It requires the support of other disciplines as well, even those that originally came about as offshoots of anthropology, such as ethnic studies, cultural studies, gender studies, etc., only to emerge later as separate disciplines in their own right. In general, we can agree on the proposition that anthropological education should extend our understanding of human evolution, the range of civilisations, the well-being of humanity, and, specifically, cultural diversity. There are other issues, such as war, disease, human conflict, inequality, and unequal development in time and space that are increasingly being adopted as the standard topics of anthropological curricula. Thus, in many countries, anthropology is included in the educational and pedagogical curricula in order to teach such issues. However, as the first volume's themes aptly illustrate (*Learning Fields Volume 1: Educational Histories of European Social Anthropology,* edited by Draklé, Edgar and Schippers), national traditions differ vastly in both the content and context of what they consider important and what they deem wholly irrelevant.

Most of the contributors are from the West (the U.K., U.S., Germany, the Netherlands, and Italy), countries with longer democratic educational practices than in Central and Eastern Europe where for decades official Marxist-Leninist schooling determined the nature of education. Not surprisingly, then, more interests have been generated in recent years in Western universities about teaching practices than in the East. For this reason alone, the book may be criticised for providing a platform for Western-dominated theories, less concerned about other cultures and anthropological traditions. While this criticism may be of some concern, I should like to call attention to the fact that *Learning Fields Volume 1: Educational Histories of European Social Anthropology* offers an excellent selection of articles on national anthropological traditions across the European continent as a whole. In this volume – also an outcome of the Teaching Anthropology Network's meetings – many contributors present a non-Western European view. Another justification is that to date most anthropological volumes on education have been published by and for American scholars, with no or very few European contributions included. This edited collection manages to carve a space for European scholars to discuss their own work. Finally, I should emphasise that the plethora of teaching practices perhaps makes for a somewhat uneven selection. The volume's strength lies in its selection of special-case anthropological studies on, for example, Italian ethnodrama and its use in anthropology, humanistic group methods in the U.K., the uses of exhibits in academic practice in the Netherlands, ethnomusicology, digitised techniques, reflective and reflexive practices, and the uses of visual aids and film techniques.

Hopefully this pioneering volume will generate further collections in the coming years. There is a great need to understand what takes place when anthropologists offer their knowledge and material to students, colleagues, informants, and to the general public. These different educational contexts require different anthropological sensitivities and understandings of what takes place between the teacher/anthropologist and the student/non-specialist. Our knowledge and understanding of these settings is rather rudimentary and needs to be tested and refined as well as challenged. I believe that the time is ripe for more reflection and a greater sharing of ideas that reveal our teaching practices and the parallel learning processes that accompany them. I cannot but hope that in the near future similar volumes will appear, volumes that will either reinforce or, alternatively, challenge the many theories offered here, and by so doing assist in the development of fresh and sound ways of sharing anthropology with others. If colleagues take up this challenge, then these volumes will include chapters describing not only European educational settings and practices, but also African, Asian, Latin and South American methods and approaches to teaching. This, too, is what anthropology is all about.

László Kürti

Introduction

Learning Fields, Disciplinary Landscapes

David Mills, Dorle Dracklé and Iain Edgar

Amidst the diverse professional lives of European social anthropologists, teaching and training are important common denominators, to which we devote a great deal of time, energy and creativity. Yet this work is not always a cause for pride or even debate, but instead can become a 'fugitive activity' (Huber 2001). Whilst we may care deeply about our students, our courses and our educationnal role, we do not always see these as topics for scholarly inquiry or sustained critical attention. If 'anthropologists are inclined to think of themselves first and foremost as researchers' (Hannerz 2002), then teaching comes in a rather bedraggled second. We pay surprisingly little ethnographic attention to the ways in which we impart, embody and reproduce our own anthropological skills and perspectives to our students.

For Bourdieu, attention to the scholarly mode of production is a key tenet of a critical sociology. His view is that much of what academics do remains invisible to them because they are 'like fish in the water in the situation of which their dispositions are the product, but also because the essential part of what is transmitted in and by that situation is a hidden effect of the situation itself' (Bourdieu 2000: 14). Like fish, academics find it hard to articulate just how they learnt to swim rather than sink.

One reason for our studied lack of attention to pedagogy may be the ambivalent attitude we have towards the classroom as a site for the teaching and reproduction of anthropology. In a discipline motivated to understand the construction of social knowledge, the university classroom has often been 'out of bounds' as a research site. Ethnographies of anthropology departments are usually oral narratives, often apocryphal, and best told behind closed doors. Empirical ethnographic research in this field has either focused on academics themselves (Becher 1989) or on graduate students (Delamont, Atkinson and Parry: 2000). The same sense of reserve is visible when it comes to discussing teaching. Course outlines, reading lists and teaching styles are one's own, sometimes jealously guarded, business. The research seminar is part of the disciplinary public sphere in a way that the classroom is not.

One way of challenging this lacuna is to point out that the classroom is just another of the many fields of anthropological practice. We make the link in our title: 'learning fields'. As a discipline we have cogitated on our research habits – excessively, some would say – and the way they inform our writing. Might anthropology also benefit from exploring the relationship between teaching and writing? The field metaphor is an easily convertible currency within social anthropology. We talk of developing a field of study and research, of going to the 'field', of doing fieldwork. This volume, building on the historical and institutional perspectives offered in its sister volume (Dracklé, Edgar and Schippers [eds] 2002), pays ethnographic attention to the variety of 'learning fields' that exist within European social anthropology.

One of this volume's aims is to celebrate and critically reflect on the range of current educational practices and innovative pedagogic philosophies and methodologies being adopted by social anthropologists. Enthusiasm is not an easy trope for social scientists. Their disciplinary instincts tend to be rooted in a judicious mixture of critique and caution. Original thinking, innovative approaches to research and critical reassessments of debates all depend on academic practices of conversation. Bibliographies are carefully edited acts of remembering: acknowledgments of whose ideas have mattered and why. Academics nurture and preserve intellectual traditions through developing a sense of a disciplinary 'canon', which is maintained and sometimes challenged through teaching. Disciplinary futures depend on the attentive transmission of disciplinary pasts.

Such attitudes can prevent us from seeing teaching as a potential moment of disciplinary innovation. Indeed, it can be hard to be proactive about teaching at all, when weighed down by administrative 'loads', and the prosaic demands of squeezing in office hours, coaxing recalcitrant photocopiers, and attending meetings. Involvement in teaching can often be at the expense of one's research profile. People talk of 'freeing up' time for research, of 'buying themselves out' of teaching commitments. Teaching, according to this dominant logic, is the unacknowledged test-bed for ideas; a place to think half-formed thoughts privately.

There are, of course, good reasons to be wary of the rhetoric of 'innovation' and 'change' in relation to teaching. All too often this is the language of the commercial market-place, the ideology of the 'new'. Change often involves challenging power relations. Welcoming innovation can be a way of legitimating forgetfulness, a disregard for past solutions and insights. As a result, many academics are suspicious about the curious new occupational hybrid of the 'educational developer', a position that has an increasingly influential presence in many university institutions particularly in the U.K. They are often beholden to a utopian narrative of teacher self-improvement and progress that shies away from the larger political questions about changes within our Higher Education systems – why and for whom.

The conventional academic wisdom that research comes first is far from universally espoused. Commitments to teaching vary, often along the fault-lines of gender, age, and disciplinary status. Yet many are passionate about their teaching and reject professional and professorial conservatism. They use the classroom as a site to explore and innovate both with the form and content of courses, exploring new methodologies and approaches. This book demonstrates the variety of such initiatives by European anthropologists, and how their work is often built upon important traditions of innovation. In what follows we seek to provide a sense of the politics that surround such innovations and the history that lies behind them.

Histories of Anthropology and Education

Disciplinary concern with the way in which social anthropology is learnt by, and taught to, students is not new. It is not just the 'reflexive turn' that has prompted this interest in teaching. Back at the beginning of the twentieth century two British professional societies launched a committee to 'encourage the systematic teaching of Anthropology' to those about to work in the British Empire (Temple 1914). UNESCO supported an international review of the teaching of anthropology in the 1950s (Levi-Strauss 1954), whilst the Association of Social Anthropologists of the U.K. and Commonwealth (ASA) held a conference on teaching Anthropology in the late 1950s. Levi-Strauss draws on a number of French and European cases to exemplify what he calls the 'difficulty of solving the problems of anthropology teaching on the basis of experience gained' (1954: 101). Indeed, he goes on to argue that the present state of teaching is 'confused' if 'enthusiastic', and suggests that rather than draw conclusions by induction, it makes most sense to see where the discipline is heading. Despite fifty years of hindsight, his ideas, such as following theoretical training with two years of practical courses, retain their freshness and perspicacity.

American scholars have long documented the situation of Anthropology within U.S. universities (Hoebel 1955, 1958; Kroeber 1954; Voegelin 1950) and discussed its teaching (e.g. Leighton et al. 1951, Laurie and Whiting 1954). A major seminar series was led by the Berkeley Anthropology department in the early 1960s, supported by the Wenner Gren Foundation and National Science Foundation. This brought together a variety of U.S. and European anthropologists in a series of ten themed teaching symposia, held in both the U.S. and Austria, and led to the production of a major volume on the teaching of anthropology (Mandelbaum et al. 1963). European anthropologists involved included Raymond Firth, John Beattie, Kenneth Little, Meyer Fortes, and Gutorm Gjessing. The final volume received little critical attention, and was not reviewed in any of the major disciplinary journals. This lack of attention might be attributable to the lack of any clear canon or comparative text against which it could be assessed. As Mandelbaum notes, writing about teaching has 'appeared only sporadically', and being 'scattered in diverse sources', forced each writer to 'begin afresh without much benefit from the experience and observations of his colleagues' (ibid.: 2). This lack is corroborated by a search in British journals – occasional articles on teaching by early social anthropologists (e.g. Myres 1946, Evans-Pritchard 1959, Firth 1963, Little 1960) rarely conform to the accepted genres of research-based work. Despite the headaches that the notion of 'canonical' texts present, they do act as a scholarly archive that can be engaged and interrogated. Many senior British and European anthropologists have written their own introductions and textbooks explicitly designed for inducting those new to the discipline, but these are personal and sometimes quirky affairs, written with little reference to either the processes of learning or to comparative texts. Indeed Pocock (1975: ix) points out the risk of 'petrification' that can occur when a discipline becomes a 'subject' to be taught to the young and is reduced to 'text-books', set courses and select bibliographies'. Pocock's view that anthropology must be 'lived at the same time as it is learned' captures his valuable insistence on the irreducably phenomonological aspect of learning, but also reveals his lack of enthusiasm for an over-structured or formalised approach to teaching. In this view, one's anthropological education rests on a personal rite of passage rather than on a broader disciplinary commitment to education.

Another reason for the scholarly amnesia that surrounds teaching is that disciplinary histories are either told as a history of ideas or as a history of anecdotes. Both approaches make for bad history. Disciplines are more than the sum of their ideas: it is as important to examine the political conditions of intellectual work as it is to record scholarly legacies and influences. Teaching, and debates over teaching, are rarely openly acknowledged as formative aspects of an academic discipline's intellectual history. This invisibility of teaching is part of the larger disregard for the role of university institutions in enabling and shaping the form that intellectual life can take. As Bourdieu suggests, it is from the 'social history of educational institutions and from the (forgotten or repressed) history of our singular relationship to these institutions that we can expect some real revelations about the objective and subjective structures that always, in spite of ourselves, orient our thought' (Bourdieu 2000: 9). The importance of analysing the histories of anthropological pedagogy across Europe has been convincingly demonstrated in the first volume of this series (Dracklé, Edgar and Schippers 2002). The contributors uncover a 'hidden history' of pedagogy, describing the educational concerns that influenced the post-war development of European social anthropology.

If there is not a recognised literature on the teaching of anthropology, there is an important literature on the anthropology of education more generally. Diverse U.S. contributions include Spindler (1955) whose work applies anthropological insights to education, and Mead's famous accounts of socialisation in Samoa (Mead 1928). There is a valuable British tradition of ethnographies of secondary schooling (Lacey 1982, Lambert 1982, Willis 1977). There is also a valuable history of feminist research on pedagogy, as exemplified by contributions to Lather (1991). There have been some interesting cross-overs with the discipline of education. The work of the anthropologist Jean Lave on 'legitimate peripheral participation' – learning through apprenticeship – has been particularly influential within education, especially in refining the concept of knowledge as being produced within 'communities of practice' (Lave 1988, Lave and Wenger 1991). Pelissier (1991) provides a review of this literature. This work has been taken up by 'sociocultural activity theorists' within education (Engestrom et al. 1999), notable for the links they make between individual motivations and cognitive processes and the larger context of learning (Edwards 2000). Its one drawback is that it has developed with little attention to other theories of practice (e.g. Bourdieu 1977). Yet social anthropologists and educationalists do not necessarily use the same language, and have very different disciplinary canons to nurture. A provocative example of this is the advocacy of 'phenomenography' (Marton 1986, Saljo 1988) as a new qualitative research method within education. Seeking to distance itself from ethnographic approaches, it brings together a mixture of phenomenology and symbolic interactionism to investigate variation within the learning process.

One aspect of teaching anthropology that is not touched upon in this volume is the training offered to newly minted teachers of anthropology. Raymond Firth once expressed the opinion that 'formal training of the kind given to schoolteachers is not wholly appropriate to the kind of intellectual development which it is the job of the university teacher to stimulate' (Firth 1963: 138), and to this day anthropologists often feel that generic higher education teaching courses are inappropriate for their own disciplinary needs and expectations. One of our intentions in this volume is to provide a set of practical 'how-we-did-it' examples of approaches to learning and teaching that will be useful for others attempting similar initiatives.

One possible bridge between anthropological and educational debates about learning is occurring through the acronym SOTL – the Scholarship of Teaching and Learning. This is a term that comes from the U.S., and is inspired by Boyer's influential *'Scholarship Reconsidered'* (1990), which argues for a research-based approach to teaching and learning across the university. Recent reviews (Healey 2000, Huber and Morreale 2001) discuss the implications of this approach for disciplinary teaching styles, with Huber making an anthropological case for studying the teaching styles of different disciplines, pointing out that 'most disciplines work with a traditional set of pedagogic practices but are only now developing a critical discourse about them' (Huber 2001: 28). The value of comparing teaching styles is undeniable, but not enough empirical research has been done on how academics actually view their learning and teaching activities to justify the label adopted. There is also the risk that the tag will be adopted by universities to justify making the scholarship of teaching secondary to research.

My Furrow or Yours?
A Comparative Approach to Learning Fields

This volume has come about through a very anthropological habit of compari-son. The meetings of the Teaching Anthropology Network of EASA initially dwelt on the seemingly very different intellectual and institutional traditions of teaching across Europe. However in this comparison of field-notes, social anthropologists in these countries realised they would have to grapple with the consequences of higher education policy convergence and 'harmonisation' across Europe. The World Trade Organisation's ambitions for 'progressive lib-eralisation' through the GAT's trade rounds is intended to create a global market for higher education. The movement towards a mass university system is a Europe-wide phenomenon, and has been accompanied by reductions in funding and resources. Issues of employment, training, and the teaching of applied and transferable skills to students are all being given prominence by policy-makers. The exponential growth in the use of technology in higher education poses sim-ilar challenges. The 1999 Bologna declaration has led to the development of European-wide credit accumulation and transfer schemes. Finally, national gov-ernments are increasingly prioritising teaching quality within universities, and funding formulas are beginning to reflect this situation, with special funding tar-geted at 'innovative' learning and teaching strategies. Each of these developments is having implications for the anthropological classroom.

The book's contributors address three broad aspects of these convergent and contradictory developments: anthropologies of higher education, com-puter-mediated learning, and experiential learning. The first set of contributions put the critical tools of anthropology to work by showing how changing classroom practices link to issues of reform and change within the purpose and delivery of higher education. In this regard they expand on con-cerns raised in the first volume in this couplet. The second set of contributions explores the use of a variety of media, and in particular com-puter and information technologies, within teaching. The last theme dwells particularly on classroom interactions, on practice-based learning and the importance of highlighting experience within learning.

All take the classroom as an important field for anthropological analysis and practice. Whether using the classroom as a prism through which to think about the effects of disciplinary and institutional reform, as a site in which to investigate the role of new media and computer technologies within teaching, or simply to thinking creatively about the very process of learning, the class-room becomes a 'learning field' in a number of ways.

Anthropologies of Higher Education: policy, practice and politics

The first theme brings together authors who demonstrate the ways in which the university classroom is an ethnographic magnifying glass; one that can be used to understand complex issues of higher education policy and institutional change – be they a focus on widening participation, skills, employment, or student exchanges. University-based anthropologists are often surprisingly ignorant of the fast-changing nature of an increasingly global higher education 'market' and its likely impact on academic practice. The contributors to this section keep their ethnographic wits about them as they describe their involvement with particular courses and initiatives, and how these link into the larger political economy of European higher education. Shore and Wright (1997) adopt the term 'policy fields' too as a way of conceptualising the influence of policy on the organisation of these systems, and in relation to which the 'learning fields' of this volume need to be understood.

In making these connections, the contributors are seeking to take up Bourdieu's challenge to make visible the conditions of the academic labour process and the way this contributes to the 'scholastic mode of thought'. The corollary of the 'scholastic fallacy' (Bourdieu 2000) – academia's predilection for creating universal truths from very particular situations – is that university teachers are often unaware of the knowledge economy of the educational activities they are themselves engaged in.

These chapters are best read in conjunction with other research on the changing political structures of higher education. There is a growing anthropological literature on the changing management cultures of higher education, and how they are affecting teachers and teaching within Europe (see Strathern 2000, Shore and Wright 1999, Coleman and Simpson 2001, Gledhill 2001, Mascerenhas-Keyes with Wright 1995). The watershed in Britain for this latest set of reforms was the Dearing report on Higher Education in 1997, and along with the Bologna declaration (1999) there have been similar reports/commissions in other European countries. The historical reproduction of anthropology in the U.K. is explored by Spencer (2000), whilst the political economy of the U.S. university sector and its implications for learning and teaching anthropology is explored by the contributors to Basch et al. (1999).

The pedagogic aim of integrating students' biographical experience with the study of anthropology is a core theme of the first chapter by Simon Coleman and Robert Simpson. Reflecting upon their experience of teaching an anthropology degree in a newly established campus affiliated to Durham university, they argue that the use of autobiographical and reflexive methods by students during their research fieldwork can generate an anthropological 'worldview' in which students' own cultural experience is acknowledged and theorised.

Sue Wright's chapter concentrates on the theme of developing anthropological reflexivity as an educational strategy. She distinguishes between educationalist and anthropological meanings of the concept of reflexivity, and shows how she built in a powerful reflexive dimension in a new 'independent learning' module. The core of the module was student engagement in 'self-initiated and negotiated' study on a subject of their choice. An aim of the course was to develop student empowerment through their analysis of the power relations of their own university. The structuring of learning opportunities within U.K. academia became an analytic foreground instead of being the more usual implicit background.

Shawn Landres and Karen Hough report on a unique workshop in Oxford at which postgraduates from eighteen British social anthropology departments discussed their experience of studying and being trained as researchers. This chapter provides an insight into aspects of research training and skills provision that postgraduates see as being of particular importance. Lists of 'poor practice' and 'good practice' are a salutary reminder to those training research students.

E.U.-funded international exchange programmes for students and teaching staff have been around for a number of years. Alex Strating reports on his extensive experience of supervising students on such programmes (ERASMUS, SOCRATES) over ten years, focusing on student needs and the problems encountered during study stays abroad. He draws our attention to the way students studying abroad tend to seek out precisely those courses that are not on offer at their home universities. Although convergence amongst systems of higher education in Europe has, to date, been minimal (for example, in the matter of the equivalence of curricula, scheduling of the academic year, etc.), a number of ideas are nevertheless emerging in this area. Strating calls on us to display greater flexibility with regard to possible exchange programmes, while making constructive proposals for a more active role for EASA in preparing future student exchanges at the European level.

Mediated Learning

These articles are united by their focus on the use of media (both new and old) in the teaching of anthropology. Debate over the use of ICT in the teaching of anthropology is highly polarised. Its protagonists enthuse about the liberatory pedagogic potentials of these new media, supplementing and transforming classroom dynamics. Those against them dwell darkly on the close link between technological developments and knowledge commodification, hinting at the 'digital diploma mills' that on-line degrees might presage (Noble 1998). Such suspicions are confirmed by the narrowly commercial agendas espoused by contributors to a British Government think-tank report on technologising higher education (OST 1999).

Most of the chapters adopt a tone of measured enthusiasm, but seek to contextualise and historicise such developments within a historical knowledge economy. However, all would benefit from being read against a more critical overview of the debates, such as that provided by Robins and Webster, who dispute any talk of an 'information revolution' and insist that information 'has long been a key component of regulation in the modern nation state and in capitalist economies' (1999: 94).

Anthropological views of CIT in teaching are less all-embracing and more contradictory. Communication technologies like e-mail packages and web-browsers are now part of everyday academic practice, yet their use resides alongside an objectifying construction of 'technology' as something explicitly and epistemologically separate. Recent research has shown that whilst anthropologists will acknowledge their use of ICT, they also distance themselves from it, justifying their lack of use of ICT within teaching by emphasising the 'human' aspect of anthropology where personal relations and socialisation are privileged (Halstead, Mills and Simpson nd).

Technological developments such as virtual learning environments (VLEs) do present challenges to the conventional lecture and tutorial model, but this should never be an all-or-nothing dogma. The real challenge is in the detail – finding and evaluating appropriate ways of integrating these new resources into the learning process. In most cases, this means supplementing rather than displacing existing classroom-based learning. Whether this is successful depends as much on how people understand and define the social space that technology occupies as it is to do with their knowledge of the particular tools under debate. Escobar (1994: 211) cautions against easy technological determinism with his reminder that technologies are 'cultural inventions' that 'emerge out of particular cultural conditions and in turn help to create new ones.'

Lenie Brouwer and Marjo de Theije relate their experience of seminars that they have organised over several years to develop VLEs and educational websites with anthropological content. The article provides a useful 'warts-and-all' narrative of the process of introducing ICT into teaching, describing the pleasures and pitfalls. As well as providing concrete examples, they have a host of useful suggestions and advice to those wishing to pursue their own initiatives in this field.

David Zeitlyn's chapter on the University of Kent's Experience Rich Anthropology (ERA) project illustrates the potential transformative nature of computer technology for anthropological learning. The ERA project allows educators and researchers to create multidimensional learning resources through integrating written analysis, sound, music and visual images all within the same virtual resource base; suddenly the study of Bemba adolescent girls' initiation dances can be seen, heard and thought about simultaneously, thus communicating a much richer ethnographic experience for students.

Sarah Pink deals with the design and use of electronic hypermedia in teaching practice. In her chapter she discusses her own experience of CD production based on two concrete examples. This medium allows anthropological and educational hypermedia texts to be combined in a way that brings together written words, audio material and video sequences. The interactive nature of the media in question allows website- or CD/DVD-users to set their own pace of learning and to develop their own ways of dealing with the themes involved. Sarah Pink furthermore recommends involving students in designing and producing these hypermedia resources, thereby imparting key skills.

Not all the chapters focus solely on ICT. Beate Engelbrecht and Rolf Husmann develop an overview of the possible uses and value of 'ethnographic films, related documentaries and indigenous/community films for teaching anthropology'. This chapter, like most in the book, offers considerable practical advice, in this case on choosing and integrating various kinds of film into courses at different levels. It also theorises the epistemological, analytical and methodological issues involved in the use of film in teaching.

Mary Bouquet argues that museums and archives are exceptionally exciting and inspirational places for teaching. Her contribution reminds us that, since its inception, anthropology has been taught using a variety of media, materials and technologies. Objects play an important part in the learning process, especially where students are able not only to contemplate them from behind glass cases but also to handle and to develop a tactile relationship with them. The structural overhaul of modern museums is also a moment for reflection and discussion, allowing students to acquaint themselves with the variety of historical exhibition techniques. In this way, the reflexive character of presentational and interpretative modes regarding both foreign and domestic cultural forms comes into greater relief. The musealised form of culture engenders a bridge between 'them' and 'us'. By taking museums as learning media one finds oneself right at the very heart of anthropology.

Experiential Learning

This final set of contributions highlight the possibilities of innovative group-work, imagework and performance-based approaches for the learning of anthropology. They are drawn together by their sustained attention to the performative and experiential aspects of learning anthropology. Links between theory and practice are often tenuous in many anthropological classrooms, and there is a long history of contention over the appropriate forms of practical experience within the anthropology curriculum. Levi-Strauss, writing in 1954, cautioned against 'a paltry three weeks in a village' and 'hasty practical courses' as harmful, and sometimes amounting to a 'kind of anti-training' (Levi-Strausss 1954: 120). More recently, there has been opposition within British academia to undergraduate anthropological fieldwork *per se* (Sharma 1989, Ingold 1991 and Watson 1995).

Other anthropological traditions take an opposing view, where undergraduate field-schools, placements and other forms of practice-based learning are commonplace. This emphasis on inquiry-based, research-based and practice-based learning is captured in the Boyer Report on Undergraduate learning which has been influential within the U.S. (The Boyer Commission 1995). These chapters reveal that the 'learning field' of our title is not merely a metaphorical connection, and that the classroom can indeed become a research field-site, as students draw on their own and each others' resources, experiences, knowledge and skills.

Stella Mascarenhas-Keyes reflects upon a decade of running a week-long, practice-based, multidisciplinary methods course in the U.K. This course, run by the Group for Anthropology in Policy and Practice (GAPP), seeks to develop a learning community in which team-work and student-centred learning strategies lead to high levels of group interaction and participation.

The course, drawing together postgraduates and practitioners, gives participants skills in producing policy-related project proposals, derived from 'real-life' case-studies. These proposals are then assessed by specialist panels. The course aim is to create for the participants the actual experience of team-based project work in applied anthropology.

Dorle Dracklé's paper sets out an approach to education that draws on Rogerian themes of education as empowerment and of the teacher as facilitator. She introduces Cohn's theory of Theme Centred Interaction (TCI) that sees the classroom situation as a continual engagement between the individual, the group interaction, the topic and the various contexts that implicitly structure the learning situation. Dracklé's idea of 'living learning' involves the teacher enabling and developing the life of the group through giving attention to emotional and political dynamics. She advocates the use of group contracts, suggesting that they facilitate beneficial group processes that in turn allow participants to take responsibility for their own unique learning.

A common theme running through these chapters is one of providing students with experiences that help them to understand the process of both creating and transgressing cultural difference. A dramatic example of this intention is presented in Giuliano Tescari's chapter. Tescari reflects upon many years of recreating, through an extended drama and role-play, something of the actual experience of participating in the annual Mexican Huichol Indian shamanic pilgrimage to 'hunt' the psychedelic peyote plant. This is an ambitious project, based on Tescari's research in that society and inspired partly by Victor Turner's performance-based educational methodology.

Whilst Tescari's chapter focuses on ethnodrama as a way of bringing the experience of the cultural 'other' into the pedagogic domain, Andrew Russell's chapter reflects upon a 'move' in the other direction: taking the students into a 'foreign' field. Russell reports on the results of a study trip to India in 1995; accounts of the importance of the experience for the students reveal both the personal growth outcomes from the tour as well as the increase in their cultural empathy, one of anthropology's prime and perhaps unique educational goals.

The generation and recreation of 'experience' is a theme in Iain Edgar's chapter on the use of imagework in the educational process. Using an array of visualisation techniques derived from humanistic psychology, Edgar illustrates how the imagination, in its various manifestations of spontaneous fantasy, memory and dream, can be used to develop educational experience. This approach is congruent with Pocock's (1975) concept of a 'personal anthropology' in which students are helped to connect their lived experience with anthropological theory. Making explicit our own constructed and cultured selves is as much an educational aim as is understanding the culture of others.

For Tina Ramnarine, personal experience is the key to the imparting knowledge of ethnomusicology to students. She argues for the importance of learning through direct participation in musical performance. At the School of Anthropological Studies at Queen's University Belfast, ethnomusicology courses integrate both theory and practice. 'Learning by doing' here takes on a whole new dimension, involving both public performances given by student ensembles and student participation in living musical traditions during periods of undergraduate fieldwork.

These chapters' contributors share a common ambition: a passion to make student experience, both of their cultural selves and of those previously far away 'other peoples', usually unheard and hidden from view, a key pathway to learning . Novel teaching strategies are used to overcome some of the limitations of traditional pedagogy in relation to the use of experience within the classroom. We hope the contributions will encourage the further use and dissemination of 'experience-near' educational practices.

The notion of 'learning fields' captures the central theme running through this volume, but this volume can only begin to scratch the surface of the diversity of practice. Increasingly much of this work is now being made publicly available via the web. We hope that this book, and the growing set of experiences, resources and literatures that it highlights, will contribute to making the world of education a central concern of both future anthropological enquiry and practice.

Acknowledgements

We should like to acknowledge the very considerable help given by Leon Jamei as English language editor for this volume. His work has been funded by the European Association of Social Anthropologists (EASA) whose support we should also like to warmly acknowledge. Thomas Schippers, our co-editor for *Learning Fields Volume 1: Educational Histories of European Social Anthropology,* has also assisted with some parts of this second *Learning Fields* volume. Jon Mitchell, previously Publications Officer of EASA, played an important role in arranging for the volume's publication with Berghahn Books and we are indebted to him. Lastly, we should like to thank Marion Berghahn and Sean Kingston of Berghahn Books for their timely and supportive assistance.

References

Basch, L., Saunders, Wood, L., Wojcicka, J., and Peacock, J. (eds) 1999. *Transforming Academia: Challenges and Opportunities for an Engaged Anthropology.* Washington: American Anthropological Association.

Becher, T. 1989. *Academic Tribes and Territories: Intellectual Enquiry and the Cultures of Disciplines.* Milton Keynes: Society for Research into Higher Education/Oxford University Press.

Bourdieu, P. 1977. *Outline of a Theory of Practice.* Cambridge: Cambridge University Press.

Bourdieu, P. 1984. *Homo Academicus.* Stanford: Stanford University Press.

Bourdieu, P. 2000. *Pascalian Meditations.* Cambridge: Polity Press.

Boyer, E. 1990. *Scholarship Reconsidered: The Priorities of the Professorate.* Princeton, NJ: Carnegie Foundation for the Advancement of Teaching.

Boyer Commission, 1995. *Reinventing Undergraduate Education: A Blueprint for America's Research Universities.* Mellon, CA: Carnegie Foundation.

Coleman, S. and Simpson, B. 2001. 'Anthropology Inside Out: Identity and Agency in the Reproduction of a Discipline.' *Anthropology in Action* 8(1): 1–5.

Dearing, R. 1997. *Higher Education in the Learning Society: The National Committee of Enquiry into Higher Education.* London: HMSO.

Delamont, S., Atkinson, P. and Parry, O. 2000. *The Doctoral Experience: Success and Failure in Graduate School.* London: Falmer Press.

Dracklé, D., Edgar, I. and Schippers, T. (eds) 2002. *Volume 1. Educational Histories of European Social Anthropology.* Oxford: Berghahn.

Edwards, A. 2000. *Researching Pedagogy: A Socio-Cultural Agenda. An Inaugural Lecture.* Birmingham: University of Birmingham.

Engestrom, Y. 1999. 'Activity Theory and Individual and Social Transformation', in *Perspectives on Activity Theory*, eds Y. Engestrom, R. Miettinen and R.-L. Punamaki. Cambridge: Cambridge University Press.

Escobar, A. 1994. 'Welcome to Cyberia. Notes on the Anthropology of Cyberculture.' *Current Anthropology.* 35(3): 211–31.

Evans-Pritchard, E.E. 1959. 'The Teaching of Social Anthropology at Oxford.' *Man – The Proceedings of the Royal Anthropological Institute* (Note 180, July 1959): 121.

Firth, R. 1963. 'Aims, Methods and Concepts in the Teaching of Social Anthropology', in *The Teaching of Anthropology*, eds D. Mandelbaum, G. Lasker and E. Albert. Berkeley: University of California Press.

Gledhill, J. 2001. 'Facing the Future: Anthropology and the Transformation of the University.' *Anthropology in Action* 8(1): 49–55.

Halstead, N., Mills, D. and Simpson, E. nd. *Research paper: Using CIT in Learning and Teaching Anthropology.* Birmingham: Centre for learning and teaching Sociology, Anthropology and Politics.

Hannerz, Ulf. 2002. Foreword to *Intellectual and Pedagogic Histories of European Social Anthropology: Teaching Social Anthropology Across Europe*, eds D. Dracklé, I. Edgar and T. Schippers. Oxford: Berghahn.

Healey, M. 2000. 'Developing the Scholarship of Teaching: A Discipline-Based Approach.' *Higher Education Research and Development* 19(2): 169–89.

Hoebel, E.A. 1955. 'Anthropology in Education', in *Yearbook of Anthropology*, pp. 391–5.

Hoebel, E.A. 1958. 'Anthropology, Universities and American Society.' *American Anthropologist* 60: 633–39.

Huber, M.T. 2001. 'Disciplinary Styles in the Scholarship of Teaching and Learning – Reflections on The Carnegie Academy for the Scholarship of Learning and Teaching', in M. Huber and S. Morreales (eds), *Disciplinary Styles in the Scholarship of Teaching and Learning: Exploring Common Ground.* Melmont, CA: The Carnegie Foundation, in association with the American Association for Higher Education.

Huber, M.T. and S.P. Morreale, (eds) 2001. *Disciplinary Styles in the Scholarship of Teaching and Learning: Exploring Common Ground.* Melmont, CA: Carnegie Foundation, in association with the AAHE.

Ingold, T. 1991. 'Fieldwork Projects in Undergraduate anthropology.' *Anthropology Today* 7(2): 22–3.

Kroeber, A.L. 1954. 'The Place of Anthropology in Universities.' *American Anthropologist* 56: 754–67.

Lacey, C. 1982. 'Freedom and Constraints in British Education' in R. Frankenberg (ed) *Custom and Conflict in British Society*, Manchester: Manchester University Press.

Lambert, A. 1982. 'Expulsion in Context: A School as a System in Action', in R. Frankenberg (ed.) *Custom and Conflict in British Society*. Manchester: Manchester University Press.

Lather, P., (ed.) 1991. *Getting Smart: Feminist Research and Pedagogy with/in the Postmodern*. London: Routledge.

Laurie, N.O. and Whiting, J.W. 1954. 'A Technique for Teaching Ethnology', *American Anthropologist* 56(3).

Lave, J. 1988. *Cognition in Practice*. Cambridge: Cambridge University Press.

Lave, J. and Wenger, E. 1991. *Situated Learning: Legitimate Peripheral Participation*. Cambridge: Cambridge University Press.

Leighton, A., Adair, J., and Parker, S. 1951. 'A Field Method for Teaching Applied Anthropology'. *Human Organisation* 10(4): 5–11.

Levi-Strauss, C. 1954. 'The Place of Anthropology in the Social Sciences and the Problems Raised in Teaching It', in *The University Teaching of Social Sciences, Sociology, Social Psychology and Anthropology*, UNESCO. Paris: UNESCO.

Little, K. 1960. 'Research Report No 2: Department of Social Anthropology, University of Edinburgh', *Sociological Review* 8: 255–66.

Mandelbaum, D. 1961. 'International Symposium on the Teaching of Anthropology', *Current Anthropology* 2: 508–9.

Mandelbaum, D., Lasker, G., and Albert, E. (eds) 1963. *The Teaching of Anthropology*. Berkeley: University of California Press.

Marton, F. 1986. 'Phenomenography – A Research Approach to Investigating Different Understandings of Reality', *Journal of Thought* 21(3): 28–49.

Mascarenhas-Keyes, S. with Wright, S. 1995. *Report on Teaching and learning Social Anthropology in the United Kingdom*, Social Anthropology Teaching and Learning Network, Sussex University: Anthropology in Action.

Mead, M. 1928. *Coming of Age in Samoa*. London: Cape.

Myres, J.H. 1946. 'The Place of Anthropology and Ethnology in Education', *Man* 46: 93–94.

Noble, D.F. 1998. 'Digital Diploma Mills: The Automation of Higher Education'. *Monthly Review* 49(9): 38–52.

Office of Science and Technology 1999. *Foresight: Universities in the Future*. London: Office of Science and Technology.

Pelissier, C. 1991. 'The Anthropology of Teaching and Learning', *Annual Review of Anthropology* 20: 75–95.

Pocock, D. 1975. *Understanding Social Anthropology*, London: Hodder & Stoughton.

Robins, K. and Webster, F. 1999. *Times of the Technoculture*. London: Routledge.

Saljo, R. 1988. 'Learning in Educational Settings: Methods of Enquiry', in P. Ramsden (ed.) *Improving Learning: New Perspectives*. London: Kogan Page.

Shore, C. and S. Wright, Eds. 1997. *Anthropology of Policy – Critical Perspectives on Governance and Power*. London, Routledge.

Shore, C. and Wright, S. (eds) 1999. 'Audit Culture and Anthropology: Neoliberalism in British Higher Education', *Journal of the Royal Anthropological Institute* 5: 557–75.

Sharma, U. 1989. 'Fieldwork in the Undergraduate Curriculum: Its Merits', *British Association for Social Anthropology in Policy and Practice* 3: 3–4.

Spencer, J. 2000. 'British Social Anthropology: A Retrospective', *Annual Review of Anthropology*, 29: 1–24.

Spindler, G. 1955. *Education and Anthropology*. New York: Russell Sage Foundation.

Strathern, M., (ed.) 2000. *Audit Cultures: Anthropological Studies in Accountability, Ethics and the Academy*. London: Routledge.

Temple, S.R. 1914. 'Anthropological Teaching in the Universities', *Man* 14–15: 57–72.

Voegelin, E. 1950. 'Anthropology in American Universities', *American Anthropologist*, 52: 350–91.

Watson, C.W. 1995. 'Case Study: Fieldwork in Undergraduate Anthropology – For and Against', *Innovations in Education and Training International* 32(2): 153–61.

Willis, P. 1977. *Learning to Labour: Why Working Class Kids Get Working Class Jobs*, Farnborough: Saxon House.

Part 1

Anthropologies of Higher Education: Policy, Practice and Politics

1

Knowing, Doing and Being
Pedagogies and Paradigms in the Teaching
of Social Anthropology

Simon Coleman and Bob Simpson

British higher education is currently adopting a new set of procedures for the review of university teaching. These latest shifts were initiated in the wake of Lord Dearing's report on the future of higher education in the U.K. (1997). One of the problems highlighted by the report was an absence of transparency and accountability in the delivery of teaching programmes, leading to a lack of national standardisation. In response to these concerns, the U.K. Quality Assurance Agency for Higher Education (QAA) was established with a 'mission' to 'promote public confidence that quality of provision and standards of awards in higher education are being safeguarded and advanced' (QAA 2000: 1). To achieve their mission the QAA has developed and begun to implement a thoroughly revamped approach to quality assurance through 'academic review'.

One thing that has become clear as a result of the developments described above is that academics must adjust to the fact that competence and good practice in themselves are worthless unless accompanied by *tangible evidence* of the effectiveness of that practice. Academics are asked to specify what constitutes graduate competence in their particular discipline; it is then the job of reviewers to determine whether, on the evidence available, these particular disciplinary objectives have been realised. Entering into this process requires academics to make explicit the substance of what was hitherto taken to be self-evident, and to commit to paper what a student will know, be able to do and, rather more elusively, 'be', at the end of a programme of study.

The achievement of proficiency in the art of disciplinary self-representation is likely to be more easily attained by some subjects than by others. For chemical engineering, say, one might assume that it is relatively straightforward to slip into an auditable apparel comprised of neatly stitched-together inventories of knowledge, skills and competencies. At the other end of the spectrum are those disciplines, such as anthropology, for which the same exercise is proving altogether more discomforting. In institutional terms anthropology is very small compared, for example, to sociology or psychology. Paradoxically, however, the subject matter of anthropology is vast, covering no less than human social, cultural and biological diversity across space and time. Furthermore, many anthropologists would argue that anthropology is not defined by a prescriptible content but rather by a certain approach or apperception that is by its very nature boundary-crossing and voracious in its synthesising.

A small constituency and sprawling subject matter might have worked well when higher education was content to operate with rather more liberal values and diffuse objectives. In the present climate it predisposes practitioners to a sense of vulnerability and misfit.[1] However, it is not our aim in this chapter to enter into detailed discussions about the rise of audit culture and the impacts that this has had on anthropology.[2] We are more interested in looking beneath the task of disciplinary self-representation in order to explore just what constitutes an anthropology student's experience of knowing, doing and being. To embark on this task we need an 'anthropology of anthropology' that begins with the experience of students and teachers of anthropology, rather than with the imperatives of quality assurance. The key question which this reflexive exercise must address concerns the kinds of people (as opposed to assemblages of key skills) that the study of anthropology helps to create (Coleman and Simpson 2001). Although few graduates of anthropology will get to work under the designation 'anthropologist', for many of those who pass through the discipline, the opportunity to consider their own society and culture in relation to others is likely to produce a significant 'value-added' dimension to perception and action, albeit not one that is easily measured (Simpson 1997).

We assume that anthropologists not only have distinctive ideas about how social worlds are constructed and hang together, but also potentially have specific pedagogical strategies for communicating these ideas. In their survey of anthropology teaching and learning in the United Kingdom, Mascarenhas-Keyes and Wright (1995) identify two distinct philosophies informing undergraduate curricula. These they refer to as 'substantivist' and 'imaginationist'. The former refers to a strategy aimed at providing students with 'mastery of a substantive body of ethnographic material and anthropological theory' (1995: 17). The latter refers to cultivating an anthropological apperception by the imaginative use of ethnography and anthropological theory. Arguments for this dual approach to teaching and learning are themselves twofold. First, anthropology should incorporate a variety of pedagogical strategies that engage the student in dialogue between self and the anthropological other, alongside the gaining of substantive anthropological knowledge. Second, it is absurd to divorce anthropological teaching experiences from a student's learning experiences. Anthropology is about the contextualisation of knowledge, action, belief, meaning and language, and any strategy that fails to understand and incorporate student understandings into this process misses a crucial pedagogical opportunity. Thus, to integrate education into other parts of student life is not just sound pedagogically, it is also sound anthropologically. Although in practice the philosophies will tend to blur, particularly as there are likely to be advocates of both in every department, the 'imaginationist' tendency has the potential to lead to a radical rethink of the content and pedagogical strategies of social anthropology.

In the account that follows we present observations regarding the use of teaching methods designed to engage and activate the student's own experiences as both biography and narrative. We draw on our own experience over the last decade as teachers of anthropology at the University of Durham, U.K., with pedagogical responsibilities primarily at its Stockton Campus (Queen's). Students at the Stockton Campus are for the most part classified as 'non-traditional' in terms of the routes they have followed into education. They are studying for degrees in Human Sciences (BA and BSc) and Health and Human Sciences (BSc) that have as their disciplinary core the study of anthropology.

A Popular Option?

The scramble to generate a 'learning society' in Britain, combined with a high level of disenchantment with studying the natural sciences, has resulted in a growing interest in social science and humanities courses (Institute of Manpower Studies 1993). In most British universities the numbers of students taking anthropology has doubled or tripled over recent years. Furthermore, as the increased flexibility that 'modularisation' allows comes into effect, anthropology is not only likely to be taken by a broader range of students than before, but also might be combined with surprising mixtures of other subjects.

These developments imply that the public profile and influence of the subject could grow over the next few years, echoing a development that has already taken place in the United States (Baba 1994). However, they also raise the question as to whether departments know what it is that students are looking for and whether students' aims are shared by lecturers themselves. Drawing from a survey, Wright and Sharma (1989) note: 'Anthropologists often say that they study other societies in order to gain insight into their own society and experience, but some recent students felt that they had not in fact been encouraged by their teachers to make that connection.' Of course, canonical texts are necessary in any discipline worthy of the name, and there is always likely to be a generation gap between much course material and current research. However, the important question is whether the teaching of anthropology can make texts of whatever era come alive by giving an indication of how such works provide readers with an anthropological world-view, moreover one that is, at least in part, applicable beyond particular geographical and intellectual confines. As Carrithers notes in describing the work of Geertz, the writing of ethnography is peculiar in its frequent deployment of 'personal experience' in the construction of ethnographic texts (1992: 149); one would have thought that the job of bridging the gap between disciplinary language and the world of the reader was already half-performed in many anthropological texts.

Making students feel excited about reflecting upon ethnographies and anthropology as a whole must be more than a simple recruitment drive for postgraduate study. The number of academic posts simply does not exist to absorb the numbers of students produced, while applications of anthropology in the field of development are specialised and relatively few. When asked what use the discipline is on the job market, many professional anthropologists are likely to talk of the values of a liberal education, literacy and perhaps numeracy (Whisson 1986). They are unlikely, for understandable reasons, to be able to give specific answers to employers who may require concrete evidence of specific and transferable skills acquired. Shore (1996: 2) claims that the discipline's poor public image prompts graduates to abandon the label of 'anthropologist' when working in the non-academic sector. Compared with such disciplines as English, anthropology lacks the benefit of having been taught at schools. Nor does it give the impression of being a well-established subject such as classics, typically characterised by employers and lecturers alike as being a good 'training for the mind', even if specific knowledge of Latin declensions is likely to be no more (and probably a lot less) useful in a business context than an understanding of segmentary lineage systems. One author of this paper vividly remembers being told some twenty years ago by a careers adviser at school, on announcing that he wished to do anthropology at university: 'Oh, my wife studied anthropology. I should think you could do better than that.'

From the outside, anthropology remains an esoteric subject taught by relatively few people who pad inconsequentially around 'ivory tower' institutions. In the media, anthropologists are depicted as eccentric recorders of the bizarre, the distant and above all the exotic (cf. Peterson 1991). As Shore points out (1996: 3), most academics write for one another rather than for the public beyond the academy. The confining of the discipline to the university world has tended to be perpetuated – again, for perfectly understandable reasons – by the Association of Social Anthropologists of the Commonwealth (ASA), which has membership concentrated largely among those explicitly involved in teaching and researching the discipline on a professional level. However, the question remains unanswered as to how or whether anthropological knowledge and skills are applicable beyond the academy, or indeed whether it is possible systematically and overtly to transfer the skills and knowledge of the discipline to other professions or, more broadly, to the development of wider forms of life-style and world-view.

Current or recent debates on the epistemology of anthropology do not help us in attempting to gain a strong profile for the discipline. A social science subject that does not claim to provide the alleged predictive power of economics or even sociology, and which has been much concerned with self-deconstruction over the past few years, can seem trivial to students as well as outsiders – as likely to vanish as the tribes featured in a 'Disappearing World' series. Overall, anthropology is having to respond to micro- and macro-political and economic developments (*see* Gledhill 2000). Modularisation encourages potential fragmentation of degrees from within universities, while the 'globalising' of people, culture and forms of knowledge reduces the ability of its practitioners to talk with exclusive expertise about distant others. Yet such developments need not be seen only as problems to be overcome in the reproduction of the discipline. They might rather be viewed as part of an opportunity to broaden the subject's influence through teaching strategies as well as research and writing. The challenge is to suggest some of anthropology's strengths in relation to other disciplines; to indicate that the subject is of use beyond the academy, without compromising its place within the university world; to indicate above all that texts can be read and constructed with multiple agendas: they are contributions to academic debate, but also means to bridge the gap between the individual reader or writer and the worlds they live in or write about.

Appropriate Pedagogies?

We propose to make our case through the use of a quasi-ethnographic method – a description and analysis of the university within which we teach and research. University of Durham, Stockton Campus, U.K. (Queen's) started life as University College Stockton (UCS) in 1992. At that time it was a novel cross-sector collaborative venture between a polytechnic (Teesside, U.K.) and an 'old' university (Durham, U.K.). With reorganisation of the U.K. higher education sector in the early 1990s and the re-designation of polytechnics as universities, cross-sector collaboration ceased to have meaning and the parent institutions decided to dissolve their partnership, with custody of their now quite large offspring passing entirely to the University of Durham. The result has been substantial further development in terms of infrastructure and numbers of staff and students involved, but it is one that is 'of' Durham rather than strictly being 'in' Durham. The distinctions are more than merely geographical. While Durham is the third oldest university in England, Queen's represents one of the most significant single additions (along, perhaps, with Lincoln) to the university world in Britain in recent years. Whilst Durham students have tended to come from middle-class, often Southern backgrounds, with a record of high achievement at A-level, Queen's was constructed partially in order to attract local, often working-class students from the Teesside conurbation, which at that time had one of the lowest take-up rates for higher education in Europe (Beynon et al. 1994).

In the early days, the mission of Queen's corresponded closely with the efforts of the then Conservative government to increase the proportion of the population who were educated to degree level (Benn and Fieldhouse 1993). Such policies were formulated against the backdrop of an economy in the throes of being restructured, with redundancies and high levels of unemployment an inevitable consequence. Under such conditions, education and training were seen as the key to a change of career. The broad theoretical framework upon which many of these developments were hung was Torsten Husén's notion of the 'learning society' (1974; cf. 1986). Husén's vision was of people having access to lifelong learning, with a variety of institutions supporting formal and informal education.

One of the more radical consequences of attempts to realise the 'learning society' has indeed been the dramatic increase in the number of mature students entering higher education. A high proportion of Queen's students are 'mature', ranging from their mid-twenties to mid-sixties. Many are the first of their family to go to university, and will previously have held jobs or brought up children with little or no expectation of going into higher education. Thus the Durham and the Stockton campuses are akin to academic moieties, complementing each other in the formation of alternative approaches to providing an anthropological education. The Durham department is located in an Edwardian building near the centre of the city. It is overlooked by the city's Norman castle and cathedral, and overlooks the river Wear – a location for student rowing competitions and heritage tours. The Queen's building, meanwhile, is situated on the banks of the Tees, on the former site of a now-defunct shipyard. Alongside the removal of past industrial pollution a new, 'cleansed' landscape of apparent post-industrial opportunity has been created. Over ten million pounds sterling were provided by the Department of the Environment via the Teesside Development Corporation to build the first phase of the university campus. This project was followed by a second teaching building completed in 1998 and a research building completed in 2001. New housing and business premises have also been located on the site, and the river combines a canoe slalom with a stretch of water that has potential as an Olympic-standard rowing course. The original Queen's building resembles a large ship, about to be launched into the water. It was for a time used in the evenings by Star Trek fans, who liked its 'space-age' appearance and who at their meetings would imaginatively convert it into the USS *Resolution*. Such a similarity was not lost on the advertising agency employed to design campus recruitment materials: 'It's Durham University, Jim, but not as we know it' proclaimed one advertisement depicting the College-as-starship.

While the degree offered at Durham to students is described as 'Anthropology', those taught at Queen's are termed 'Human Sciences' or 'Health and Human Sciences', and modules at the latter originally transformed stock anthropological subjects into more vernacular form: kinship, for instance, became split into such modules as 'Sex, Reproduction and Love', and 'History and Change in the Family'. Only in their final year have students from both departments come together to take selected modules at Queen's or Durham. Admittedly, much that goes on at Queen's would be duplicated in any anthropology department in the country: lectures are given, seminars and classes taken, essays written, and books such as *The Nuer* read and reflected upon. As at Durham, biological and social anthropology modules are taken by most students throughout all of their three years. Yet the Human Sciences programme in Stockton also has a more pronounced policy of making explicit links between academic study and the rest of students' lives. Students are indeed encouraged to make themselves objects of study. At the simplest level, staff attempt as far as possible to draw on Western as well as non-Western material in quoting and analysing case-studies during lectures and seminars. Visits to local sites such as Beamish Industrial Open-Air Museum or a local Theravada Buddhist monastery are designed to aid reflection on the political economy and culture of the local area. Students are encouraged to bring material pertinent to their own lives to classes, and to present such material to others in short presentations. Essays are often left open to allow the exploration of personal experiences in terms of anthropological literature. Recently, for instance, a Catholic priest produced a paper on celibacy; a former salesman wrote a structuralist analysis of oral myths told to him in the pub; a divorced man reflected on changing constructions of fatherhood and paternity in contemporary society.

Lest the impression be gained that we spend all our time running encounter groups, it is important to stress that many students choose subjects that are deliberately far removed from their personal experiences. The point is, however, that there is a significant body of students who are intentionally using our degree programme as an opportunity to reflect on their own lives through the intellectual lenses of modules on such topics as kinship, social change, cultural classification, and so on. Fundamental is the fact that students are given a number of opportunities, culminating in a third-year dissertation, to carry out carefully supervised research that might well carry them directly into areas which are of personal interest and possibly local concern. In these endeavours, textual knowledge is juxtaposed at an early stage with considerations of methodology and the practical mastery of managing fieldwork projects in groups as well as singly. In Sharma's terms (1991: 10), the aim is to add an 'anthropological dimension' to activities to which the student is already committed.

To Do or Not to Do:
Fieldwork in the Undergraduate Curriculum

In recent years, a certain amount of debate has been evident concerning the carrying out of project-work/fieldwork in undergraduate anthropology degrees. Sharma (1991: 9) talks of how anthropologists have tended to mystify their methods of investigation, and it is certainly the case that conveying the experience and utility of fieldwork has proved a difficult task at this level. Thorn and Wright (1990; Hyatt 2001) argue, nevertheless, that project and placement activities help to move learning from the classroom into the 'real' world, thus giving theory and methodology tests of relevance. Students are thereby encouraged to become active learners with transferable skills, rather than passive ingesters of knowledge. In contrast, Ingold denies that fieldwork should be part of undergraduate anthropology courses (Ingold 1989). Some of the reasons he gives are pragmatic, such as the fact that this kind of work requires intensive supervision on the part of staff and much energy and attention on the part of the student. More broadly, he states (ibid.: 2): 'It is unfortunately the case that the specific character of anthropological field-work – the search for participant understanding through long-term immersion in an alien setting – places it beyond the bounds of the under-graduate degree.' To Ingold, students with limited time and material and an imperfectly grasped conceptual frame cannot be expected to bridge the gap successfully between collecting and analysing data. His view is that the knowledge of anthropology can be taught to all, with the skills of the discipline being conveyed only to those likely to become professionals.

Ingold is right to argue for the utility in their own right of anthropological texts. Nor can the day-to-day difficulties and demands of arranging practical research projects be denied. Indeed, the work involved with these projects looks set to acquire another tier of complexity as extensive requirements for ethical and risk assessment become the norm. However, it is more difficult to accept his apparent assumption that a divorce between acquiring knowledge and gaining skills within anthropology is to be recommended, even at the undergraduate level. Wright and Sharma (1989) and others have pointed out that carrying out research projects, however limited, can help students to read ethnographies differently, not least as they gain some understanding of the problems involved in collecting, analysing and presenting data. For many of the students who engage with such projects, there is a realisation that beneath the polished ethnographies they are required to read lies a craft (Epstein 1967), which it is usually the object of the craftsman or craftswoman to conceal. Furthermore, learning anthropology is not simply a matter of assimilating knowledge, it is also a question of applying such knowledge in contexts beyond those of the classroom.

Jean Lave's notion of 'situated learning' is relevant here. For her (Lave and Wenger 1991: 65), learning is not so much about the direct internalisation of knowledge as about its indirect transmission, which occurs when a person becomes a member of a sustained community of practice. Developing an identity within a particular social setting and becoming knowledgeably skilful are seen as part of the same process, with the former giving meaning to the latter. Subjects are constituted by their relationships with and activities in the world. Thus, in our teaching we should try to be mindful that learning is part of a wider life course. The student experience of university involves the partial objectification of self and de-objectification of knowledge, and this is a dual process in which knowledge is both an academic currency and a means to understand oneself.

At issue is a far broader question concerning the role of anthropology and what its practitioners feel they do. In one sense, the answer is obvious: anthropologists reproduce and expand their discipline through research produced and consumed within the academy and in ways that contribute substantially to the image of anthropologists as investigators of exotica. Yet students are both part of the academy and part of the public. Antikainen et al. (1996: 1) make the obvious point that people construct and conceive their lives partly through their educational experiences, and the latter provide not only ideas but also language through which to understand and formulate such experiences. In our next section, we shall examine this idea in some detail with reference to biographical research methods in undergraduate field research.

An Anthropology of Self

The use of biographical and life history methods in sociology and anthropology has a long pedigree. However, their deployment in teaching at undergraduate level is a relatively recent departure. In sociology, the use of biography reached an enhanced respectability in undergraduate teaching in the wake of a more reflexive and ethnomethodological shift in the early 1970s. Peter and Brigitte Berger's *Sociology: A Biographical Approach* (1972) proved to be something of a watershed in this regard. More recently, further re-evaluation has come about through the impetus of feminist scholarship and a critique of androcentric research methodologies (Ribbens et al. 1991). Uses of autobiography were popularised by David Pocock's *Introduction to Social Anthropology* (Pocock 1975; Pocock and MacClancey 1999) in which he made his famous invitation for aspirant anthropologists to reflect upon their 'personal anthropology' and in so doing render the 'self' as the means to data generation *par excellence.*

When this pedagogical strategy works well, the results can be satisfying and impressive for teacher and student alike. Take the case of Joyce, a former student at Queen's. A grandmother and the wife of a retired miner, she came to university in her mid-fifties. Her graduation in 1995 was the realisation of an aspiration to acquire an education that had been thwarted when, in her teens, she had been channelled by social and gender conventions into early marriage and pregnancy. Attending university in mid-life was a considerable challenge. It came on the back of her divorce and remarriage and a period that had seen the once-thriving coalfields and pit-villages of East Durham decimated. Joyce had been actively involved in the 1985 national miners' strike and in its aftermath: pit closures and the gradual deterioration of coalfield community and culture.

Within a substantivist curriculum there might be little opportunity to express, apply or explore Joyce's rich fund of experience. However, the use of autobiographical and reflexive methods, particularly in courses on methods and kinship, served to open up rich veins of insight which in Joyce's case leavened her experience of the more conventionally taught and assessed aspects of her degree. Connections could be made between her own experience of gender, history, class, culture, boundaries, identity and the like, and the way that these are talked about and theorised in relation to communities in India, Papua New Guinea or Latin America. 'Experience' began to feed into 'knowledge' as much as 'knowledge' fed into 'experience'.

Below is an extract from a journal kept by Joyce as part of her 'Methods and Analysis' module.[3] The entry was prompted after attending a lecture on language, metaphor and classification, and concerns a recollection from her childhood concerning the local expression 'whatcher marra'.

> Wherever I went in Hepley Colliery, as a child, with my father, he used this phrase repeatedly. Perhaps I am idealising the past in my recollections for I remember my father ... as a tall strong man who held a small girl's hand tightly as they walked along the busy colliery streets (he retired sick just before his death at 53 years).
>
> On a ritual basis, both grandmothers, who live in Hepley, were visited daily according to my father's pit-shift pattern. My mother, older sister, and myself always accompanied my father on these visits, along with 'whatcher marra'. It was a strange phrase which I hardly hear now. But what did it mean when he exchanged it with all the men he met? Perhaps it was a secret sign similar to those used in Enid Blyton's Famous Five books. It certainly appeared to belong to men. I never heard a woman say it. My mother never used it, nor my sister, and I. It did not belong to aunts, shopkeepers, nor the people who lived in the nearby towns of Hartlepool and Sunderland. ...
>
> Perhaps it was used only by men who wore caps on their heads, or did it accompany men who drank beer in public houses named the 'North Eastern' or the 'Big Club'? Well, my dad drank beer and wore a brown checked cap but beer belonged to a Friday night only, as Saturday night drinking was not allowed because he had to attend chapel on Sundays.
>
> The phrase went with us everywhere. It went down to Hepley beach banks where wild flowers grew alongside stone coal-washed sand and a cold black sea. ... Payday and the Miners' Welfare Hall went hand in hand with 'whatcher marra'. The phrase accompanied men and their families everywhere within the community. It belonged to Hepley Colliery.
>
> In the 1950s Hepley Colliery was thriving, which meant, at that time, employing over 6,000 men. The community was tight-knit with all men closely linked through work at the colliery. The phrase 'whatcher marra', I discovered when I grew older, was a sign belonging to those who worked alongside one another down the pit. Other pitmen used it, those in Easington, Shotton and Blackhall, for all colliery villages were in walking distance from Hepley. It was a sign of friendship, comradeship, trust, strength and a way of saying 'what cheer friend' or 'hello friend' or 'hope you are keeping fine'. Indeed, it was a greeting used by the pitmen of the Northern coalfield.

Recollections and memories such as these, involving the discussion of a phrase that becomes the metonym for a wider culture, are anthropologised in ways that would not have been possible without the experience of the Human Sciences programme, and enabled Joyce to produce an excellent ethnography of the Durham coalfield in decline as her undergraduate dissertation. The dissertation focused on male and female roles and the domestic division of labour in a community formerly structured along rigidly segregated gender lines and powerfully underpinned by male occupational prowess and identity. The document she produced was not a history, psychology or sociology of the Durham coalfield, but an *anthropology* of it and, what is more, an anthropology in which a female participant-observer was placed at its centre.

The benefits that emerge from a pedagogic strategy of the kind we advocate are to be seen when it comes to questions of self-confidence, self-presentation and personal empowerment. All of these are extremely slippery outcomes to evaluate but are ones that must be taken up as part of our 'anthropology of anthropology', if for no other reason than that they are a source of fascination and reflection for people such as Joyce. She is interested in her self and her environment in ways that she sees as having been unimaginable before.

An Anthropology of Home?

Joyce's example is one of many that could have been identified to illustrate the way students combine perspectives gained from an anthropological 'world-view' with reflections on their own past. While we would argue for the value of such work and its justification in an anthropological context, we are also aware of a number of unresolved issues associated with encouraging reflexive research projects in anthropology courses.

Maurice Bloch (see Houtman 1988) has argued that social anthropologists should be wary of carrying out fieldwork in the West. He claims that, once it is established in a department, such research is likely to become all too popular because of its relative 'ease' of execution. While other social sciences customarily study Europe and the U.S., only anthropology makes a point of carrying out research within regions, such as Madagascar, that would otherwise be neglected. Finally, it is necessary, Bloch argues, for anthropologists to emphasise that the world is more surprising than economists, political scientists, philosophers or sociologists ever dreamed.

Bloch is absolutely correct to emphasise the value of anthropology's comparative dimension, and to note that anthropologists study the parts of human diversity that other scholars cannot reach. However, to argue that certain areas of the world have been 'covered' by other social scientists and therefore do not need to be studied by anthropologists is to surrender any idea of our discipline's uniqueness of approach and form of analysis. To make rigid distinctions between contexts of study may also be misleading in the context of a 'globalising' world. Ulin (1991) discusses the notion that the growing interest in European society as a place to conduct fieldwork should be understood as an outcome of the transformation of the world system of political economy since the Second World War. He agrees (1991: 8) that anthropology should not abandon its comparative mission, but adds that it is possible and necessary to conduct critical and reflexive work in Europe. Nor, we add, should we blindly adopt the assumption – common within sociology and economics – that 'the West' is a homogeneous cultural entity.

The kinds of project carried out by Queen's students may not constitute anthropological fieldwork as conceived of by Ingold or Bloch, but they do often study aspects of our society that might not otherwise be covered by any of the social sciences. Indeed, one of the spurs for Joyce to undertake the fieldwork she did was Bulmer's (1978) observation that the history of the Durham coalfield had been written from the perspective of men, but that a women's history had yet to be written. Such research need not be culturally monochrome but can include a comparative dimension by juxtaposing the student's data collection and analysis with ethnographic information drawn from elsewhere in the world.

Approaches such as these have the potential to confer pedagogical as well as broader intellectual benefits. Carrying out work on local communities is a powerful means of bringing home the truth of the maxim that the construction of the other is a political as well as an epistemological act (Fabian 1983). Bourdillon asks (1995: 23) how many of us would allow undergraduates into our own homes to allow them to write about our own way of life; in fact Queen's undergraduates often study their own lives as well as those close to them (although not, so far, the lives of their lecturers). Students often see the dangers of presenting cultures or groups of people as homogeneous or passive when they are asked to describe communities that they have lived in for many years – it is easy to refer to 'the Nuer' or 'the Germans' but less easy when one is referring to known individuals. Whisson (1986) refers to the well-known Turnerian notion of anthropology being about going to a far-off place in order to understand a familiar place better: here, we are describing a pedagogical strategy whereby students are encouraged to perceive and write about places that are familiar, but to do so through an anthropological lens that defamiliarises and even, to some extent, objectifies them. In this way, subject-object, participant-observer distinctions are blurred in a way that can be helpful if it serves to bring the techniques and worldview of anthropology to life.

Thus we return to the notion that anthropology can offer some important personal value-added perspectives over and above the acquisition of a degree. Some students claim that they can understand and explain personal experiences in ways that grant the possibility of self-directed change, and further that they can begin to place local circumstances in an explanatory context of global political and economic transformations. This latter point is all the more poignant when one considers the social and economic changes that many of our students have lived through. It is not that they might one day travel abroad in search of a 'field', but rather more likely that the so-called 'field' will come to them in the form of Fujitsu, Nissan or Komatsu, and a variety of other global concerns that have been keen (for the time being) to fill the vacuum left by the drastic contraction of local industry.

We do not pretend that the ideals of a reflexive teaching methodology always become reality. For every Joyce there is another student whose work remains anthropologically naïve, lapsing into self-indulgent description or folk psychoanalysis. Interesting though such works might be as genres of modern life, they show little evidence of the anthropological penny having dropped. Undoubtedly, some of the work is very bad for the reasons Ingold describes – theory and practice remain unintegrated and the demands of the exercise are simply beyond some students. However, the main point of the exercise is to produce a useful learning experience rather than a piece of publishable work. In the second year 'Methods and Analysis' module, in which key research project work takes place, students are indeed encouraged to reflect upon the failures inherent in their research work, rather than pretending that their work has been unproblematic. This exercise is crucial in getting students to realise that much of anthropology is about a practical craft and not about mystic revelation.

There is a rather worrying question concerning just what students do with their anthropological awareness. Some have reported that the taking of a degree in the Human Sciences and the personal changes that this precipitates have sometimes made them feel strangers in their own homes, unable to integrate themselves into former ways of life. Pelissier (1991) also talks of this issue in relation to education among minority and working-class communities in the U.S. She notes how, given the cultural incongruities that may be evident between home and school, students learn to be competent actors, adapting behaviour and language to relevant contexts in order not to appear out of place. A similar strategy is used by Queen's students where their degree work might rouse suspicion and even resentment among relatives and friends. One group of students told of how they described themselves to friends and relatives as 'going to college' rather than to university for the simple reason that the former suggests a familiar, vocational-type activity whereas the latter is seen as highbrow, élite, intellectual activity and smacks of people, particularly women, getting above their station. In another instance, a mature student had kept his student identity quiet for over a year before he decided 'to come out' to his friends.

Finally, there is a danger that conducting an anthropology of home is an open invitation for students to lapse into self-indulgence. Students might come away with the idea that they are justified in describing themselves and nothing more, without reference to a broader field of anthropological scholarship. Anthropology thus loses its centrifugal tendencies and becomes entirely centripetal: an applied problem-solver that can ensure the automatic validity of one's beliefs. Undoubtedly, for some students emic and etic frames of analysis are easily and dangerously confused, as in the case of one of our undergraduates who wanted to write a dissertation on space aliens – not the social and cultural phenomenon of current widespread interest and belief in aliens, but whether or not they actually existed!

Anthropologies: a Mixed Economy of Learning

When measuring the impact of anthropology on the wider world, we tend initially to think of such direct action as advocacy and participation in development projects. In practice, however, whilst relatively few anthropologists are involved directly with these activities, virtually all professional anthropologists are engaged in teaching of some sort. Day-to-day encounters with large classes of novice anthropologists have considerable potential to affect public and private lives, especially given that many students are actively seeking means of relating ethnographic knowledge to everyday existence. The majority of those whom we teach will never become professional anthropologists, and we surely need to think more seriously about how to enable them to apply the experience of taking a degree in anthropology to their future lives. While Queen's has had some very particular features (e.g. the age of its students combined with their relative rootedness in the local area, as well as distinctive assessment procedures and course delivery), in other respects it is the same as any other anthropology department in the country: its students wish to take a subject that involves personal engagement as well as academic interest, but they also wish to gain employment at the end of their degree.

We are not advocating that the teaching of anthropology should become a form of extended workshop on personal development and careers guidance, nor that anthropology should abandon its fundamental project of understanding ways of life for their own sake. We are saying, however, that we should be flexible enough as researchers and teachers to have multiple agendas. Our students will be facing a mixed economy of work as many of them leave the academy after their brief three-year apprenticeship in anthropology. As social scientists, we should be able to create a mixed economy of learning wherein multiple techniques and approaches to learning anthropology give insights into the various applications of the discipline beyond the spatial and temporal confines of higher education. Our models and practices of pedagogy can combine the study of anthropological classics, the writing of essays, and the assimilation of knowledge through texts about 'others' with forms of teaching and learning that encourage self-reflection and analysis through cross-cultural comparison. If project-work involves active engagement in learning the pitfalls and pleasures involved in constructing anthropological knowledge through fieldwork and analysis, such a situation should be seen as a vital pedagogical opportunity, not a time-consuming liability. It is essential that these pedagogical threads and their outcomes are woven into current efforts to construct an appropriate disciplinary representation of anthropology in higher education. Present circumstances should prompt us not into forcing anthropological ideas and practices into generic agendas, but into asserting the explicit value of the methodologies and worldviews that we can call our own.

Notes

1. At the time of writing there is a conflict ongoing between the QAA and the U.K. anthropological community concerning whether, for the purposes of subject review, anthropology is placed in the same unit as sociology. Anthropologists and sociologists feel unhappy about what they perceive as a bureaucratic decision which pays little heed to the actual content of either discipline (see Mills 2001 for background to this debate).
2. See Shore and Wright (1999) and responses by Mills (2000) and Richardson (2000); also see Strathern (2000).
3. Part of the assessment for the 'Methods and Analysis' is based on a research journal kept throughout the research project in which students record not only the events which occur in the running of the project but their reflections on them.

References

Antikainen, A., Houtsonen, J., Kauppila, J. and Huotelin, H. 1996. *Living in a Learning Society: Life Histories, Identities and Education.* London: Falmer Press.

Baba, M. 1994. 'The Fifth Sub-Discipline: Anthropological Practice and the Future of Anthropology', *Human Organisation* 53(2): 175–86.

Benn, R. and Fieldhouse, R. 1993. 'Government Policies on University Expansion and Wider Access, 1945–51 and 1985–91 Compared', *Studies in Higher Education* 18(3): 299–313.

Berger, P. and Berger, B. 1972. *Sociology: A Biographical Approach.* Harmondsworth: Penguin.

Beynon, H., Hudson, R. and Sadler, D. 1994. *A Place Called Teesside: A Locality in a Global Economy.* Edinburgh: Edinburgh University Press.

Bourdillon, M. 1995. 'Invasion of Privacy?', *Anthropology Today* 11(1): 23.

Bulmer, M. (ed.) 1978. *Mining and Social Change.* London: Croom Helm.

Carrithers, M.B. 1992. *Why Humans Have Cultures.* Oxford: Oxford University Press.

Coleman, S. and Simpson, B. 1999. 'Unintended Consequences? Anthropology, Pedagogy and Personhood', *Anthropology Today* 15(6): 3–6.

Coleman, S. and Simpson, B. 2001. 'Anthropology Inside Out: Identity and Agency in the (Re-) Production of a Discipline', *Anthropology in Action* 8(1): 1–5.

Dearing, R. 1997. *Higher Education in the Learning Society: The National Committee of Enquiry into Higher Education.* London: HMSO.

Epstein, A.C. 1967. *The Craft of Social Anthropology.* London: Tavistock.

Fabian, J. 1983. *Time and the Other: How Anthropology Makes its Object.* New York: Columbia University Press.

Gledhill, J. 2000. 'Finding a New Public Face for Anthropology', *Anthropology Today* 16(6): 1–3.

Houtman, G. 1988. 'Interview with Maurice Bloch', *Anthropology Today* 4(1): 18–21.

Husén, T. 1974. *The Learning Society.* London: Methuen.

Husén, T. 1986. *The Learning Society Revised.* Oxford: Pergamon Press.

Hyatt, S. 2001. '"Service Learning," Applied Anthropology and the Production of Neoliberal Citizens', *Anthropology in Action* 8(1): 6–15.

Ingold, T. 1989. 'Fieldwork in Undergraduate Anthropology: An Opposing View', *British Association for Social Anthropology in Policy and Practice (BASAPP)* 3: 2–3.

Institute of Manpower Studies. 1993. *Shortlisting the Best Graduates.* Brighton: Institute of Manpower Studies.

Lave, J. and Wenger, E. 1991. *Situated Learning: Legitimate Peripheral Participation.* Cambridge: Cambridge University Press.

Mascarenhas-Keyes, S. and Wright, S. 1995. *Report on Teaching and Learning Social Anthropology in the United Kingdom.* London: Anthropology Teaching and Learning Network.

Mills, D. 2001. '"We'll Show Them a Real Discipline", Anthropology, Sociology and the Politics of Academic Identity', *Anthropology in Action* 8(1): 34–41.

Mills, M. 1999. 'Audit Culture and Anthropology – Comment', *Journal of the Royal Anthropological Institute* 6(3): 521–23.

Pellissier, C. 1991. 'The Anthropology of Teaching and Learning', *Annual Review of Anthropology* 20: 75–95.

Peterson, M. 1991. 'Aliens, Ape-Men and Whacky Savages: The Anthropologist in the Tabloids', *Anthropology Today* 7(5): 4–7.

Pocock, D. 1975. *Understanding Social Anthropology.* London: Hodder & Stoughton.

Pocock, D. and MacClancy, J. 1999. *Understanding Social Anthropology* (revised edition). London: Athlone Press.

Quality Assurance Agency, 2000. *Handbook for Academic Review.* Gloucester: Quality Assurance Agency.

Ribbens, J. and Oxford Polytechnic Students, 1991. *The Personal and the Sociological: The Use of Student Autobiography in Teaching Undergraduate Sociology.* Oxford: Sociology Subject Committee, Oxford Polytechnic.

Richardson, P.D. 2000. 'Audit Culture and Anthropology – Comment'. *Journal of the Royal Anthropological Institute* 6(4): 721–22.

Sharma, U. 1991. 'Field Research in the Undergraduate Curriculum'. *British Association for Social Anthropology in Policy and Practice* 10: 8–10.

Shore, C. 1996. 'Anthropology's Identity Crisis: The Politics of Public Image', *Anthropology Today* 12(2): 2–5.

Shore, C. and Wright, S. 1999. 'Audit Culture and Anthropology: Neo-Liberalism in British Higher Education', *Journal of the Royal Anthropological Institute* 5(4): 557–75.

Simpson, B. 1997. 'Anthropology, Vocationalism and the Undergraduate Curriculum', *Anthropology in Action* 4(2): 23–5.

Strathern, M. (ed.) 2000. *Audit Cultures: Anthropological Studies in Accountability, Ethics and the Academy.* London: Routledge.

Thorn, R and Wright, S. 1990. 'Projects and Placements in Undergraduate Anthropology', *British Association for Social Anthropology in Policy and Practice* 7: 4–5.

Ulin, R. 1991. 'The Current Tide in American Europeanist Anthropology'. *Anthropology Today* 6(6): 8–12

Whisson, M., 1986. 'Why Study Anthropology?', *Anthropology Today* 2(1): 23–5.

Wright, S. and Sharma, U. 1989. 'Practical Relevance of Undergraduate Courses', *British Association for Social Anthropology in Policy and Practice (BASAPP)* 2: 7–8.

2

Politically Reflexive Practitioners

Susan Wright

The attempt to move from élite to mass higher education in Britain in the 1990s has been accompanied by two primary discourses about its aims and 'best practices'. One discourse comes from policy-makers who see the purpose of higher education as the production of 'flexible' workers who will perform well in the new post-Fordist organisation of work and in the global knowledge economy. The second discourse comes from educationalists concerned to improve student learning and the quality of teaching. Both emphasise 'reflection': sometimes they use 'reflection' interchangeably with 'reflexivity'.

I encountered these uses of 'reflection' and 'reflexivity' in the early 1990s when I approached my university's[1] educational developers for ideas to improve my course design and teaching. They were using terms which were central to my identity as an anthropologist. Since the 1970s, 'reflexivity' has been the focus of debates about the production of anthropological knowledge. Feminist anthropologists used the notion of 'reflexivity' to discuss how anthropological understanding was generated through fieldwork. Critical anthropologists (including feminists) reflexively examined how their own Western assumptions underpinned the construction of anthropological knowledge. Their aim was to expose and transform the political relations in which anthropology was located (Scholte 1969). Since the 1980s, with the literary turn, the focus has narrowed onto the narrative structures, tropes and problems of representation in ethnography – a stunted form of reflexivity which deflects attention from the political context in which anthropologists work (Nencel and Pels 1991: 19). Given the importance of debates about reflexivity in the politics of anthropological practice, how should I respond to educationalists' use of 'reflexivity'? With joy of recognition in a sea of otherwise unfathomable concepts? With caution and reserve until I had worked out what they were doing with 'my' term? Or, as I suggest here, with a 'discipline-specific' approach to educational development? In other words, I aimed to incorporate a specifically anthropological concept of 'reflexivity' into the design of an interdisciplinary course, with results that may make a contribution to educational development generally.

If 'reflexivity' has particular valency for an anthropologist, the new change-agents of higher education in Britain – the new professions of university managers, policy-makers and educational developers – also use other terms which generate a similar response of misrecognition amongst academics.[2] For example, the key instrument for transforming higher education – audit – has been framed in terms of 'quality'. Staff could never be opposed to 'quality' in their teaching, pastoral care or administration of students, but, more than this, 'quality' is a term over which staff themselves have a sense of pride and ownership. Yet by turning 'quality' into a tool of policy, the word acquires meanings and implications for our practices which run counter to our sense of professionalism. These meanings have not simply been imposed on us from 'outside' by the new managerialists; policy procedures have caused them to infiltrate our everyday practices. In the first round of Teaching Quality Assessment in Britain, the demand to demonstrate 'quality' was passed from government agency to university to quality control teams, and via heads of department to individual lecturers. It was the latter who disciplined themselves as the agents responsible for setting and achieving targets to demonstrate the quality of their teaching. Achievement of these targets in each department was audited by teams of peers from each subject drawn from other universities. The audit procedures collapsed distinctions between 'inside' and 'outside'. We were attracted by 'warm' words we hold dear, only to find that, through them, we became involved in auditing ourselves and implementing procedures which might have deleterious effects on our teaching and conditions of work (Shore and Wright 1999, 2000, 2001).

Alert to the way that 'weasel words' were playing a crucial role in the transformation of higher education institutions, I sought to try and work out what was happening to the meanings of 'reflection' and 'reflexivity' and how I would try and assert my own meanings, derived from critical anthropology, in the development of my own teaching. The first part of the chapter compares meanings of 'reflection' and 'reflexivity' in sociology-inspired educational literature and in anthropology. The second considers what I tried to convey to my students by 'reflexive learning' and what I learnt about my own practice in the process. In the third part of the paper I turn the phrase 'reflexive practitioner' away from students and back onto teachers. I consider how staff can use 'political reflexivity' to analyse the institutional and policy context and the myriad and fast-moving changes within which they are operating in order to work out how individually and collectively we might respond to changes in higher education in our own terms.

Educationalists' Concepts of Reflection

Many educationalists derive their interest in reflexivity from sociology, and notably the work of Giddens (1984, 1994) and Beck (1992, 1994). Although these authors sometimes write together, their ideas of reflexivity differ sharply from each other, as well as being different in important respects from those of anthropologists. To Giddens (1984), reflexivity is an important quality of the human actors who are under sociological study. He argues that actors can understand what they do as they do it, and they use this reflexive ability continually to monitor and adjust their behaviour in the flow of day-to-day activities. Their knowledgeability as agents takes two forms. First, their 'practical consciousness' enables actors to know how to 'go on', even if they may not be able to explain this knowledge as propositional beliefs or even give it 'direct discursive expression'. Second, Giddens argues that human actors also maintain a continually adjusted theoretical understanding or 'rationalisation' of the grounds for their activities, which they can explain. Actors are knowledgeable about the circumstances of their own actions, and their lay theories help constitute the institutions studied by social scientists. In time social scientists' theories seep back into the very events that they study and become entwined in lay peoples' everyday practices. Giddens calls this mutual interpretive interplay between social actors and social scientists a 'double hermeneutic'. In this sense sociology is a reflexive enterprise. While anthropologists might agree with this argument, where they would differ, as discussed below, is seeing social scientists themselves (and not just the objects of their study) as positioned actors, and using reflexive monitoring of their own practices as a crucial research tool.

For Giddens, reflexivity was an important route into his structuration theory. He argued that through reflexive monitoring of their social practices, actors drew on, changed and reproduced structured sets of rules and resources. His concern was to overcome the impasse of conceptualising society either as made up of autonomous subjects or as consisting of people who were objects of structural forces they could neither understand nor control. For Beck (1994), in contrast, it is a reified society that is regressive, rather than individuals. He argues that reflexivity is an important response to late modernity. To him, early forms of modernisation involved disembedding 'traditional' society and creating industrial social forms. Now, industrial side-effects (pollution, nuclear, chemical and genetic technologies, impoverishment) are breaking up the premises and contours of modern society. Modernity is disembedding modernity. Beck considers this transformation to be a creative process, out of which new social forms will emerge, but one which has been unnoticed by formal, democratic, institutional politics, and has happened without crises or political debate. He terms this initial transition to late modernity 'reflexive' in the sense of an unconscious reflex action. Only later does society, and its ability to deal with unpredictable threats and risks, become the subject of public, political, and scientific 'reflection' about itself (Beck 1994: 6). Scott, an educationalist writing in a similar vein, argues that modernisation of the early twentieth century had an 'other' in the form of 'traditional' society, which it was in the process of modernising. By the late twentieth century that process was complete – in Giddens' terms 'modernity destroys tradition' (1994: 91). Late modernity only has itself to interrogate and therefore becomes reflexive (Scott 1995: 116). Both Beck and Scott speak of 'society', as an entity and an actor, being reflective or reflexive about itself, examining its own radical transformation and its ability to respond to the risks of late modernity.[3]

Barnett, another educationalist, also argues that reflection and reflexivity (he uses the two interchangeably) are important to cope with late modernity. Like Giddens, he sees reflexivity as a quality of individuals, not of society, but unlike Giddens, he is not concerned about the interplay between individual actors, social systems and structures. For Barnett, the aim of education is 'self-realisation' of students as autonomous individuals. Barnett describes a world where distant events impact on a locality unpredictably, where traditions have lost their authenticity, and where abstract and expert knowledge, which has replaced tradition, also puts people at risk. In this world, he argues, people only survive by questioning fundamental categories of knowing and action, including their own. Such questioning produces the potential for radical new orderings, new insights, new sources of action and knowledge (Barnett 1997: 92).

Such 'critical self-reflection' is the third and most important ingredient (along with critical thought and critical action) in producing 'critical beings' which, Barnett argues, is the true purpose of higher education. In his view, the modern world needs higher education to be 'an emancipatory process in which students, by means of their own powers of self-reflection through their lifespan, come increasingly into themselves, maintaining their critical distance from the world around them while acting purposively in it' (1997: 101). 'Coming into themselves' or 'self-realisation' is central to Barnett's idea of critical reflection. He is arguing for education to regain its earlier liberal agenda of personal development of the individual. Of the eight forms of reflection that Barnett outlines,[4] three especially contribute to this 'self-realisation': individualistic pursuit of one's own projects as a route to 'self-discovery'; disturbance and interrogation of one's taken-for-granted thinking, to identify ideological delusions, to reach for profoundly new interpretations and to transform the self; and awareness that the educational principles instilled in individuals (a concern for truth, a search for precision in communication, scrupulousness in analysis, ability to see from a range of viewpoints) are the basis of liberal human values of tolerance, wisdom and reasonableness. Ultimately, 'reflection...looks to the formation of at least a stratum of society that understands itself as embodying these human qualities' (1997: 96).

Barnett feels that his ideal 'critical' questioning of established ways of ordering, knowing and acting is rarely achieved. He argues 'although the banner of critical thinking flies over the university' (1997: 93), higher education has sold it short. Universities have succumbed to 'the big battalions in the wider society' (1997: 93) that do not want 'critical' reflection which 'goes beneath surface reality'. They want 'instrumental' reflection which takes the form of self-monitoring and merely fulfils the demand of the modern world for flexibility and adaptability. Self-monitoring makes people effective in a world of unforeseeable change by knowing when to jettison a taken-for-granted world-view and take on another. These qualities, he argues, far from the ideal of 'criticality', meet the goals of economic competitiveness, organisational efficiency and institutional responsiveness. On the surface, by taking on 'reflection', higher education appears to be fulfilling its 'own deep agendas of personal development, enlightenment, empowerment and emancipation' (1997: 92), but, he argues, this merely masks the real intent of 'a social project' which 'is being driven by an agenda of instrumental reason' (1997: 91). To Barnett, 'reflection', as found currently in higher education, is 'a wolf in sheep's clothing' (1997: 92).

Although I endorse Barnett's ideas of criticality in principle, it may not just be the rather vague 'battalions' that are impeding their achievement. There seem to be two problems inherent in Barnett's own concept. First, it is difficult to see how the aim of creating a stratum of society whose identity is based on endorsement of liberal human values of tolerance, wisdom and reasonableness is compatible with continual questioning of established ways of ordering, knowing and acting. Barnett does not explore this contradiction. The liberal autonomous individual is a stable centre from which Barnett views the world, but which is not itself explored. Similarly, Beck treats society as a given category. Giddens (1984) explores the interplay between individual actors and social structures, for methodological reasons 'bracketing' one whilst focusing on the other, without exploring the conceptualisation of either. Anthropological reflexivity would aim, in contrast, to critique received categories such as individual and society.

Second, and most important for the argument developed in this chapter, Barnett's approach to reflection focuses on the interior of the self. To him, education is a process of introspective dialogue with oneself, in pursuit of 'self-realisation'. In his list of eight forms of reflection, Barnett does include four related to 'the world'. Three of these he describes as more 'instrumental' than 'critical'. The fourth, 'reflection on social formation', for example through community-based learning, involves students' dealing with the 'inner disturbance' caused by their entering the language and perspectives of people they encounter in unfamiliar social interactions. This is an example of how, in his attempts to move the focus outside the ambit of the self, Barnett treats 'the world' as a resource for new ways of reflecting critically on the self. I will distinguish this latter, very self-centred, introspective idea of 'reflection' from an anthropological notion of 'political reflexivity'.

Anthropological Ideas of Reflexivity

The derivation of reflexivity in anthropology is very different. In the 1970s, a reflexive approach to fieldwork became one where the anthropologist uses the self as an instrument for research, with the aim of understanding more, not simply about themselves, but about the society under study. If the aim of fieldwork is 'the careful eliciting of unfamiliar rationalities' (Hastrup 1987) and the exploration of how they 'work' in the construction of persons, social relations and institutions, then the generation of data is through the field-worker as a positioned actor within the society, interacting, building relationships and experiencing social events. Anthropologists use a diary to reflect on their responses to observations and encounters in the field, and on the way those responses seem to be perceived by those with whom they are working. Through this daily discipline, anthropologists hope to identify their own taken-for-granted assumptions, in contrast to those of the society they are studying. This is not just a private exercise. Nor is it a descent into ever-more exquisite self-consciousness (Strathern 1987). The anthropologist's own cultural assumptions and disciplinary concepts and procedures are not just exposed to her or himself. The anthropologist's behaviour and questions are 'read' and commented upon by the people in the field of study and are a basis for eliciting comparisons. Unexpected comments or events may 'surprise' either side (Willis 1997: 190) and confound the anthropologist's assumptions and theoretical starting positions. Such surprises open up space not only for indigenous exegesis but for cross-cultural discussions in which 'informants' may quiz the anthropologist as much as the other way round. Each side is only understanding the 'other' by bending the gaze of the other back on the self and considering reflexively their own taken-for-granted cultural logics. When studying 'at home' this kind of reflexivity places the anthropologist at 'the explosive centre of a semiotic paradox' – the more you think you know, the less perceptive you are (Hastrup 1987).

Feminist and other anthropologists who engaged in reflexive fieldwork in the 1970s were often called narcissistic. In the Greek myth, Narcissus was reflective not reflexive (Disalvo 1980). He fell in love with the flattering reflection of an idealised and grandiose self-image in the pool of his own imagination. He only had a relationship with himself, not with any outer world. Unlike the anthropologist, Narcissus had no 'other' to mediate his relationship with himself. In contrast, the anthropologist first tries to create sufficient distance from the personal 'I' to regard the social 'me' as an object and reflect on his or her own behaviour and reactions. Second, the fieldworker perceives the self as an object in the discourse of others. How are they regarding your behaviour and attitudes, what does this reveal about their categories and concepts, and what, in contrast, does it reveal about your own? This 'bending back' upon oneself of the gazes, both of the distanced self and of others, in order to expose the interaction between your and their rationalities and interpretive processes, is the hallmark of reflexive fieldwork (Babcock 1980).

Central to the idea of reflexivity in fieldwork is to see the anthropologist as a positioned actor. Interactions in the field are not just between personalities but between social persons carrying cultural histories and engaged in power relations (Okely 1994, 1996). Indigenous understandings of international history and of current world order may place the researcher in the category of imperialist or oppressor – a classification which may be confirmed or confounded by the power relations surrounding the specific fieldwork encounter. Local gender, kinship, social and symbolic classifications will also be stretched to locate the fieldworker in some way. Yet none of these positions need be fixed: the point of reflexive analysis is to be able to negotiate continually that positioning and to use oneself to reveal how boundaries and hierarchies operate (Fernandez 1983: 324, Okely 1992). Thus reflexivity is inherently political. Unlike Barnett's instrumental idea of reflection which makes the individual into a self-monitoring agent fulfilling the demands of the economic and political order, 'political reflexivity' aims to make the anthropologist an analyst of that order, and able to work out how to act upon it. It was this kind of 'political reflexivity' that I sought to engender in my students. By this I mean an ability to analyse daily encounters, their reactions to them, and signs of how other actors seemed to expect them to act, in order to uncover the detailed ways in which boundaries, hierarchies and power relations operated in the institution in which their learning was taking place. I aimed for them to perceive how they were positioned within the daily processes of this institution, and for them to be able to use this knowledge actively: if this positioning was constraining their ability to learn, how could they use their knowledge to negotiate a more conducive environment?

Reflexive Learning

In the mid-1990s I was given responsibility for designing a new interdisciplinary one-term, undergraduate course which had been given the title 'Independent Study'. The idea was that it would give final-year students an opportunity to initiate their own project, which could include library-based or empirical research for a dissertation, a placement in an organisation, a report, a film, or any combination of these. This was the first time I had been allocated work-time to research course design and engage in the 'scholarship of teaching' (Boyer 1990, Healey 2000). I contacted other universities with Independent Study courses. With the help of the university's staff development officers, I delved into the education literature (e.g., Brown and Pendlebury 1992; Graves 1993; Marshall and Rowland 1993; Murray and Gore 1994). I engaged in the task as if it were a piece of anthropological research, approaching the somewhat familiar environment of higher education as a strange world of educational concepts and institutional systems. This account is based on 'fieldnotes' I made throughout the project in all my encounters with students and staff as course convenor for the first two years.[5]

Whilst the course I designed was based on a lot of borrowing of good ideas from elsewhere, its original contribution was the way I clarified the sometimes vague concepts of 'independent' and 'reflexive' learning and worked out how to turn them into practice. Independent, I took to mean self-initiated and negotiated study. If students were to exercise initiative and generate their own project, they needed to have the security of working in a clear structure. I asked them to produce a project proposal during the preceding term, using a set of headings. These included a description of the issue they wanted to explore (substantive objectives); a statement about the academic abilities and practical skills they would acquire in the process (learning objectives); an indication of the concepts and theories, from more than one discipline, that the project would explore, supported by a preliminary bibliography; methodology; plan of work; resource implications; working arrangements with an organisation if relevant; and proposed products for assessment. One of the meanings of 'negotiated study' was that students were responsible for finding a member of staff willing to tutor them, and to discuss their draft proposal with them. They then discussed the proposal with me as course convenor. Once all three of us were satisfied that the project was viable and sound, the proposal was signed. The proposal was a version of a 'learning contract' (Baume 1991; Brown and Baume 1992; Stephenson and Laycock 1993).

One of the issues for students to negotiate was the assessment. The assessment was in two parts. Eighty percent of the available marks were for the 'products' of the project, which should total a maximum of eight thousand words. Students could divide the weighting and words between a number of products on the ratio of 10 percent for one thousand words. They might wish to devote all 80 percent to one eight thousand word dissertation; or they might wish to divide the 80 percent between a report for an organisation (say 50 percent, i.e., five thousand words) and a reflective essay (30 percent, three thousand words). If they produced a film, made an audio-visual presentation or gave a lecture, which carried, say, 40 percent of the marks, that would leave another 40 percent, therefore four thousand words, for a piece of written work. The most important issue was that there should be congruence between the work involved in the project and the assessment, both in terms of the kind of products and the weighting between them. The course booklet contained a statement of the criteria that would be used to assess their work and students were encouraged to identify how, between all their pieces of work, they would cover all the criteria. Students said these negotiations over the congruence of and criteria for their assessment increased their awareness of what they were aiming to achieve both substantively and in terms of their learning objectives.

The other 20 percent of available marks were allocated to a dossier of learning. This was one of several new forms of writing being tried by anthropologists at the time (Crème 1999). The dossier was intended to encourage students first of all to reflect on their own process of learning. The educational literature on 'reflective learning' argues that students learn most effectively if they plan their work, begin to carry it out, periodically take stock of their progress, plan the next phase, carry it out, then reassess again. Such an approach is based on versions of Kolbs's learning circle. The dossier of learning was both a tool for and a record of reflective learning. The first item in the dossier would be the project proposal. I encouraged students, with their tutor, to look back periodically at the proposal, discover that the work was maybe taking them in an unpredicted direction, assess whether this was appropriate, and record the reasons, before planning the next steps. More importantly, I emphasised that although the project proposal contained a preliminary statement of substantive and learning objectives, I expected these to be refined, radically changed, or even only become really clear as the project progressed. Each of these periodic reviews resulted in a note in their dossier which revised and updated the original proposal. Apart from these formal documents, some students kept diaries. Some students included documents that recorded important stages in their work. For example, an organisation tried to cancel one student's placement at the last moment. Copies of all the faxes involved in renegotiating access, with a commentary on the negotiation strategy, went into the learning dossier. The dossiers ended with a short essay reflecting on the academic and practical (organisational, presentational) learning objectives the student had set him or herself, how they had been attained, or how others had emerged in the process of doing the work.

The impetus to develop a 'reflexive' approach to their learning came from a support group which I convened for the students to share experiences. Initially students used it as a forum for swapping skills. For example, one nervous student set herself the challenging task of learning how to give a lecture to her peers on her chosen topic, nineteenth-century representations of the rural poor. Another student had vast experience of audio-visual presentations from her previous employment, and tutored her. The support group also became an effective forum for generating the critical distance needed for students to become aware of their learning processes. Often students said they had not had the words to express their learning experiences in their diary, until they found a way to explain them to their peers. For example, one student, who was analysing fairy tales from the perspectives of three disciplines, explained how in other courses she had just stood inside her own discipline and borrowed ideas and concepts from other subjects. Now for the first time she had got inside the logic and premises of different disciplines. She understood the incompatibility of their approaches and out of that creative conflict, explained how she was developing her own analysis. First in discussion, and then in her diary, she 'bent back' her gaze on her own experience and identified how disciplinary concepts and boundaries worked.

A further dimension of 'reflexivity' derived from discussing what was involved in 'negotiated' learning. One of the most important issues that emerged was the level of courage needed by students, not just to negotiate with outside organisations, but with even the most friendly staff members. It was through these discussions that 'reflexive learning' began to mean not just introspection about how their experiences were disturbing assumptions and causing them to think in new ways (similar to Barnett's idea of critical reflection). More than this, students began to develop 'political reflexivity' by examining the environment in which they were learning and especially the power relations involved. Each student experienced this in a different way. Some students who were doing placements quickly found that despite formal agreement, their presence in the host organisation was provoking sensitivities which affected their access or ability to do their project. We explored how the way they were inserted into the organisation, the identity of their sponsor, or even the topic of their study was inadvertently exposing how the organisation worked – its boundaries, hierarchies and relations of power – and used this information to renegotiate their positioning. Many students had occasion to explore the power relations surrounding their own process of learning within the university. For example, one student whose project had been inspired by a second-year course, offered to present the results of her work in the form of one in a series of 'guest lectures' for that course. This would be one of her items for assessment. She had in mind a date when she would be ready to give such a lecture. The course organiser received her idea with great enthusiasm but 'suggested' a much earlier date for the presentation. The student accepted this as unalterable; but then came to me in panic as she would not have completed the work in time for the earlier date. She had to be supported to return to the course organiser with her well-argued case for an alternative arrangement. The member of staff later said to me, with a wide grin, 'I wanted her to do one thing, and she wanted to do something else, and she won'. He then added, 'that's fair enough, that's how it should be'. He was pleased with the interaction with the student, a little surprised, and very impressed. I do not think he realised how much courage and planning had gone into the interaction on her part. She however, identified this as one of the major learning outcomes: she had found out enough about how the organisation worked and what administrative and curriculum considerations would be shaping the course organiser's thinking, in order to work out where room for flexibility existed and how to influence him successfully.

Here was a major learning outcome for me. This and other examples revealed to me the surprising degree to which students who have carefully thought out the best ways of achieving their learning needs can be deflected by staff in well-intentioned, friendly and subtle ways. The extent of students' perception of disempowerment only became evident when, after overcoming a fear that they would be perceived as confrontational and after successfully finding a way to negotiate, students' confidence was visibly enhanced. These examples also made me realise that when students have accepted that they have the right and ability to negotiate, they enable staff (me included) to see the subtle ways some of our well-intentioned interactions and embedded practices may disempower. I had suggested to them that independent and reflexive learning meant 'being in the driving seat of your own learning'. I had not anticipated the way I would have to draw on anthropological fieldwork skills to help them read from interactions and encounters the ways in which interpersonal and institutional forms of power operated in the university, and through such 'political reflexivity' work out ways in which they could negotiate successfully to pursue their own well-considered learning processes.

Academics as Reflexive Practitioners

During fieldwork we usually analyse reflexively what our own positioning and actions reveal about social processes in order to dampen down our impact on the fieldwork situation. At home, in our own higher education institutions and policy field, we can use reflexive analysis with the aim of maximising change. The kind of reflexive analysis developed by students in independent study enabled them to gain an insight into their learning environment and act upon it. Academics, similarly, could use reflexivity to analyse their positioning within a policy field, better understand the emergent power relations in the new higher education, and work out how to negotiate with, and act on, their fast-changing conditions of work.

However, this has been anthropology's reflexive blind spot. Anthropologists have rarely brought their reflexive fieldwork techniques to bear on the conditions of production of their own discipline, and especially on their teaching and its institutional context (exceptions are Lather 1984, Strathern 2000). Anthropology is not alone in this, as testified by the difficulty that staff from a variety of disciplines experienced in considering, in a reflexive mode, the politics of their interactions with Independent Studies students. In the 1980s and 1990s anthropologists shifted their focus away from reflexivity in fieldwork and towards self-questioning the construction of academic texts. Other disciplines in the social sciences and humanities became similarly transfixed with the reflexive production and reading of texts. *Writing Culture* (Clifford and Marcus 1986) deflected attention from teaching culture. Hopper (1995) argues that through this period, academic culture remained blissfully unaware of its own construction. He argues that instead of focusing on reflexivity at the level of individual texts, academics should turn their attention to the conceptual frames and social and cultural processes that shape university culture. This includes the processes of construction of academic knowledge through teaching and research, the formal and informal arrangements of universities, and the external policies and funding of universities. In a way similar to that argued here, Hopper, a social theorist, says we should each use our own subject's tools and resources to analyse and reflect on our own discipline. He recommends reflexivity as an intersubjective, social, and political project to be carried out both at the personal and textual level and the institutional and collective one.

In order to engage in such a project, academics would have to see themselves as just one category of actors in the higher education policy field,[6] contesting amongst themselves and against others the meaning and purposes of education. We will have to be self-critical about the way we deploy key words such as reflexivity, and with what effects, as against the ways other actors in the field – educationalists, university administrators and policy-makers – use the term, maybe with different intentions and effects. Nor is there a neat symmetry between categories of actors and their uses of key terms. One actor can move through different uses of reflection and reflexivity within one statement or text. For example, 'reflection' features strongly in the Department for Education and Employment's Enterprise in Higher Education programme that supported my development of the Independent Studies course. This programme funded semi-autonomous projects in a number of universities which resourced staff and students to develop new forms of teaching and learning. Rather than being overtly directive, Enterprise in Higher Education purported to 'go with the grain' of staff and student interests, and hoped that some of the resulting work would concern students' development of the skills needed for a 'flexible' work-force and staff's development of an institutional culture able to cope with change.

The Enterprise in Higher Education summary report *Mastering Change* moves through a number of uses of 'reflection'. First it converts Barnett's concept of 'critical reflection' into an instrument for managing change in universities.

> Reflection is far from instinctive. It needs to be forced in every way possible. It must be built into agendas and required in reports....The personal habit of critical reflection is essential. It is the basic building block of an institution which is able and willing to respond appropriately to changing needs. This is because personal change is at the root of all organisational change (DfEE 1997: 36).

The report argues that the main method for 'forcing' organisational change ('forcing' in the sense of accelerated plant growth rather than coercion through sanctions or violence?) is by building the 'personal habit of critical reflection' into daily structures and activities. The report asks, 'In the world of education, where the language of lifelong learning is common currency, how many teaching staff write a personal learning log, setting aside regular time for reflection?' (DfEE 1997: 38). Its method for encouraging critical reflection among staff is similar to that proposed for staff development by Brookfield (1995) and to the one I encouraged as a process of learning among my students. In designing the Independent Study course, it was important to consider how the meaning of a learning log alters if it is no longer a personal or research diary and if it becomes an item for assessment, but the report does not consider how a 'personal learning log' is transformed once it becomes a tool for management.

Second, the above quotation from the report implies that reflection is a process of introspection resulting in personal change and, simplistically, that the sum of such individual changes will result in organisational change in the direction desired by management. Later, the report takes a different stance. It recognises that allocating regular time for reflection may give staff the space to analyse and act on their circumstances, with no guarantee that their actions would be in the direction sought by DfEE:

> The habit of reflection … is the best way to make the most of changing circumstances and the best way to be prepared for the future. Reflection is the basis of self-aware-ness and can also help identify unseen opportunities. It can make the difference between acting as a victim and choosing a proactive response' (DfEE 1997: 39).

This second view echoes the approach I adopted with Independent Study students to analyse and act upon the conditions of their learning. Such a reflexive approach may also enable staff to analyse how their conditions of work are affecting their teaching practices and professionalism.

Schön (1987), concerned with the training of professionals, argues that their hallmark is that they are 'reflective practitioners'. Barnett (1992: chapter 11) argues that Schön's work is relevant not just for training professional practi-tioners such as lawyers, engineers and architects, but for any form of learning: it is also relevant for the education of higher education teachers. Schön argues that, contrary to the assumptions of technical rationality which underpin the modern university, professionals do not draw on a store of professional knowledge to apply rules instrumentally to types of situations. Real-world problems present themselves as messy and indeterminate, and professionals first engage in a discipline-specific process of naming and framing the prob-lem. Second, they deploy 'artistry' in handling uncertainty, uniqueness and conflict. This artistry has two facets. First, 'knowing in action' is a competence like recognising a face in a crowd, riding a bicycle, or catching a ball. These skilful judgements, performances and actions are undertaken spontaneously without antecedent reasoning and without being able to state afterwards the rules or procedures that have been followed. A *post hoc* explanation would probably be inaccurate, and if it were followed as a blueprint, would get a pupil into difficulties. It is even more difficult to render an account of the sec-ond facet, 'reflection in action'. This is occasioned by a surprise problem that does not fit the categories of 'knowing in action' and pushes the practitioner beyond established rules, facts, theories and operations. The practitioner reflects in the midst of an action in order to make corrective interventions and adjustments that reshape what he or she is doing without interruption. The practitioner responds to the unexpected or anomalous by restructuring strate-gies of action, theories of phenomena, and ways of framing the problem, and then makes on-the-spot experiments that put new understandings to the test.

Schön's account rings true as a description of processes of teaching in higher education, albeit one which, pleasingly, does not over-simplify the complexities of professional encounters. There are two ways in which Schön's account of *reflective* practitioners falls short of the *politically reflexive* approach advanced here. First, a politically reflexive practitioner would seek to interrogate his or her own professional practices and generate a language for analysing their underlying concepts and assumptions. Schön seems to think that this is impossible. Second, the surprises Schön describes are merely slight changes among the clients; the institutional environment of Schön's practitioners is a stable 'given', organised in terms of characteristic units of activity, familiar practice situations, a common body of professional knowledge and an uncontested value system. In contrast, a teacher who is a reflexive practitioner in higher education would be forced by the speed of changes, to problematise the institutional environment, and question how national policies, the university's procedures, classroom interactions and their own values interact in ever-changing ways in the processes of teaching and learning in which they are involved.

Conclusion

Many educationalists, sociologists and anthropologists are concerned with how to equip students to analyse and make interventions in a supercomplex and fast-changing world. Strathern (2001) has argued that anthropology's holistic approach to data and its focus on real-world exemplars increases the possibilities of tracing the supercomplex network of interacting factors, intersecting knowledges and unpredictable flows of events that characterise the modern world. I suggest that another anthropological concept, 'reflexivity' can be applied to this pedagogic challenge to help students understand and act upon the political order of which they are a part. In addition, a politically reflexive approach gives academics themselves the potential to grasp and act upon the supercomplexity of interacting factors in higher education.

Within the policy field of higher education, multiple meanings of reflection and reflexivity are in play. Much of the literature on students' learning draws on Kolb's learning circle which gives importance to periodic reflection in the sense of taking stock. Schön's reflective practitioners incorporate reflection into their professional actions without pause, as part of what he calls their artistry, their ability to adjust to problems that do not fit expectations and established theories and practices. Barnett has an even 'deeper' meaning of reflection, which involves scrutinising the disciplinary concepts and personal assumptions that frame one's thinking, in order to unsettle and radically reform established ways of ordering, knowing and acting. This is exemplified by the Independent Studies student who realised how disciplinary knowledge and boundaries operated and how she could work across them in a new way.

These approaches to reflection are limited by their attempts to hold something stable in a fast-changing and supercomplex world. Schön's individual is adaptive to new problems but within a stable environment of professional practice. In higher education, in contrast, the institutional and policy environment, and very notions of professionalism are in turmoil. Barnett's stable centre is the liberal autonomous individual, who engages in introspective dialogue in pursuit of self-realisation. For Beck, on whose work Scott and other writers on higher education draw, it is society that is the given category that reflects upon itself. In contrast, anthropology examines how both persons and social relations are constituted by ever-changing cultural rationalities and power-relations. Reflexivity, as a fieldwork technique, is concerned to use scrutiny of the self as a historically and socially positioned actor interacting with others in the field, to reveal how social categories, boundaries, hierarchies and institutions work. This reflexive analysis is used immediately to negotiate one's positioning in the field, and in the longer term to try to develop new relations of knowledge production in anthropology. In the Independent Study course, students gained some experience of political reflexivity in order to analysis their learning environment and work out how to negotiate with and act upon it in pursuit of their learning aims. If anthropologists, in their role as staff in higher education institutions, similarly turned their political reflexivity back on themselves and applied their fieldwork skills to analyse and act upon their own conditions of work, Schön's reflective practitioners might be transformed into politically reflexive practitioners. However, political reflexivity, derived from feminist fieldwork and critical anthropology, is in danger of being lost in the aftermath of the literary turn. Despite their subtitle, Clifford and Marcus have been far more successful in developing the poetics than the politics of anthropology.

Shore and I have argued (1999) that a political reflexivity of higher education involves first the critique of key terms in educationalist and policy discourses and a discussion amongst ourselves about what we mean by them. In this chapter I have distinguished the meanings of reflection advanced by different actors in the higher education field, and suggested a distinctive meaning of 'political reflexivity' which I incorporated into pedagogic practice. There are many other words, such as quality and accountability, which are key to current changes in higher education policy and practice and which are candidates for similar treatment. Second, political reflexivity provides a method for analysing the ways these terms work and, as suggested in the DfEE document above, for finding and using the available spaces for being proactive – and optimally for 'regulatory capture'. This would involve using ourselves as research tools and analysing our own experience reflexively to understand our fast-changing conditions of work and to be proactive in changing them. Can anthropologists use political reflexivity to create the space to work out how changes in higher education are affecting our teaching, and instead of being drawn in by policy-makers' use of attractive warm words, work out what we want our key concepts to mean and how we will convey those meanings through our teaching practices? To do so we have to overcome anthropology's blind spot and bring the reflexivity of fieldwork to bear critically on our teaching.

Acknowledgements

I am grateful to Professor Marilyn Strathern for an early discussion of the ideas that have been developed in this chapter, and especially for the insight about how policy-makers feed back to us warm words we hold dear. An earlier version of this chapter was presented as the keynote paper to the National Network for Teaching and Learning Anthropology's annual conference 'Anthropological Reflections on Pedagogic Culture and its Institutional Organisation', held at the University of Sussex, 14–15 November 1997. Participants at that conference provided much helpful feedback. I wish to thank Dr Stella Mascarenhas-Keyes, Dr Phyllis Crème, Dr David Mills, Professor Julie Marcus and Professor David Jary for their comments on drafts of this chapter.

Notes

1. I was then a Lecturer in Anthropology a British university.
2. Bourdieu's 'misrecognition' is an apt term for the process: 'political strategies for mobilisation can be effective only if the values they pursue or propose are presented in the misrecognisable guise of the values in which the group recognises itself' (1977: 22).
3. This language seems strange to an anthropologist. Not only does it make modernity a social entity and an actor, it turns the heuristic contrast between modern and traditional into two real social formations, it suggests that living in the late-modern world is a uniform experience, and it suggests that previously people lived by fixed traditions which provided unchanging norms. Giddens for example equates tradition with nature, as both 'lie undisturbed, created independently of human activity' and 'remain outside the scope of human intervention' (1994: 76–7).
4. Barnett's (1997) eight forms of reflection are:

   Reflection on disciplinary competence: an inner dialogue with the rules and voices of the discipline, until the student comes to see the world through a particular set of cognitive spectacles.
   Educational reflection: a concern for truth, a search for precision in communication, scrupulousness in analysis, ability to see from a range of viewpoints, and awareness that these are the basis of liberal human values of tolerance, wisdom and reasonableness.
   Critical reflection: students will resist the pain of divesting old conceptions of the self and freeing ourselves from ideological delusion, but this is the route to emancipation, transformation, liberation.
   Reflection as metacompetence: self-reflection as a transferable skill. The ability to read situations and call forth appropriate competences in order to respond efficiently to instrumental agendas.
   Reflective practitioner: Schön's idea that professionals first evaluate which response to choose from myriad possibilities, and then through 'reflection in action' continually interrogate and imaginatively reconstruct their actions as they are unfolding. Barnett (1992: 185) argues these attributes are relevant for all forms of HE not just professional education.
   Reflection as self-realisation: individualistic pursuit of one's own projects as a route to self-discovery.
   Reflection as social formation: self-realisation cannot be achieved in isolation but has to draw on others. Through community learning or study service, students

enter the language and perspectives of those they encounter, experience inner disturbance caused by unfamiliar social interactions, and engage in self-reflection 'of a demanding kind'.

Societal reflection: as in policy studies, an attempt to develop strategic thinking oriented to purposive interventions, but in the process, the world is objectified as a stage for action and 'self-reflection becomes a mere self-monitoring'.

5. There were five students in the first cohort and thirty students in the second.
6. For discussion of policy as a field of anthropological research see Shore and Wright (1997).

References

Babcock, B. 1980. 'Reflexivity: definitions and discriminations', *Semiotica* 30(1–2): 1–14.

Barnett, R. 1992. *Improving Higher Education. Total Quality Care.* Milton Keynes: Open University Press/Society for Research into Higher Education.

Barnett, R. 1997. *Higher Education: A Critical Business.* Milton Keynes: Open University Press/Society for Research into Higher Education.

Baume, D. 1991. 'Learning Contracts in Use. An Example from the Diploma in Higher Education by Independent Study in the School for Independent Study, Polytechnic of East London'. *The Cambridge Forum – Reclaiming Higher Ground*, 13 August.

Beck, U. 1992. *Risk Society: Towards a New Modernity.* London: Sage.

Beck, U. 1994. 'The Reinvention of Politics: Towards a Theory of Reflexive Modernisation', *Reflexive Modernization: Politics, Tradition and Aesthetics in the Modern Social Order.* In eds. U. Beck, A. Giddens and S. Lash. Cambridge: Polity Press.

Brookfield, S. 1995. 'Changing the Culture of Scholarship to the Culture of Teaching. An American Perspective'. In *The Changing University?*, ed. T. Schuller, Buckingham: Society for Research in Higher Education and Open University Press.

Bourdieu, P. 1977. *Outline of a Theory of Practice.* Cambridge: Cambridge University Press.

Boyer, E. 1990. *Scholarship Revisited.* Princeton, NJ: Carnegie Foundation for the Advancement of Teaching.

Brown, G. and Pendlebury, M. 1992. 'Assessing Active Learning'. *Effective Learning and Teaching in Higher Education,* Module II, Part 2. Sheffield: CVCP.

Brown, S. and Baume, D. 1992. *Learning Contracts, Volume 1, A Theoretical Perspective.* Birmingham: Standing Conference on Educational Development (SCED) Occasional Paper no.71.

Clifford, J. and Marcus, G. (eds) 1986. *Writing Culture: The Poetics and Politics of Ethnography.* Berkeley: University of California Press.

Crème, P. 1999. 'A View from the Outside: New Student Writing in Social Anthropology'. Occasional Paper No. 3, Birmingham: National Network for Teaching and Learning Anthropology.

Department for Education and Employment 1997. *Mastering Change. Learning the Lessons of the Enterprise in Higher Education Initiative.* Sheffield: DfEE. Higher Education and Employment Division.

Disalvo, M. 1980. 'The Myth of Narcissus', *Semiotica* 30(1–2): 15–25.

Fernandez, J. 1983. 'Afterword: At the Centre of the Human Condition', *Semiotica* 46(2–3): 323–30.

Giddens, A. 1984. *The Constitution of Society.* Cambridge: Polity Press.

Giddens, A. 1994. 'Living in a Post-traditional Society', in *Reflexive Modernization: Politics, Tradition and Aesthetics in the Modern Social Order,* eds. U. Beck, A. Giddens and S. Lash. Cambridge: Polity Press.

Graves, N. (ed.) 1993. *Learner Managed Learning. Practice, Theory and Policy.* Leeds Metropolitan University: Higher Education for Capability.

Hastrup, K. 1987. 'Fieldwork among Friends: Ethnographic Exchange within the Northern Civilisation', in *Anthropology at Home*, ed. A. Jackson. London: Tavistock.

Healey, M. 2000. 'Developing the Scholarship of Teaching in Higher Education: A Discipline-based Approach', *Higher Education Research and Development* 19(2): 169–89.

Hopper, S. 1995. 'Reflexivity in Academic Culture', in *Theorising Culture*, eds B. Adam and S. Allan. London: University College London Press.

Lather, P. 1984. 'Critical Theory, Curricular Transformation and Feminist Mainstreaming', *Journal of Education* 166: 49–62.

Marshall, L. and Rowland, F. 1993. *A Guide to Learning Independently.* Buckingham: Open University Press.

Murray, K. and Gore, C. 1994. 'Differing Approaches to Independent Study', in *Developing Student Capability Through Modular Courses*, eds A. Jenkins and L. Walker. London: Kogan Page.

Nencel, L. and Pels, P. (eds) 1991. *Constructing Knowledge. Authority and Critique in Social Science.* London: Sage.

Okely, J. 1992. 'Anthropology and Autobiography: Participatory Experience and Embodied Knowledge', in *Anthropology and Autobiography,* eds J. Okely and H. Callaway. London: Routledge.

Okely, J. 1994. 'Thinking through Fieldwork', in *Analysing Qualitative Data,* eds A. Bryman and R. Burgess. London: Routledge.

Okely, J. 1996. *Own or Other Culture.* London: Routledge.

Scholte, B. 1969. 'Towards a Reflexive and Critical Anthropology', in *Reinventing Anthropology,* ed. D. Hymes. New York: Random House.

Schön, D. 1987. *Educating the Reflective Practitioner.* San Francisco: Jossey-Bass.

Scott, P. 1995. *The Meanings of Mass Higher Education.* Milton Keynes: Open University Press/Society for Research into Higher Education.

Shore, C. and Wright, S. eds. 1997. *Anthropology of Policy. Critical Perspectives on Governance and Power.* London: Routledge.

Shore, C. and Wright, S. 1999. 'Audit Culture and Anthropology: Neo-liberalism in British Higher Education', *Journal of the Royal Anthropological Institute* 5(4): 557–75.

Shore, C. and Wright, S. 2000. 'Coercive Accountability: The Rise of Audit Culture in Higher Education', in *Audit Cultures,* ed. M. Strathern. London: Routledge.

Shore, C. and Wright, S. 2001. 'Changing Institutional Contexts: New Managerialism and the Rise of UK Higher Education plc', *Anthropology in Action* 8(1): 16–21.

Stephenson, J. and Laycock, M. 1993. 'Active Learning in Field Work and Project Work', in *Effective Learning and Teaching in Higher Education*, Module 7, Part 1, Sheffield: Committee of Vice Chancellors and Principals.

Strathern, M. 1987. 'The Limits to Auto-anthropology', in *Anthropology at Home*,
    ed. A. Jackson. London: Tavistock.
Strathern, M. (ed.) 2000. *Audit Cultures*. London: Routledge.
Strathern, M. 2001. 'Blowing Hot and Cold', *Anthropology Today* 17(1): 1–2.
Willis, P. 1997. 'TIES: Theoretically Informed Ethnographic Study', in eds S.
    Nugent and C. Shore. *Anthropology and Cultural Studies*. London: Pluto Press.

3

Studying Social Anthropology in the U.K.
A Report from the Field

J. Shawn Landres and Karen Hough

Academic social anthropologists in the U.K. have paid increasing attention to the importance of teaching in postgraduate courses, both for course-based master's degree programmes and for research-oriented doctoral programmes. This reflects not only increasing public attention to the ethics of anthropological research and the government's growing concern with 'quality control', but also considerable frustration on the part of postgraduate students themselves, who have become more vocal in demanding guidance from their mentors (Watson 1999: 3, 19ff). When the National Network for Teaching and Learning Anthropology initiated a wide-ranging series of projects to assess and improve training methods, it included among them one workshop dedicated to gathering the viewpoints of students themselves.[1]

The Marett Project was conceived by Drs Marcus Banks and Roger Goodman of the Institute of Social and Cultural Anthropology (ISCA) in the University of Oxford. Its two stated aims were 'a pooling of experience of graduate teaching in anthropology from those most directly concerned – the students themselves', and 'the gathering of factual information on course design and structure from departments around the country'. Underlying these objectives was Banks and Goodman's belief that a 'grassroots' perspective on teaching and learning would provide an important new perspective, untainted by the prejudices and biases of teaching staff (Banks and Goodman, 1997). As such, Drs Banks and Goodman assigned responsibility for the Marett Project to five ISCA postgraduate students whose background reflected the diversity of courses and subdisciplines at the Institute. Student representatives from all but three of the eighteen postgraduate social anthropology departments in the U.K. attended the three-day work-shop, held at Lincoln College, Oxford, in March 1998.

The workshop attempted to address the postgraduate experience as com-prehensively as possible. Students discussed recruitment and admission; the effect of different personal and professional backgrounds; progress and mon-itoring, including student-supervisor relationships, research and field methods training, and examinations; post-fieldwork write-up and presenta-tion of research; and funding.

Three themes emerged from the workshop. Firstly, attendees noted the diversity of teaching methods in departments across the U.K. but simultane-ously criticised the lack of transparency within degree programmes and a general disinclination towards curricular innovation. Secondly, participants almost unanimously expressed dissatisfaction with the current provision of research methods courses. Thirdly, although academia is decreasingly either a career option or even a top choice for postgraduate anthropology students, postgraduate courses have not yet sufficiently addressed the implications of this change for teaching and training.

Transparency and Accountability in Social Anthropology Courses across the U.K.

Participants expressed concern over the variability of the standards of teach-ing and learning anthropology in Britain. While discussions revealed a valued diversity in departmental approaches – from the highly theoretical and spe-cialist to the informal, practical and business-oriented – they also revealed the universal absence of any consistent and effective interdepartmental commu-nication that would make this diversity meaningful, particularly with regard to curricular innovation and best practice. Moreover, the sense of 'tradition' or of a 'school' in some departments – and not necessarily those with which such terms are usually associated – too often results in closed-mindedness and self-serving research that reproduces knowledge rather than creates it.

As one participant pointed out, the presentations and discussions revealed intriguing differences between the official, 'representative' narrative of teach-ing provided by each department, on the one hand, and, on the other, the unofficial, 'operational' lived reality of learning in each department. What the departments claim to teach is often quite different from what students say they are taught.

Problems with transparency and accountability emerge at the very begin-ning of postgraduate courses. At the university recruitment level, students noted frequent discrepancies between what is offered and what is actually delivered: there was a general consensus that students often do not get what they believe to have been advertised, such as adequate access to facilities, tech-nology, and personal and academic support. At the departmental level, as well, there is insufficient clarity and specificity in the admissions procedure, and information often comes too late to be as useful as it could be. Specifically, workshop participants wanted to see more information on funding opportunities for students, including sources available at or before the outset of the course and sources that are available to continuing students. Moreover, participants felt strongly that potential applicants and candidates should be kept aware of staff status, in order to avoid making choices based on the presumption of access to a specific faculty member, who may prove to be unable to take on more students, to be on research leave or sabbatical, or to be otherwise unavailable. Returning to the theme of comparability addressed earlier, students stressed that all of this information should be provided in sufficient time to allow them to make informed choices among offers from different universities.

To be sure, departmental literature and student experience correspond on a wide variety of issues. These include the importance of access to foreign-language training, as well as the need to provide postgraduates with the opportunity to teach at the undergraduate level. 'Interdisciplinarity' is seen as a universally good thing; faculty members do encourage their students to seek complementary courses in other university departments, such as cultural geography, history, psychology and sociology. Finally, students and staff alike agree that conversion courses for students with a non-anthropological background remain an important element of postgraduate programmes.

However, workshop participants also reported major disparities between what their departments offered – or often merely advertised – and what they in fact experienced. By far the greatest area of concern involved the provision of research training and field methods courses (which we discuss below). However, students also reported that computer and technical skills training is often inadequate, as is audio-visual training, particularly in visual anthropological methods. Moreover, the practice of interdisciplinarity seems not to have filtered up to the staff level, resulting in an absence of interdisciplinary contact with other related departments and a consequent failure to understand and incorporate diverse methods.

General concerns reflected an apparent ambiguity over agenda-setting and curricular innovation. Theory and methods courses often have an air of resignation about them: rather than having been developed from genuine departmental commitment, often they have been imposed by the quasi-governmental U.K. Economic and Social Research Council (ESRC), the British Government's funding council for Social Science.[2] Students said that such courses tend to be sloppily designed and taught with remarkably little enthusiasm. Moreover, the efforts of the ESRC and other 'outside' bodies to standardise a 'national curriculum' were seen as inhibiting innovation, rather than encouraging emulation of best practice.

Throughout the various sessions, participants reiterated a need for greater transparency and accountability in student-staff relations. By 'transparency', they meant the consistent practice of explaining to students, by whatever means appropriate, the whys and wherefores of the processes and procedures involved in entering, proceeding through and completing postgraduate training in social anthropology. Indeed, in preparation for the Marett Workshop itself, students from each participating programme requested basic information and materials to share with their colleagues. Many students reported that their departments were unable to provide much of this material. Students expected that in addition to the usual gamut of university and departmental prospectuses and brochures, departments should provide prospective students with departmental admissions guidelines and information about fellowships available from the department and the university. Furthermore, admitted students ought normally to receive preparatory materials, such as pre-course summer reading lists, university induction materials, departmental induction materials, and departmental and university student handbooks. Upon arrival, new students should receive copies of any postgraduate 'bill of rights', as well as teaching handbooks (guidelines for instructors), lecture lists and course syllabi, university and departmental course/supervision assessment forms, prior examination papers and other assessment exercises, and titles and abstracts of the previous five years of master's and doctoral dissertations.

In discussing 'accountability', participants in the Marett Workshop referred to the responsibility – financial, legal and moral – that staff members not only do bear, but also should feel that they bear, towards the students on their courses. While participants recognised that the academic enterprise should not be reduced to legalistic contractualism, they nonetheless felt that staff members too often fail to recognise that they have important obligations to students who have invested time and money – indeed years of their lives – in their courses.

In the session on students' backgrounds prior to anthropology, non-British and non-European students noted that beyond the timetabling of assessed essays or examinations, they frequently had no idea what grading methods would be used or by what standards they would be judged. Moreover, they often had the impression that departments profit from their overseas student fees but do not provide value for money – although a number of students wondered whether departments actually get the extra money they 'earn'. Students felt that greater dissemination of this critical information from staff to students would easily correct such problems. These concerns resurfaced in discussions about induction sessions and other procedures by which students are integrated into the department. Not only do students need more information than they currently receive – about grading methods, assessment procedures, navigating the bureaucracy and the like – but they need better quality information. Too much is left to informal pub sessions, which as one student pointed out, raises a significant barrier for students from a variety of cultural backgrounds. Information should be delivered in written and oral form, not only by staff members, but also by advanced students who can offer important perspectives.

With respect to teaching and supervision, students appreciated the diverse methods of informal teaching via work-in-progress seminars, coffee mornings and informal socialising after departmental seminars. Of particular note in this regard is the programme at the University of Hull, where students reported that they have great flexibility in tying modules to their own specific interests and current areas of research. There are many cross-departmental meetings with other disciplines, which widen the scope of anthropological inquiry. Students can take language modules and teacher-training courses. This is all complemented by a 'system' of informal learning, in which students organise interest groups and conferences that centre on their own research; these are given much support and encouragement from members of staff.

While much has been said, and much remains to be said, about who supervises the supervisors, a number of points were raised that merit repetition here. Participants in the Marett Project Workshop stressed that supervisors ought to feel a sense of personal responsibility towards their students, and that they and their students ought to agree with one another on their mutual expectations at the outset of their working relationship. A number of participants commended notions of 'student-supervisor contracts', as currently used at Belfast, as well as student-supervisor codes of practice. Supervisors should be prepared to provide regular feedback to their students on how they are doing. Beyond that, participants stressed that students have the right to expect supervisory support on their applications for funding and jobs.

A number of issues that arose centred upon large departments, departments with a tradition of 'formality' and excessive professional and social distance between staff and students, and departments where there is a lack of contact between fellow postgraduates. Students in these types of departments often suffer from feelings of isolation. This was of particular concern to students in departments that rely, perhaps too greatly, on 'informal' learning methods, without thinking through the implications of such 'methods'.

Quality of Research Training and Methods Courses

Perhaps the single greatest set of concerns expressed by the participants in the Marett Project Workshop revolved around the provision of research training and field methods courses. Students felt that the continuing influence of the U.K. (ESRC) on these courses is a decidedly mixed blessing: on the one hand, ESRC insistence on methods courses sets an important national standard; on the other hand, staff feel that the ESRC criteria are imposed on them and so teach with a notable lack of commitment. The ESRC aside, students described as pervasive across departments two extreme attitudes: either the belief that methods cannot be 'thought about' but must simply be 'done' in the field, or, conversely, an over-emphasis on anthropological theory without an accompanying consideration of the methodological issues at stake. Moreover, where methods courses are provided, there is often an over-emphasis on quantitative and statistical approaches at the expense of qualitative ones; this is primarily the case at institutions where there is no specific anthropological methods course and where students take 'appropriate' courses elsewhere in the social sciences faculty or division.

Various weak points mentioned in research methods courses included sending students into the field without adequate discussion; dull, dry lecturers (often not anthropologists) teaching courses; failure to provide a reading list; and an overly heavy emphasis on 'thinking' rather than 'doing'. The following examples of 'poor practice' were reported at a variety of departments and institutions:

1. Lack of teaching enthusiasm due to perceived 'imposition' by the ESRC.
2. Absence of strictly anthropological methods and/or an assumption of 'cookie-cutter' conformity across the social sciences.
3. Where the course is faculty- or division-wide, the absence of anthropology lecturers.
4. Excessive lecturing, as opposed to discussion or practice.
5. Courses that are too short and lack structure.
6. Absence of any kind of intellectual coherence – courses that jump around from week to week and in which lectures vary vastly in quality.
7. Courses that lack reading lists and/or fail to require adequate pre-lecture preparation.
8. Courses that are too vague and/or that depend too much on the reminiscences of the instructor.

In general, courses that rely too heavily on lectures rather than discussion, as well as courses that put too much distance between 'theory' and 'method', between 'thought' and 'practice', came in for the strongest criticism.

By contrast, successful courses shared the following attributes: they emphasise the use of all available computer technologies; they encourage comparison of methods; they incorporate guest speakers into the programme; they maintain a balance between formal presentations and student discussion; and they stress both the internalisation of methods ('thinking') and practical examples and experience ('doing'). 'Best practice' courses were reported to include the following elements (see Appendix):

1. Computer-based skills (searching for data, using bibliographic databases).
2. Publication and presentation skills, for both academic and general audiences.
3. Participant-observation techniques, ethnomethodology, and participatory/rapid rural appraisal.
4. Interview techniques, for structured and unstructured encounters.
5. Preparation of grant proposals.
6. Techniques of textual criticism.
7. Ethical issues.
8. 'Emotional' coping strategies.
9. Audio-visual training.
10. Ongoing field-note production and analysis.
11. Awareness of statistical methods.

12. Awareness of ethnographic methods – critical reading of existing ethnographies.
13. Pragmatic advice from post-fieldwork students and other recently returned fieldworkers.

Overall, the most successful courses were those that took a hands-on, applied approach that highlighted links with existing ethnographic and theoretical literature.

Marett Project Workshop participants made a critical link between the success of the research training and field methods courses, and the success of the student's field research itself. The application of methods after or during theoretical learning, and substantial critical engagement with the course materials were seen by workshop participants to be the most beneficial not only to the student, but also to the people who are the objects of anthropological study. Conversely, lectures alone or lack of adequate or effective research methodology create distance not only between student and teacher, but also between fieldworker and community, and lead to ineffective results.

Careers Guidance

Participants in the Marett Project Workshop were extremely sensitive to the fact that anthropology graduate students face at best an uncertain future, and they were critical of departments which failed to recognise the implications of the changed professional landscape. To be plain: it is simply no longer appropriate to speak of 'when the government finally funds universities' or 'when the children of the baby boom grow up and universities have to hire new lecturers to accommodate demand'. It is simply not going to happen, and departments must stop assuming not only that their students will or even want to work in academia, but also that these students will even end up in a job that is recognisably 'social anthropology', or 'applied anthropology', or even 'development' or 'advocacy'.

Participants in the Marett Project Workshop linked their discussion of research training and field methods courses to problems in postgraduate employment opportunities. Workshop participants criticised a general lack of departmental support for students intending to remain in academia, in particular, the absence of supervisory and departmental support for students preparing grant and job applications, as well as the failure of departments to provide opportunities for students to publish their work and, to a lesser extent, to participate in conferences.

However, of greater concern was the failure of departments to respond to the changing career landscape. Students noted that the future of the discipline of social anthropology depends on its application – most importantly on extending its application as broadly as possible. Outside the traditional arenas of academia, development and advocacy work, students identified a number of areas in which training in social anthropology might prove useful. These include mediation, arbitration and negotiation; foreign and diplomatic service; international consulting; journalism; and social policy. In order to prepare students for work in these and other fields, workshop participants argued that it would be necessary to open disciplinary boundaries and to widen the relevance of social anthropology. Most importantly, this requires teaching staff not to consider alternative forms of anthropological practice as subordinate to 'pure' or 'objective' academic theory.

Students had high praise for specialised courses such as the Oxford Brookes' MA in the Social Anthropology of Japan and the Goldsmiths' MA in Applied Anthropology and Community and Youth Work, which appear to be designed for students who wish to bring anthropological skills to bear in non-anthropological settings. According to its brochure, the Brookes' MA aims, among other things, 'to develop a critical awareness of the limitations of some of the assumptions currently made about intercultural relations in the world of business and trade'. Similarly, the Goldsmiths brochure asserts that its MA 'is endorsed by the National Youth Agency as a professional qualification in Community and Youth Work'.

Other innovations are beginning to take into account the changing professional landscape. Based on reading through catalogues provided by workshop participants – with the attendant risks that these courses may not actually exist or may be implemented with varying degrees of success – we have identified some 'best practice' examples of departmental and institutional innovations:

1. The department at Belfast offers a course called 'Anthropology in Practice' whose first objective is 'to develop awareness of how anthropology might provide skills that have practical applications away from the academy' and which also aims 'to analyse the relationship between anthropology and other disciplines and professional areas'.
2. The department at Durham offers a course in 'Business Anthropology' (Course # 223041), which focuses both on intercultural communication and on the anthropology of organisations. The course listing also indicates that the department has made available a booklet on 'Careers in Business Anthropology'.
3. The department at Edinburgh offers a course entitled 'Vocational Anthropology'; the course description's first sentence begins: 'Today the majority of anthropology graduates are engaged in part- or full-time careers outside the faculty....'. The course incorporates 'practical exercises, group projects and discussions', as well as guest speakers.
4. The department at Swansea provides a booklet that describes the relevance of social anthropology 'as a basis for a career'. It lists six different career paths – regional expertise, general education, development work, museum and media work, social work and public health – before mentioning the possibility of teaching social anthropology in colleges and universities.

5. Of particular importance to students seeking actual, rather than abstract, career models, the School of Oriental and African Studies produces a glossy alumni newsletter. While the newsletter encompasses all of SOAS's departments, not just anthropology, the articles and alumni self-reports in this magazine none the less reveal and reinforce the variety of careers outside academia that are available to social science PhDs.

On the practical level, students suggested that departments and universities should participate in consultancy networks and should establish ties with various types of non-governmental organisations. Students should visit development projects and should have access to guest speakers from as wide a variety of organisations as possible, from multinational corporations to lobbying and pressure groups to international human rights agencies.

In addition to emphasising academic career paths as superior to other paths, departments and universities tend to assume that non-academic anthropologists will end up in development or in some form of advocacy work – certainly something with a tinge of the moral high ground. However, as the course description at Edinburgh recognises, 'anthropologists do not have all the solutions to the world's problems' and that anthropologists 'should be willing and able to work as members of [a] multidisciplinary team without disciplinary prejudice'. Beyond implying that social anthropology PhDs may well prefer a career in international business or investment banking to one in social work, this also means that departments cannot give moral or intellectual preference to one career path over another, but instead encourage, indeed require, students to engage critically with their post-graduate aims no matter what they might be.

Conclusion

The Marett Project revealed the diversity of both teaching and assessment methods across anthropology departments in the U.K. Simultaneously, it brought to light an internal dichotomy between what departments claim to teach and what students believe they are taught. Participants in the workshops rightly urged that the teaching of anthropology should be subject to the same critical and analytical approaches with which anthropological research itself is undertaken.

Marett Workshop participants agreed that they favoured three general changes to the current state of affairs. First, they advocate improvement in the research methods course, including additional practical guidance. Second, they seek clarification of supervision guidelines and improved student-staff interaction generally. In addition, they favoured alteration and/or abolition of exams in favour of continual assessment methods. Third, they call for expanded student-student networking, both within departments (between taught-course and research-course students) and among departments (as in the Postgraduate Network of the Association of Social Anthropologists).

The Marett Project provided an essentially 'bottom-up' critical appraisal of the way that the teaching and learning of anthropology is experienced by postgraduates in Britain. It provided important comparative data about the standards of teaching and learning anthropology and the means to improve them. As the forces of national standardisation loom nearer and 'customer-service' approaches become increasingly popular, the role of students in the evaluation of teaching and learning anthropology will become ever greater. Whether or not this role is welcomed by departments and staff, the discipline can only benefit from careful consideration of the experiences and views of this critical constituency.

Notes

1. This essay originated as a paper presented to the Workshop on Teaching and Learning Social Anthropology in Europe, fifth Biennial Conference of the European Association of Social Anthropologists, Frankfurt, September 1998. We would like to express our thanks to our colleagues on this project: Drs Marcus Banks and Roger Goodman, and the three other student organisers of the workshop: Alison Brown, David Odo and Heather Pesanti. While we take full responsibility for the interpretations and conclusions reached in this paper, we wish to acknowledge our dependence on the excellent 'field-notes' and reports written by Alison, David and Heather during and after the Marett Workshop.
2. Since this paper was written the ESRC has restructured postgraduate training into a compulsory taught one year master's research training followed by a three-year Ph.D. requirement. This format is known as a 1 + 3 model.

References

Banks, M.J. and Goodman, R. 1997. 'Graduate Teaching and Research', National Network for Teaching and Learning Anthropology Workshop Proposal. Oxford: Institute of Social and Cultural Anthropology.

Watson, C.W. 1999. 'Introduction: the Quality of Being There', in *Being There: Fieldwork in Anthropology*, ed. C.W. Watson. London: Pluto Press.

Appendix: A Research Methods Course Wish List

According to Marett Project Workshop participants, the ideal research training and field methods course would include all of the following elements:

1. Training in P.R.A. (Participatory Rural Appraisal)/Rapid Rural Appraisals.
2. Identifying and working with key informants and gatekeepers.
3. Taking oral histories (supplemented by classroom role-playing).

4. Research ethics.
5. Computer-based research.
6. Publishing.
7. Mapping.
8. Preparing kinship charts.
9. Practical participant observation.
10. Working with focus groups.
11. Interview techniques (supplemented by mock interviews).
12. Presentation skills (academic conferences, non-anthropology and non-academic audiences).
13. Comparison and critical assessment of different methods.
14. Analytical techniques – how to 'think' in and out of the field.
15. Classroom guest speakers, including post-fieldwork students and other recently-returned fieldworkers, representing the variety of anthropological field methods.
16. Understanding and using statistical analysis.
17. Writing dissertation proposals.
18. Writing grant applications.
19. Critical evaluation of completed doctoral dissertations ('literary criticism').
20. Emotion-dealing with emotion (especially frustration) in the field.
21. Taking fieldnotes – comparing on-the-spot, end-of-the-day, and after-the-fact fieldnotes.
22. Evaluating critical thinkers and formative texts in social anthropology.
23. Museum ethnology – exhibition preparation.
24. Visual research methods.

4

Away from Home
Some Reflections on Learning Anthropology Abroad

Alex Strating

In 1989, the Executive Committee of the EASA decided to set up, as it was formulated in their proposal, 'a consortium of anthropology departments which are prepared to establish a system of generalised exchange at the level of undergraduate teaching'.[1] Eventually twenty-seven universities joined this programme.[2] The idea was that 'every department would send between one and ten second- or third-year students to other departments, while each participating department might expect to receive a similar number of students'.

Every year each participating department had to send in an application indicating the number of outgoing students and the number of months they expected these students to study abroad. During the first years of the programme, the participating universities, or in fact the anthropology co-ordinators at those universities, generally tended to vastly overestimate the number of students they expected to send abroad during the coming year. All co-ordinators assumed that 'their' students would queue up for a period of study abroad and they applied for ten, sometimes twenty exchanges. In reality, only very few students actually applied for an exchange proposal.[3] During the second general co-ordinators' meeting of the network held in Aix-en-Provence (1993), this was a topic for serious debate, as the network was due to be evaluated by Brussels' Inter-university Co-operation Programme (ICP) administration on the basis of its 'performance', i.e., on the relation between the planned and the actual exchange figures. Since only 20 percent of the expected number of students had actually gone abroad, the co-ordinators tried to determine the causes for the apparent lack of enthusiasm on the part of the students.

Money, Information, Language and Calendars

An important factor that prevented students from participating in the exchange network was (and still is) the amount of money offered by the ERASMUS/SOCRATES grant, which proved generally insufficient to cover the extra costs of travel and living abroad. Only students with parents who were willing to contribute to the extra costs of studying abroad or students with sufficient savings could participate.[4] This problem was brought home every year by students' reporting on their exchange experiences during meetings we organised in Amsterdam for students who were thinking of a stay abroad. Although returning students usually emphasised the positive sides of participating in an exchange experience, they all bitterly complained about the meagre grants they received from the E.U.

Another problem was the lack of information about the curricula of the partner institutions and their policies with regard to the number of students that they were willing to host. Apparently most students did not just opt for a period abroad as such, but wanted to have more detailed information about available courses and staff members, as well as about practical matters like accommodation, language of lectures, possibilities for extra language training and the calendar of the academic year. Most students wanted documentation on these issues well in advance of any decision on whether to participate or not.

As the co-ordinators only had fragmentary information about their partner institutions they often could not supply what students were seeking. The general co-ordinator of the network, Hastings Donnan, and the staff of the International Liaison office of The Queen's University of Belfast, solved part of this information problem, when in 1992 they published the *EASA Register of ERASMUS Courses in Social Anthropology*, a guide in which all relevant information for students and staff was presented. After 1992 two updated hard copies of the guide were published, and in 1994 the guide was available on diskette. The information about partner institutions was also improved as a result of the network meetings that were held between 1990 and 1996 in Amsterdam, Aix-en-Provence, Copenhagen and Perugia. During these meetings topics like 'network performance', credit transfer, differentiation between undergraduates and graduates, and linguistic requirements were discussed, also enabling the co-ordinators to talk to each other in person and to discuss the possibilities for the exchange of specific students.

A third difficulty for the exchange programme was related to language problems. Although there were financial provisions made within the ERASMUS programme for linguistic training before departure or after arrival, few students used these facilities. The stay abroad (between a minimum of three months and a maximum of one year), was for most students too short to invest time seriously in linguistic training. So most students opted for a university in a country of which they had (more or less) mastered the language or for a university offering courses in English. In some anthropological departments, staff members were even willing to lecture in English if foreign students were attending. Although this increased the opportunities for students, it still meant that they could only choose from a very limited number of courses. As a result of the limitations related to linguistic skills, departments in Great Britain as well as departments that offered a series of courses in English, tended to attract a disproportionately large number of exchange students. This sometimes caused some reluctance among the British academic administrators to continue participation in the programme.

Finally, the various academic calendars sometimes made it difficult for students to study abroad. Of the twenty-seven universities in the EASA network, twenty had a semester-based system, six had a trimester-based system and one offered a full-year programme. In 1995, the start of the academic year ranged between 20 August and 25 October, and the end of the academic year ranged between 10 May and 15 July. This meant that students, who did not want to spend a whole year abroad, were often unable to plan their programme efficiently for that given year. They would lose time because a semester/trimester abroad would partly overlap with the trimester/semester at home, making it impossible to complete a full year's work-load. This situation was complicated even further by the fact that several universities had compulsory examinations, which limited students' options.[5]

As a result of the improved information within the network, the intensification of contacts between the co-ordinators, the willingness of some departments to offer courses in English (or sometimes French), and notwithstanding the inadequate amount of the grants and the problems with the academic calendar, the number of students participating in the exchange network increased substantially. In 1995–96 ninety-nine students participated in the EASA-ERASMUS exchange network and studied abroad at another university for a period of between three and twelve months. According to an administrator of the University of Amsterdam's International Office, this anthropology network then ranked at the top of the European league in terms of numbers of students actually studying at another university.

Attractions of Anthropology Abroad

According to my own experience as an exchange co-ordinator, few students participate in exchange programmes just because they want to spend some time away from home. Although there are students who use the exchange programme as a 'sponsored holiday', enjoying life in another country and city without any serious interest in the study of anthropology, they are the exception. Most students have very specific ideas about universities and departments where they want to study and usually their preferences derive from the ambitions they have within the field of anthropology. Globally there are three, often overlapping, considerations important to students with respect to the country and university they want to attend.

The first consideration is related to the fieldwork requirements that are part of most anthropology programmes. Some students opt for a country rather than a specific university because they want to do fieldwork as an exchange student or plan to do future fieldwork there. For example, some students from Amsterdam did M.A. fieldwork in Northern Ireland, Germany and Scotland while participating in the network, whereas students from Denmark, Finland, Germany and Scotland did fieldwork in the Netherlands during their stay at the University of Amsterdam. This result of informal agreements among co-ordinators had two advantages for students: they had some financial support and staff members of the host university could help them locally, even acting on occasion as fieldwork supervisors. More frequently, students did not actually do fieldwork during their stay abroad, but used the opportunity to prepare for it. They were able to benefit from local libraries, archives and specialists to develop their research projects on the basis of much better resources than those available at their home universities.

A second consideration for students in opting for a specific country and university is to improve their linguistic skills. Usually they would have some basic knowledge of the language. As far as I know, no students ever went to a country of which they could not speak the language at all or where the university did not offer courses in English. In other words, anthropology students do not use the exchange programmes exclusively to learn a new language. The host-university had to have other attractions than just its local language. Of course, the language issue is very often related to research plans and this not only means that students might have plans for research in the country of the host-university, but also that they plan to do research in countries with the same language as that of the host-university. For example, a student from Amsterdam who wanted to do fieldwork in Latin America would go to Spain or Portugal, or a student with an interest in French-speaking Africa would go to France or Switzerland.

The third consideration is related to the content of the programme offered by the various anthropology departments within the network. This is probably the most important issue as many students will look for courses that are not offered at their home university. In general, they tend to look out for courses on theoretical approaches, topics or regions that are not part of their home curriculum, as each anthropology department usually only covers a limited number of such areas. Students who are dissatisfied with the programme at their home universities will look for courses that suit their interest elsewhere. Every exchange co-ordinator has met students with questions concerning the possibilities of going to a foreign department where they can attend courses on theories of consumption, economic anthropology, ethnicity, visual anthropology, ethnomusicology, health and sickness, Buddhism, applied anthropology, Brazil, the Himalayas or urban anthropology etc. There seems to be no limit to the range of topics anthropology students are interested in and want to learn about. The exchange programmes offer many opportunities to overcome the limitations of home-university curricula.

All three considerations for participating in the exchange programme amount to one central issue: a quest for diversity. Generally speaking, anthropology students do not go abroad to attend courses that are also offered at home. Anthropology is a discipline that covers a very wide range of topics, regions and theories, although there is a common core that in one way or another is part of all anthropology programmes; but there are also all kinds of 'local traditions' and national specificities. According to my observations, it is not the common core of anthropology that exchange students are primarily interested in, but the local differences. The fascination anthropologists have for diversity and local particularities also seems to be reflected in students' attitudes towards studying anthropology abroad.

The present system of student exchange under the SOCRATES protocol favours rather rigid exchanges between a limited number of departments and thus the number of courses students can choose from are also limited. Within this system too many students cannot find courses in the programmes of their department's SOCRATES partners that suit their needs; but with some creativity on the part of anthropology departments (and their academic administrators) and with some help from the EASA, this problem might be solved in the near future. Most anthropology departments have existing exchange contracts with a few other departments, but not all exchange possibilities within these small networks are used every year, as students interested in studying abroad might not find a programme that suits their needs within this limited number of possible departments. This not only happens with anthropology exchange programmes; the total number of exchange possibilities at any given university are seldom used in full. Therefore universities are starting to open up discipline-specific exchange agreements for other students. In this way, a system of generalised exchange is being re-established, not at the level of departments or disciplines, but at that of universities. This opens new perspectives for anthropology students because universities usually have agreements with a large number of partner institutions; but here again the problem of information surfaces. In the case of anthropology, this could be resolved if, for example, the EASA took the initiative of designing and maintaining a website where every European anthropology department could list its programme, the procedure for applying as an exchange student, and information about the areas of theoretical, regional and thematic expertise. By visiting the website, students could find out which anthropology departments fit their needs and so apply, with the help of their university, for an exchange grant. In doing so, a large and flexible network could be developed allowing students to access the different fields of anthropological expertise that are scattered over a large number of European anthropology departments. As a result, the actual weakness of fragmentation would be transformed into the strength of diversity.

Notes

1. I had initially planned for my contribution to this volume to start with an analysis of the data and statistics concerning the anthropology students who participated in the European Union's exchange programmes ERASMUS and SOCRATES between 1987 and 2001. My idea was that these statistics would provide an insight into patterns of exchanges and that these patterns could be the starting-point for some interviews with local exchange co-ordinators about the anthropology students' reasons for opting for specific host universities and about student and staff evaluation of the exchanges. At the end, I expected to be able to draw some conclusions in regard to the strengths and weaknesses of the various ways in which anthropology is at present taught within the E.U.; but, it proved to be impossible to get hold of specific statistics about the movements of anthropology students. Although local exchange co-ordinators, local international offices and network co-ordinators had to report on the numbers of incoming and outgoing anthropology students every year, these data tend to vanish in the statistical result of this process under a general category labelled 'social sciences'. Apparently anthropology, as well as other social science disciplines, is not considered a relevant category for the national and European exchange bureaucracies. This was a severe setback to my plans.

   Instead of combining quantitative and qualitative data, I have concentrated here on my own experience as exchange co-ordinator and lecturer at the International School of Humanities and Social Sciences of the University of Amsterdam for more than a decade. This institution is where anthropology exchange students in Amsterdam take their courses. My main focus will be the so-called EASA ERASMUS/SOCRATES Inter-university Co-operation Programme (ICP) that was initiated in 1989. This was not the only ICP in anthropology – there have been dozens of other, more or less successful, anthropology exchange programmes during this period – but it was certainly the largest one. The story of its development can serve as a good example of the opportunities and constraints of teaching and learning anthropology within an international (i.e., European) context.

2. These universities were: Aarhus Universitet; University of the Aegean; University of Amsterdam; Universitat de Barcelona; Universitat Autònoma de Barcelona; The Queen's University of Belfast; Free University of Berlin; Brunel University; Free University of Brussels; Universidade de Coimbra; University of Copenhagen; University of Edinburgh; Georg-August Universität Göttingen; University of Helsinki; University of Iceland; University of Manchester; University of Neuchatel; Oxford Brookes University; Panteion University of Social and Political Sciences (Athens); Université de Paris VIII; University of Perugia; Université de Provence (Aix-en-Provence); Università degli Studi di Roma 'La Sapienza'; University College of Swansea; University of Tromsü; University of Zürich.

3. This was not just the case for the EASA network, smaller networks seemed to encounter the same problem.

4. In some (rare) cases, regional administrations in home countries have 'sponsored' outgoing students with extra funding.

5. In their Bologna Declaration, the European Ministers of Education decided that the structure of academic education should be harmonised in order to increase the number of students participating in the European exchange programmes. They agreed that all universities within the E.U. should work with a structure of two cycles, undergraduate and graduate (or BA–MA). They apparently assumed that the different systems of diplomas presented an obstacle for exchange. Interestingly enough I have never met a student who refrained from study abroad because of differences in diplomas or academic cycles. These were problems that were always easily resolved. The problem of the incompatibility of academic calendars seems to be a more serious obstacle, but it was not addressed in the Bologna Declaration.

Part 2

Mediated Learning

5

Anthropology and ICT
Experiences of a Dutch Pilot Project

Marjo de Theije and Lenie Brouwer

Introduction

Yes, we have finished. And realised many of our dreams! Five of our courses now have a special website and form a cumulative series of new technology applications integrated within the programme. Moreover, our pilot project has inspired other teachers and the faculty board to develop further applications and as of now the entire study programme is on-line. Indeed, looking back, 1997 seems like pre-history.

Anthropologists were relatively slow to discover the challenges of modern information technology. Although there are a few notable exceptions,[1] they apparently did not feel especially attracted to computers. Perhaps this observation should not surprise us. At first sight, it is difficult to combine the stereotype of anthropologists who study indigenous people in faraway countries, with a perspective of 'cyber-anthropologists' who also gather their data behind their home computer using the Internet. Nevertheless, this is already reality.[2] Traditional anthropological research subjects have also experienced the impact of information technology. For example, Indonesian students used the Internet, e-mail and mobile telephones to communicate with other groups and protest together against the dominant state power.

Thus, the world anthropologists' study is becoming permeated by new information technologies, as are our own working routines. Anthropologists have increasingly discovered how handy it is to use the new technology. In fact, the two writers of this chapter were about ten thousand kilometres apart from each other when they were drafting the final version, but using the platform of BSCW[3] they were able to stay up-to-date at each stage of the writing process.

The technological and cultural developments related to the Internet also have consequences for the changing demands of the labour market for the next generation of anthropologists. How do we prepare students adequately for the future? Anthropologists cannot ignore contemporary knowledge and the information society. Therefore, we ought to seek to follow these developments and find out how we can use them for our own requirements. For example, what is the advantage of information and communication technology (ICT) for academic teaching? Back in 1997 we could think of several useful applications, such as manageable collaboration projects (like this co-authored article), more supervision time, as well as the opening up of access to new information sources on the Internet for students.

For all these reasons we set out into the unknown by formulating a project for the use and implementation of ICT in a sequence of five courses over the first two years of the (four-year) anthropology course at our university. In this chapter we shall describe the form and contents of the learning path we developed. In so doing we shall also pay ample attention to the anticipated and unanticipated effects our project yielded. Our goal is two-fold. First, we want to share our experiences with colleagues involved in similar projects. When we started four years ago, very little practical information was available and we would have appreciated an article such as this one in order to learn of the mistakes and successes of others.[4] Second, this article can be read as a reflection on our role as teachers in the learning process of our students with respect to ICT.

In the first section, we give a short description of the context of our project. The second section is a summary of the original plan. Sections three, four, and five deal with the website, the use of e-mail and discussion groups, and BSCW respectively. In section six we take a look at the legacy of the project, evaluating the results and reflecting on the advantages of using ICT as well as the problems to be expected.

The Context of the Project

The Department of Cultural Anthropology is a small part of the Social Science Faculty of the Vrije University Amsterdam; it consists of about 250 students and fifteen staff members. The academic year is divided into five periods of eight weeks each. In any period, a student attends two courses of six ECTS[5] each. Generally, full-time students attend classes twice a week for each course. However, almost half of the students are studying part-time, which means they attend classes only once a week and do most of their learning at home. Students and teachers felt this limited number of contact-hours constrained the opportunities for variation in teaching and learning techniques. For example, collaboration between students, writing reports together, created huge organisational difficulties. Also, the situation offered little possibility for teachers to monitor the learning process. Therefore, we were looking for ways to shape better circumstances for the supervision of students. In 1996, the Ministry of Education, Culture and Science launched a programme to develop 'learnability projects' in order to make the educational system more efficient in terms of students' success.[6] One of the important fields of the programme was the implementation of new information and communication technologies in academic courses. Combining these two factors, the faculty board invited teachers to design projects that would meet the criteria of the ministry and thus generate the financial possibility of experimenting with other teaching methods. In the anthropology department a sequence of five new courses seemed the most obvious target for experimentation with new techniques.

These five new courses were the result of a thorough discussion that had taken place within the department in the previous years. Teachers wanted to modernise the anthropology curriculum and adjust the programme to the demands of the rapid changes in society and the labour market with respect to technology and communications. They also felt a need to integrate contemporary problems and processes into the courses to a greater extent. The outcome of the discussion was the development of the five new courses that combined theoretical and applied anthropology, each addressing a specific topic in a specific cultural region. In the first-year programme the courses 'Migration in Europe' and 'Gender and Sexuality in India' were introduced, in the second-year programme the themes and regions were 'Stagnation and Innovation in Senegal', 'Asian Tigers (the Economy in South Asia)', and 'Poverty in Brazil'.

Furthermore, in these courses a new method of learning for undergraduate students was implemented. This method can roughly be seen as our local variation of the better known method of problem-based learning. The goal of this specific form of tuition was to stimulate students to be more self-supporting and active in their learning process. Instead of passive listening to a lecture given by a teacher, students were expected to read anthropological texts by themselves, to raise their own questions and to design a path to search for the answers in collaboration with their colleagues during the whole process. In addition, writing skills were emphasised, since in all stages of the learning process students had to write reports. The assumption was that an active way of learning would increase the quality of the knowledge. The educational model thus meant a change of role for students. As a result, the student has become both the centre of the learning process and more responsible for discovery and self-learning. The same is true of teachers. They have become supervisors who closely monitor the learning process. Both the educational model and the themes of the new courses were introduced by the time we started the ICT-project in 1997 and nothing seemed more logical than to use the new courses as a test-bed for our pilot project.

Aims of the ICT-Project

The project was designed as a two-year pilot to integrate ICT into the teaching and learning practices at our department. The aim of the project was to develop an electronic learning environment consisting of four applications. First, access to the Internet to search and consult information; second, the use of e-mail to communicate with teachers, students, and to participate in (world-wide) discussion groups; third, the design of a platform for group work; fourth, developing or providing special educational materials on the Internet with reference to anthropology. The intention was to implement these different means in the courses gradually.

To realise those goals an adequate technical infrastructure was necessary. Teachers need good personal computers and relevant instruction on how to use them. The main idea was to compose a team of experts, consisting of a technical specialist, an educational specialist and an intermediary. This intermediary was supposed to be an anthropologist who communicates with her colleagues and with the technical and pedagogical experts.

However, our project had a difficult beginning. Before it was even started, a great many problems emerged. The technical conditions required to implement the project became operational rather late in the day and even then did not form a very good basis. There was a lot of trouble regarding the platform to be chosen at the faculty level, and the expert-team was never established. As far as technical assistance to the teaching staff was concerned, only a website manager could be hired.

This presented the writers of this article, the two anthropology teachers involved in the project, with a difficult decision. We could do one of two things: either wait until all the conditions were perfect or start the project with all these barriers. We decided to start the project, and see how far we would get.

The Website

The first step of the project was the creation of an educational website for two of the five courses in the series. We chose the modules which we ourselves taught: a course about migration issues for first-year students and one about Brazil for second-year students. The following year we launched the other three websites. The main role of these websites was to provide all the information on the modules in a structured format. As such, they served as a support during our teaching. Students can consult the websites on their own computers with an Internet connection independently of time and place. Another positive aspect of such websites is their flexible character. Changes in the schedule can be made very easily, and information and new links can be added and updated constantly.

In the second year of the project each of the five courses was supported by a website; because of our two experimental sites in the first year, we had developed ideas on how these sites had to be structured. We now introduced a common structure for all sites. This structure consisted of four categories: news, course outline, libraries and the Internet. Under the *News* heading we included changes in the schedule or announcements of lectures which might be of interest to students. The flexibility of this unit is a very practical feature, especially with respect to students who have missed a lesson. In the *Course Outline* we provided all the information regarding the programme, such as schedule, learning goals, end terms, working methods and literature. In pre-website times we used to print this information and distribute it in the classroom. Now we only need to publish these data on the web, to which all students have access, enabling them to make a print by themselves if they so wish. Instead of going to the *library* to find out whether the publications are available on topics students want to write about, they can consult the catalogue on the website first. This section of the website might also contain tips on other libraries relevant to course contents. Under the heading *the Internet* we set up various search machines, websites of research institutions, (electronic) journals and attractive websites of anthropologists. For the module on migration, for example, a link was created to the website of the Norwegian anthropologist Eriksen (1996), who has put many of his articles and manuscripts on ethnicity on-line.[7]

However, the impact of the introduction of ICT into the course was larger than this. The first instance of ICT in the course 'Migration in Europe'[8] explicitly used the Internet as an extra information resource for students. All kinds of migrant organisations nowadays have their own website, in which they provide information about their activities and goals. This shows that the Internet gives voice to certain social groups, but also creates an entirely new source of research material for students. Another extra resource for students is the easy access to conference papers which have not yet been printed or never will be. Furthermore, some articles that are difficult to find in libraries can be downloaded free of charge from the Internet.

In the course, one of the assignments is to find out what kind of information is available on the Internet with respect to Islam. Students had to search the Web for useful links and had to give a description of the sites they found. In the next course on Gender and Sexuality in India, students had to make their own home pages and launch these on the educational website.[8] In the second-year course about Senegal, we taught them how to put their written papers on their homepage.[8] Students liked these assignments very much and sometimes created quite original products.[8]

The most extensive website was set up in the last year of the project, for the last module of the series on 'Poverty in Brazil'.[8] Arranged in thematic categories, the site provided around one hundred links to NGOs, academic and government sites. For some students this site caused an information overload and they had difficulty in retrieving useful information from it. Other students, however, were very fast in picking out the relevant material for their specific projects. We suspect this difference is related to previous experience in using the Internet for academic purposes. In addition, of course, not all students know how to distinguish between what is important and what is not when they use printed documents either. However, we have the impression that all students need to develop a more critical view on the value of the sources that they use. The Internet offers a lot of 'rubbish' too, and students should learn to select wisely. The papers the students wrote for the course are in some cases entirely based on material found on the Internet which proved insufficient to develop good arguments for their research topics. As teachers, we should pay more attention to the critical analysis of Internet-based sources.

In the Brazil module we gave students two small assignments before they started to work on the final project. One of the small assignments was to take a topic of interest and search for information on it over the Internet. The assignment was to write a report not only on the content of the sources found, but also on the way this information was found and on what they thought was its value. Such an assignment allows the teacher to monitor the techniques used by students for selecting information.

Besides these websites designed for specific modules, we felt a need for a website that covered more general educational information.[8] Following the same structure of the other websites, this general website also provides help on scientific writing and on how the Internet works. In this Internet reader we included the instructions of all the Internet applications we use in the classes (like discussion lists, home pages and BSCW). While giving our instructions we were confronted by the fact that a vast difference in technology skills exists among students; by placing all this information on the general educational website we made it accessible to all students. This made the instruction courses easier and students were able to practise in their own time. It should be noted that not only students, but also our colleagues used this Internet reader extensively.

Since the project was started three years ago, the website has been constantly adapted to new needs and ideas. In the academic year 2000–01, the initial structure has been adapted to the official website of the Faculty of Social Sciences.[9] Now all modules offered have a website, including the ones that do not use ICT in the teaching and learning process. For the co-ordination of this website a full-time educational specialist was appointed, as well as a website manager. A team of four or five part-time student assistants is hired to put all texts written by the teachers in HTML or PDF and to maintain the site on-line.

E-mail and Discussion Groups

Students who had their own computers at home benefited most from the ICT project. Using e-mail meant better communication between student and teacher during the process of writing a paper or working on an assignment.

The part-time students – most of whom live far from the university and follow classes only once a week – were able to consult their teacher easier. At the beginning of the project, the faculty had only one room with about forty personal computers connected to the Internet. However, since then the situation has been greatly improved. In three rooms a hundred PCs are now available, and special assistants can provide help with problems. Students seem generally satisfied now.

Another important use of the Internet is for discussing issues. We thus introduced a special *Discussion List* in order to extend the classroom and to offer the means of equal participation in the discussion to all the students. As the group of full-time students consists of almost thirty members, it is impossible to let them all respond individually to a question in the classroom. For the part-time students, generally a smaller group of about ten individuals, the discussion list provided the possibility of meeting the other students on line and extending contact moments beyond the weekly meeting in the classroom. Another advantage of using a list for discussion is that one can read, reflect or respond at one's own pace (Porter 1998).

All mailing lists need specific rules for the subscribers, which are referred to as 'netiquette'. The purpose is to prevent abuse of the list, or emotional responses and to try to moderate the debate. Therefore a moderator was required to manage the list properly; in our group the web director has accomplished this task on several occasions and last year a trainee was taken on for this purpose. In order to receive the posted e-mail messages, every student has to subscribe individually to the discussion list. In our first year, we completed this subscription during classes, which cost a lot of time because students did not really understand how to do it. In the following year the web master subscribed the students, which saved a lot of trouble.

Before introducing the mailing list to our course, we talked with some Dutch colleagues from other faculties about their experiences. One point which came up very often was the question of voluntary or mandatory participation; if students are not obliged to take part in the discussion, only a few will really be apt to use it. For that reason we integrated the list in the course as an assignment; students had to respond to a rather provocative statement on the integration of migrants in Dutch society from a recent government publication. Some interesting discussions developed between the part-time and full-time students, who had never met each other before because they follow the course at different times. They not only added their own contributions to the list, but also replied to earlier contributions from other students. This was, in fact, our intention: to stimulate discussion about a topic from the course. However, most of the students only posted their answer on the list without really participating in the discussion.

Our colleagues on the project were also able to use the mailing list; however, they considered posting a statement to constitute too much work. This objection is certainly valid. If all thirty, or sometimes forty, students contribute to the list and if they also reply to other e-mails, one can end up with a great many messages in the in-box. One can create a special folder in the e-mail program in order to collect all the e-mails sent by students, but this still means a great deal of reading. As Sarah Porter, who gave a presentation at a meeting of English anthropologists on the use of discussion lists in the classroom, put it: 'technology improves the learning process, but it *does not* save time.'[10] This means that a discussion list in big courses is not the most appropriate tool. However, our colleagues on the ICT project used the list for the dissemination of course information to students during the learning process. Referring to the list's communication function, they expressed having had a positive experience.

In fact, students also used the list as an easy means of communication; it suffices to send one e-mail in order to reach all other students. For example, if they were confronted with a problem during their preparation of the literature or assignments, they posted a question on the list. Furthermore, they also put announcements about interesting meetings on the list. Finally, in the evaluation, most students expressed a liking for the medium, although part-time students seemed to be more positive than full-time students. The latter group did not feel the necessity of exchanging views to the extent that the part-time ones did; nor were full-time students particularly interested in more extensive use of the list.

After using the system of discussion lists for three years, we have to conclude that most full-time students are still not really interested in this specific medium. The communication aspect of the mailing list is not really the main intention; such a goal can also be achieved by putting the information on the website's *News* slot. We still believe in the advantages of a discussion list in order to prepare students – especially the more timid ones – more adequately for discussions. Perhaps a mailing list will function better in social settings where students do not meet or know each other, for example with distance learning. Another possible use of the list, such as asking invited speakers to contribute to a discussion group, might make it more challenging and attractive to students. Sarah Porter had a more positive experience. She also quoted some conclusions from other studies, in which students used the list so extensively that they 'developed a consciousness of the class' (Porter 1998). Furthermore, the list changed the traditional balance between instructor and students; they had an 'on-going discussion instead of lectures'. With respect to our experiences we are probably too impatient and need to experiment more.

Group-Work Platform BSCW

The final stage of the ICT project entailed the use of a platform for group-work. In the module 'Poverty in Brazil'; students are supposed to write an evaluation report on the work of a Brazilian NGO for a funding agency. The NGO works in various fields, and groups of about eight students have to study each one of them in turn, after which they are required to formulate common recommendations for the funding agency. They are therefore expected to read contributions and edit the introductions and conclusions jointly. This requires them to stay up-to-date with their colleagues' progress and to discuss developments at great length.

Only in the third year was a satisfactory means found to implement this component of the ICT project, although implementation had been planned for the second year. However, at that time, a variety of external factors resulted in the experiment's total failure. Once implemented, however, the platform proved a success.

We chose to employ BSCW as a platform because it is easy to use and stable. In fact, this decision was taken by the ICT specialist team, the educational specialist and the website manager. They installed BSCW on a local server in order to be able to adapt it to our specific needs.

For the 'Poverty in Brazil' course we created a working space and various 'folders' in which to organise the different documents. For example, there were folders in which students put the individual small assignments and a separate folder used by the teacher for additional reading materials and general tips. All of these folders were accessible to all students on the course. In addition, each group had a folder in which to place the material relating to their case study. These folders were only accessible to members of the working groups.

In all cases the teacher attached her comments to the students' work. The idea behind this was that students learn from each other's work, especially if they also have access to the teacher's observations concerning this work. Of twenty students who filled in an evaluation form at the end of the module, only one mentioned being unhappy with the fact that others could see the teacher's remarks on the individual pieces of work, considering this to be too personal.

With respect to the collaboration between students participating in group-work, we observed that not all groups (there were four groups of seven or eight students) took full advantage of the possibilities offered by the system. As such, some groups would only put their last versions on the BSCW site. This prevented their colleagues and the teacher from reacting to previous versions and led to much less integrated results. Especially the group composed of part-time students made full use of the potential of the shared work-space. They wrote comments on each other's chapters and discussed the introduction and conclusion, as well as the general theoretical and analytical frame for their report. This led to a well-balanced result.

The flexibility in the allocation of access rights makes BSCW particularly useful. It is also very fast. When teacher and students have access to the Internet from different work places, they are theoretically able to work seven days a week, twenty-four hours a day. The downside, however, as one part-time student remarked, is that university can start impinging upon students' private lives. She found herself logging in to the system so often that she had the feeling that the course was the most important part of her life for two months. The teacher also found herself logging in before going to sleep to see if students had added new pieces, and several times ended up writing comments in the middle of the night. It seems to us, however, that this is not necessarily a negative aspect of the shared work-space system. It only demands some habituation in terms of working routines of both students and teachers. Where the alternative is that students hand in written work that the teacher returns to them during the next meeting, the advantage of gains in time outweighs any possible inconvenience. As a result of these advantages, BSCW is now also being implemented in larger courses.

The Road from Prehistory to Teaching with ICT

Now that the project is finished we can look back and see that, thanks to circumstantial factors, it has fundamentally altered our teaching practices. The year 1997 seems like prehistory, and we can now hardly remember how we were teaching and communicating with our students previously. In the course of the project's implementation, we constantly adjusted our plans and ideas to the technical and social environment of the department and the faculty, but also to our own changing views on the matter.

The first adjustments resulted from the lack of a pre-existing technical and organisational infrastructure. Most of the problems and frustrations we experienced in the first phase were caused by technical factors. This is rather common with such first attempts; we also heard similar accounts from colleagues at other universities. As Schwimmer (1996: 1) has noted in his *Internet and Anthropology* article, 'be prepared for some initial frustration'.[11] Our main problems concerned:

1. Insufficient technical infrastructure.
2. Lack of knowledge on the use of computer programs, e-mail and the Internet by both students and faculty staff.
3. Lack of technical assistance. The educational and technical professionals were only hired by the time we were almost concluding the pilot project.

This precarious infrastructure had positive results, too. By starting the project in spite of the inadequate state of the technical framework, our own knowledge of ICT and our insights into the limitations and possibilities of teaching with the aid of ICT grew fast. It certainly gave us a better understanding of the problems we would be likely to encounter and how we could improve on the results. The first partial results were very useful in strategic terms, because they helped us to convince the management of our faculty to invest more time and money in the infrastructure and also to provide financial resources for the hiring of technical personnel.

Another point of constant negotiation was the involvement of our colleagues. As the two co-ordinators of the project only gave two of the five courses themselves, other teachers' enthusiasm had to be awakened in order to implement the ICT work schedules, too. In the beginning we experienced a lot of resistance amongst colleagues, some of whom even refused to use e-mail. Fortunately, in the course of the project this resistance was rapidly overcome. However, it cost us considerable time and energy to reach the current state of play. In practice, we (with the help of a student assistant) had to make the web pages for the sites relating to our colleagues' courses ourselves. Luckily, most university teachers are increasingly acknowledging that they cannot keep avoiding the implications of the World Wide Web.

A less expected problem was caused by the computer illiteracy of the students. There exist considerable differences between students with respect to the level of knowledge of the Internet. Although our experience is that students are fast in picking up the basics of new media, we also see a danger. To some extent these new technologies create new inequalities: who has access to PCs and who not, and who knows how to use them? Teachers should pay attention to these new inequalities amongst students, because otherwise they will become even more pronounced.

All these problems proved to be temporary. As the implementation of the website for all our faculty's courses shows, initial resistance has faded rapidly. Each new group of students will arrive at University with more knowledge of Internet applications than the previous, and we expect our colleagues' general 'backwardness' to soon disappear as well. Each year of the project, the problems encountered have become fewer and the results have improved. For example, the collaboration between students on the BSCW platform resulted in qualitatively better final exams compared with the work produced by previous years. Students are especially pleased about the extra supervision they receive in the written comments to their works on BSCW. The speed with which the communication happens is also highly appreciated. Our goal to increase contact time, and the quality of it, between students and teachers was reached.

The Future

Although our project is now completed, we already have new dreams and plans for the future. As far as we are concerned there are a lot of advantages to using ICT in education. Our next project will be a website for students who are writing their monographs. Another idea concerns the creation of a platform for the fieldwork students undertake. The Internet offers a lot of possibilities for anthropological use; among other things, this is because it can work with a variety of materials (photographs, sound recordings, films, videos and artefacts). Traditionally one writes a book or an article about the findings of fieldwork. Now one can use the Internet to publish writings, to exhibit artefacts and photographs, and to show videos and make sound recordings available.[12] Both the fieldwork and monograph phases of the programme offered by our department require students to carry out individual and independent work and therefore often cause time delays. A website or shared work platform may help overcome this problem. Our experience shows that the application of ICT increases the space for teacher supervision and feedback among students. ICT, as we use it, is a technological intervention that has added to already existing teaching techniques and thus is a means to increase contact time between students and teachers. This improves the overall results of the learning process.

Notes

1. E.g. University of Kent at Canterbury, The Centre for Social Anthropology and Computing (http: //lucy.ukc.ac.uk/CSAC/csac.html). See also the work of Escobar (2000 [1994] and 1995) and of the group of people who founded the Committee on Science and Technology within the AAA in 1992 (see the references in Escobar 1995).
2. Lenie Brouwer, one of the authors of this article, is currently involved in a cyber-anthropology project. She is conducting research about the use of the Internet by Muslim migrants.
3. BSCW (Basic Support for Co-operative Work) enables collaboration over the Web. BSCW is a 'shared work-space' system which supports document upload, event notification, group management and much more. To access a work-space you only need a standard Web browser. This work-space can be seen as comparable with the digital learning space Blackboard, with the difference that BSCW can be used free of charge. Furthermore, the access rights are more easily controlled in BSCW as compared with Blackboard. Accessible at: http: //bscw.gmd.de/ (date of last visit: 2001–09–09).
4. See e.g., Robbins (1996) and Zeitlyn & Houtman (1996).
5. European Credit Transfer System.
6. The final report of the project can be found on the Ministry of Education, Culture and Science site, unfortunately only in Dutch. Accessible at: http: //www.minocw.nl/onderwij/ho/nota/index.htm (date of last visit: 2003–09–09).
7. Accessible at: http: //folk.uio.no/geirthe/Network/Network.html (date of last visit: 2001–09–09).
8. Accessible at: http: //student.fsw.vu.nl/extern/mediated-learning.
9. Accessible at: http: //student.fsw.vu.nl/ (date of last visit: 2001–09–09).
10. New Technology: Epistemology, Pedagogy and Anthropology. Oxford Brookes University: 6–7 November 1998. Organised by the Network of Teaching and Learning Anthropology (University of Birmingham,).
11. See also Robbins' experiences of introducing the use of the internet in the teaching of Anthropology (1996). He reduced his frustration by hiring an assistant whose task was to help students with their Internet assignments and problems.
12. A good example is Zeitlins' 'Virtual Institute of Mambila Studies' (1995). ICT also is a useful to make tutorials, as is shown by e.g. Schwimmer's 'Kinship and Social Organization' (1995).

References

Eriksen, T.H. 1996. Website 'Engaging with the World'. Department of Social Anthropology, University of Oslo, Norway. Accessible at: http: //folk.uio.no/geirthe/Network/Network.html (date of last visit: 2002–07–08)
Escobar, A. 1995. 'Anthropology and the Future. New technologies and the reinvention of culture', *Futures* 27(4): 409–21.

Escobar, A. 2000. 'Welcome to Cyberia: Notes on the Anthropology of Cyberculture', in *The Cybercultures Reader*, eds D. Bell & B. Kennedy, pp. 56–77. London: Routledge. (Originally published in *Current Anthropology* 35(3) 1994).

Porter, S. 1998. 'Less Technology More Learning: Using Email and Discussion Lists in Teaching'. Accessible at: http: //users.ox.ac.uk/~sporter/email (date of last visit: 2001–09–09).

Robbins, R. 1996. 'The Internet in the Teaching of Anthropology'. Plattsburgh: Department of Anthropology. Accessible at: http: //www.plattsburgh.edu/ richard.robbins/internet_in_the_teaching_of_aut.htm (date of last visit: 2003–09–09).

Schwimmer, B. 1995. 'Kinship and Social Organization. An Interactive Tutorial'. University of Manitoba: Department of Anthropology. Accessible at: http: //www.umanitoba.ca/anthropology/kintitle.html (date of last visit: 2001–09–09).

Schwimmer, B. 1996. 'Anthropology on the Internet: A Review and Evaluation of Networked Resources'. *Current Anthropology* 37(3): 561–67.

Zeitlyn, D. 1995. 'Virtual Institute of Mambila Studies', Centre for Social Anthropology and Computing, Department of Sociology and Social Anthropology, The University of Kent. Accessible at: http: //lucy.ukc.ac.uk/VIMS/ (date of last visit: 2002–07–08).

Zeitlyn, D. and Houtman, G. 1996. 'Information Technology and Anthropology'. *Anthropology Today* 12(3).

6

Lessons Learnt from the Experience Rich Anthropology Project

David Zeitlyn

Anthropology defines itself in terms of the collection and analysis of primary data derived from life in human groups and the comparison of these results. In particular, the 'fieldwork experience' is seen by many anthropologists as formative and crucial for the development of an anthropological understanding. However, the conventional anthropology curriculum is formally based almost entirely on the assimilation of a body of readings in conjunction with discussion of these materials. As class sizes rise, reliance on these 'secondary' views of anthropology have increased, isolating students further from the 'primary' experience of 'doing' anthropology. In the past this was conveyed informally in small-group sessions by teachers relating their personal experience and those of their colleagues. Informal teaching and learning resources are increasingly restricted to those few students involved in a research methods course or in postgraduate work. Informal transmission of experience is being threatened by current pressures of numbers. Formalisation is a means to its survival. Changes in scale imply that existing good practice will not perpetuate since personal presentations of experience do not work in the same way in large groups. Instead techniques must be developed to convey the immediacy of experience to individual students however large and heterogeneous a group they may comprise. If these techniques are efficient they can be used to introduce the experiential-based teaching of anthropology in new places in the curriculum.

The Experience Rich Anthropology (ERA) project was funded by the U.K. Higher Education Funding Council as part of their Fund for the development of Teaching and Learning programmes. At the conclusion of the project we had contributions from sixteen researchers at six institutions. The project built on the work being done since 1985 at the Centre for Social Anthropology and

Computing, University of Kent at Canterbury. Consortium partners included Anthropology departments at universities in Belfast, Oxford, Oxford Brookes, London, Manchester, and Canterbury. A major aim of the ERA project was to enable teachers of anthropology and social anthropology to develop and construct their own teaching and learning materials from those that are being hosted at the sites of various members of the consortium.

Our intention was to promote and disseminate innovative and successful means of developing materials for both teaching and learning and, at the same time, serving as an alternative form of research output. Our principal aim was the narrowing of the gap between research and teaching. Those teaching anthropology are researchers who typically employ only a little of their research, and often only the published results, in their teaching. Anecdotes about fieldwork experience do not translate well out of the bar and tutorial (in large groups the presentation style cannot be so well tailored in response to the audience reactions – particularly important when recounting personal experience) and so are poorly placed to deal with the increase of student numbers that we have experienced in recent years. The position of visual materials illustrates this – field photos are among the largest and least exploited resources produced by anthropology. The relative accessibility of camcorders (analogue and now digital) means that a surfeit of unanalysed and subsequently under-used visual material is currently being accumulated by contemporary researchers. The methods, practices and experience resulting from the ERA projects provide some guidance and pointers to ways round the problems of maintaining and improving the role of 'other' research inputs into the process of teaching and learning.

What We Have Achieved

All of the ERA projects were produced by anthropologists at partner institutions in our consortium. The initial level of computer literacy among the project developers was minimal (apart from those based at Kent and Manchester), something that should be borne in mind when evaluating the structural and presentational aspects of the material. Consortium members were provided with a computer and the necessary development software, as well as on-line access to technical expertise in Kent. Regular consortium meetings were held for information and ideas exchange. We might note that such meetings were viewed very positively by participants given the common experience of relative isolation in a number of the institutions involved. E-mail and video-conferencing cannot compete with the benefits of being able to share complaints about administration and quality control bureaucrats while drinking beer! The quality of the results improves as a consequence.

The projects produced reflect a variety of approaches to the WWW as a learning tool. Some are styled as on-line books with supporting sound and image files, some are led by sound and/or image with supporting text, some make use of the data-searching properties of the Web, and others use expert systems for simulation work. Such variety was an outcome of a deliberate policy of the ERA team at Kent to avoid dictating to the consortium members how they should design their materials. Developers were free to experiment with their own approaches, and design and navigational issues were deliberately dealt with once the materials had been collated. Adopting this policy clearly has the advantage that contributors could design projects with particular regard to the expertise and specialism of the subject material. However, at the present state of development student end-users often exhibit a somewhat mixed response to the diverse nature of the material. To quote a student from Oxford-Brookes University:

> There is an awful lot of information and each site tends to be a bit dense – they would benefit from being broken up by a few pictures or colours or something. I got bored of trying to wade through masses of samey looking text to find interesting bits. There didn't seem to be that many intertextual links so the site map came in handy for checking out where I'd already been and where looked good to go to next. There should definitely be more pictures – I know it's a bit needy, but it really helps a lot of information to get taken in a bit easier. It's like a spoon full of sugar or something. I do think it is a brilliant thing to have this kind of stuff available on line, but as I mentioned before, unless you have a decent computer room at college you probably wouldn't bother. Slow computers and the net just don't mix well. It is definitely the learning tool of the future though. It's just a matter of time and money.

Comments of this nature are not untypical and raise issues of navigation, access and presentation, set against a background of positive enthusiasm for the environment overall. Students perceive the potential benefits but remain cautious about using material which, at first hand, would seem to involve a lot of reading from screen.

We produced a CD sampler and accompanying booklet that was distributed to staff at U.K. anthropology departments. The CD (without booklet) was distributed at the American Anthropological Association meeting in Chicago in November 1999. The website was established early in the project and contains everything (with one exception) on the CD and additional 'chapters' not available on the CD for technical reasons. The CD is necessarily frozen but the main project continues and the website enables incremental changes and corrections to be made, as has already happened.

The global project enables and encourages student criticism by giving the students access to a wider range of material than is found in standard books and articles. This can be used to encourage them to read across the grain, to come to conclusions other than those of the authors. This can help teachers encourage students to be critical by contrasting published conclusions with (some of) the material on which they are based.

We have worked with a range of colleagues around the country trying to help them to do what they want. We have not been prescriptive or proscriptive about content or general subject matter in any way or form, although some technical guidelines were proposed. The resulting collection is extremely varied and provides a good illustration of what can be done with limited technical expertise and resources (although many of the projects became quite sophisticated as the project progressed).

We hope the results have two results. First, that they are used in teaching. The parts are self-contained so teachers can use only the pieces that interest them and are relevant to the courses they teach. One section can be copied off the CD and put onto a local web server so that, for example, one week's reading is easily available to the students on a course and a single seminar is based around some ERA material. Whole courses do not need to be redesigned to use the results of the ERA project. Second, that they serve as models inspiring people to work on their own research material, hence allowing the gap between research and teaching to be narrowed. Our spring and autumn intensive schools let people loose to create their own mini-ERA projects and the participants achieved an impressive amount in three days' hard work.

Why Interactive Multimedia?

Some projects could have been achieved using conventional multimedia technology that has been with us for more than a thousand years (see Eisenstein 1979, 1997). Examples such as Zeitlyn's 'chapter' on the status of ancestors in Africa, Ian Fowler's work with the fieldnotes of Sally Chilver and Phyllis Kaberry and the Pitt Rivers Museum project on the history of General Pitt Rivers as a museum curator could have been produced on paper. The reason for using web-based technologies in such cases rests on a simple economic argument: no conventional publisher would consider publishing this material any more. It is not profitable. It is quite heartening to be able to demonstrate that some of the clearly naïve ideas of the web pioneers (of a technology enabling wider access to information) are not completely groundless. Other material cannot work in the same way on cellulose-based multimedia technology (paper) because it is not dynamic. In another ERA 'chapter', Mike Fischer developed simulations that allow students to change variables and see the effects of these changes; for them to ask questions of divination in a way akin to Mambila diviners, and then themselves make the interpretations that link a pattern of leaves in a pot to the answer to a recondite question. This exercise, we claim, puts them in a better position to understand the literature on divination.

Four Facets to Multimedia Projects

The ERA project (or each constituent part of it) can be viewed in four different ways:

Openness and Honesty

The use of multimedia as a communication device can be used as a small (I emphasise **very** small) step towards transparency. Making more source material available opens up new possibilities for criticism. For example, by making source recordings available, a colleague can demonstrate that it has been 'written down wrong' (at present transcription must be taken on trust). Many anthropologists do not like this (it should be noted, that such a protective attitude is not restricted to anthropologists). Michael Fischer (1996) has described the process of anthropological research as the production of layers of source material each resting on the preceding, but with complex interconnections between layers. More of this can be made available to our colleagues using anthropological multimedia than is possible with conventional forms of publication (including film and video among these).

Research Tool

Multimedia provides a fascinating opportunity in the interactive and negotiated process that is anthropological fieldwork. It produces an artefact that documents its own creation almost as a by-product and does so in ways that only Foucault could dream of: as a total document of the research process! However, I want to be the first to demolish that claim. It may suggest completeness but in fact is anything but. It is, however, more complete than a standard ethnographic monograph.

Publication Device

Multimedia escapes from some of the financial constraints that inhibit academic communication. A mixed economy may be possible – publishing on both paper and electronically but in complementary fashion – may be possible in which regional experts can be satisfied with large amounts of detail available electronically, thereby freeing print publication for a wider audience.

Teaching Tools

Having developed the other three facets, the production of teaching material – the use of one's own material in any teaching that one is doing – becomes greatly simplified. The ERA project sought to create teaching material from existing material that was often only in analogue format initially. This entailed a lot of hard work, but some examples such as the Day in the Life of Somié Village – where digital video was taken when in the field – proved to be a relatively easy project to complete.

In what follows I will consider some examples of what has been done as part of the ERA project.

Seeing and Playing are Different from Reading

Mambila Spider Divination

This provides an excellent example where a simulation originally developed for use in the field is also successful as a teaching tool. Students can interact with the simulation just as Mambila Diviners do, and having read the on line documentation they can attempt to use it to answer everyday questions, to choose lottery tickets, or whatever they will. They can thereby come to appreciate the point of Evans-Pritchard's claim (1937) that Zande oracles provided a completely adequate means of solving everyday quandaries.
< http: //www.era.anthropology.ac.uk/Divination/ >

John Blacking

Ethnomusicology is very hard to discuss in print media. One can transcribe and describe but cannot convey as much as sound and image in conjunction with the textual analysis. All we have done is take some published work and bring the illustrations to life! Sound recordings and video-clips now accompany the published texts of the late lamented Professor John Blacking. I note that it is easy to say that all this has been done. However, it should be stressed that first Lev Weinstock, then Suzel Reily, laboured long and hard to make this possible – for a third party to do this is very hard indeed (although, as they have demonstrated, it is possible). It would be much much easier had the work been undertaken by the author, the person making the recordings. Indeed using this sort of multimedia as an aspect of research documentation where fieldnotes are linked directly to recordings means that transforming them to teaching material may be an easy side-effect of the research process!

Visual Material that is not to Do with Film or Photography (or How We Have Underestimated the Diagram)

In a fascinating analysis that deserves to be far more widely known, Eric Livingston (1987) has analysed the significance of diagrams for Euclidean geometry. The proof is inscribed in the sequence of drawing the diagrams. By drawing them ourselves we repeat actions of Euclid himself, and can thereby participate in the same sense of conviction: a proof is a proof because we **know** we have covered all the possibilities: the diagrams show it.

This raises some fascinating issues which both set agendas for research and have pedagogic implications. It raises the possibility that multimedia (which may be nothing more than a diagram plus text) is a good educational medium precisely because it engages students in a variety of different ways. There is now quite a lot of research in human-computer-interaction and in education about these sorts of issues. I would suggest that visual anthropology has suffered because its focus is still on film to the detriment of other visual material.

Various ERA project demonstrate these points in one way or another:

A Simple Genealogical Tree Drawing Program

<http: //www.era.anthropology.ac.uk/Era_Resources/Era/Kinship>

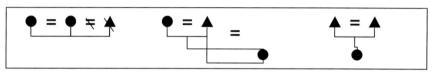

Figure 6.1a: *Nuer ghost marriage*

Figure 6.1b: *A form of incest*

Figure 6.1c: *Male homosexual marriage and 'adoption' of a 'daughter'*

In Figure 6.1 above, I have drawn (a) Nuer ghost marriage (b) a form of incest, (c) Male homosexual marriage and 'adoption' of a 'daughter'.

Why is such a programme good to use for teaching? The flexibility of the programme provides a graphic demonstration of the social construction of 'marriage'. The programme allows any two (or more) individuals to be linked in a 'union'. So, to take a controversial, and purely hypothetical example, were the ruler of a large superpower to have an illegitimate daughter, that would be the result of a second union. The students might want to discuss how a legitimate daughter (let's call her 'Mayfair' for the sake of argument) might be related to this hypothetical offspring? How do 'adulterous' relationships differ from those resulting from divorce and remarriage? Or same-sex unions. Are these significantly different from mixed-sex ones? Nuer 'ghost marriage' can also be represented – in Evans-Pritchard's classic description this is where when a man dies leaving no offspring and his widow remarries another woman. Any children that either of them may have are deemed to be the deceased man's offspring. Another revealing problem case is that of adoption. The problems of trying to represent such complex relationships with the programme provide natural starting-points for discussion of the meaning of the relationships, and how society constructs them (recall that under British law it is entirely legal for two full siblings who have been adopted by different families to wed and have children). At this point we reach the limits of what can easily be represented (though we are working on this); but to appreciate that, you need to have gathered quite a lot of basic knowledge about kinship and how it varies.

John Blacking: Venda

<http: //www.era.anthropology.ac.uk/Era_Resources/Era/VendaGirls>

Consider the following description:

The basic position and movements of most ndayo dances (-thaga) are:

1. The dancers squat (-tumba), with arms folded against the chest in the vhusha humble position.
2. They rise to a crouching position.
3. They shuffle their feet rapidly or 'jab' the metatarsal arch into the ground in time to the different multiple rhythms of each song.
4. Very often, as the dancers rise rapidly from the squat to the crouch position, they swing their arms downward. This movement makes it easier to raise the body rapidly.
5. Similarly, when they resume the squatting position, they throw up their arms, bending them at the elbow.

Such a description is helped by photographs such as Blacking was able to publish:

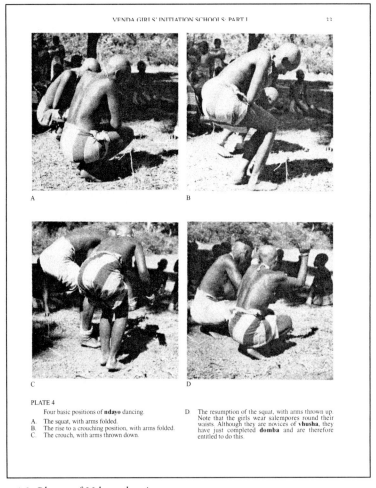

VENDA GIRLS' INITIATION SCHOOLS: PART I   33

PLATE 4
Four basic positions of **ndayo** dancing.

A.   The squat, with arms folded.
B.   The rise to a crouching position, with arms folded.
C.   The crouch, with arms thrown down.

D.   The resumption of the squat, with arms thrown up. Note that the girls wear salempores round their waists. Although they are novices of **vhusha**, they have just completed **domba** and are therefore entitled to do this.

Figure 6.2: *Photos of Ndayo dancing*

However, even the low-quality video of the dance (as we have made available: <http://www.era.anthropology.ac.uk/Era_Resources/Era/VendaGirls/Video-Clips/V_VC48.html>) is a considerable improvement over textual description or even still photographs. Similarly, a musical score with transcribed (and translated) song texts, is the basic stuff of ethnomusicology. This can now be complemented with digitised sound recordings, so students and other researchers can listen to the source of the score they are reading.

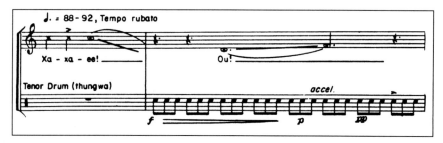

Fig.6.3: *Venda song transcript*

Simulation

In another section of the project, Mike Fischer has presented several different types of simulation, and discussed the purposes of building dynamic representations of aspects of social worlds. Examples include the Mambila divination simulation already mentioned and one where a simulation developed as a research tool is now being used in teaching. Other examples are of population and kin group composition, and how these change over time, or models of the inferences and information required in complex decision-making. The formalisation required in order to prepare a simulation (for example, by making an expert system), encourages the anthropologist to be rigorous. Simulation can give evidence that our knowledge is adequate, or, for example, that either our understanding or the indigenous account being modelled may be incomplete. Students can construct their own simulations and see them work, as well as investigating how changing the variables in classic simulations affects the outcomes: does making more food available increase population size? What are the limits to such increases?
<http://www.era.anthropology.ac.uk/Era_Resources/Era/Simulation>

Conclusions

The ERA project has given anthropologists new to the Web the opportunity to explore its potential in relation to their own teaching. Consortium members have been provided with the equipment, software and technical support to develop their projects, and other interested parties have been given some hands-on skills through open days and workshops. As far as expanding and developing the experience-grounded teaching and learning of anthropology based on the use of research data the project has met its aims. The clearest indication of this can be seen in the more recent products which have emerged from our workshops. The ways in which these anthropologists have used the Web to develop new approaches to their teaching has varied. As one would expect in a project of this nature some have been innovative in their approaches, others more conservative. It has been a deliberate policy of the ERA project team to encourage diversity and not to dictate how the web should be used. This seems an appropriate approach to take when dealing with new technologies which have yet to settle into set ways of representing ideas. It needs to be recognised, however, that with additional resources valuable insights into generic multimedia teaching and learning processes might have been forthcoming. For example, a formal analysis of participants' products may yet highlight factors which could enhance teaching and learning within such domains, and had resources been available, a touring roadshow would have been arranged to provide multimedia training for the departments in their usual surroundings. However, it became apparent as the project progressed that there were many particular and localised obstacles to the use of the Internet that need to be solved locally. Anthropologists often have been at a disadvantage in internal competitions for resources, partly because they cannot demonstrate a need. This ERA can provide.

The project has been an enlightening experience for those involved, giving anthropologists new skills and new visions. The consortium believe that this knowledge will filter through to other colleagues and institutions, and act as an example of good practice for future projects. The plans for future dissemination of the results of the project should ensure that these goals are met.

Finally by a way of a conclusion that looks to the future some practical remarks:

Think Small

A useful starting-point that is an achievable goal and yet one that produces useful results is to take a published (or publishable) paper or book chapter and then surround it with some of the material on which those conclusions were based. These may include extracts from archives, field photographs, letters, maps, video-clips and possibly field notes of edited summaries of fieldnotes. By sketching some of the extremely non-linear chain by which published conclusions are reached, a researcher can help students follow their thought processes. The researchers may even come to some new conclusions in the process since they have such privileged access to their own material, but this is coincidental. The current norm is that researchers have uniquely privileged access to their material; no one else will ever see it, so any advance on that is to be encouraged.

Eschew Fanciness and the Latest Quirks

It is still hard to achieve platform independence, and to produce material that will run straight-forwardly on most people's machines as you cannot assume much about the monitor size, font choice and display colours let alone anything more profound. This makes designing for the Web a nightmare for the more typographically inclined. Most anthropologists are not so sensitive and are more concerned to get their message across whatever it may be. Since anthropology remains a resolutely text based subject (for all my comments above), the following seems more than adequate for most anthropologists (of course some exceptions can be dreamed up but they remain just that: exceptions). What we need are texts that include links to other parts of the same texts and to other texts. Photos, diagrams and video-clips (or sound recordings) can be included to appear seamlessly, and can be cross-referred to any other item. To do this, programmes or formats such as *Flash*, *Director* and *Front-page* are not needed![1] All that is needed is easily available in generic HTML and it is this that we strenuously encourage people to use. If that is the starting-point, then any further things that may be needed can be kept to an absolute minimum.

Copyright, Ethics and Confidentiality

Making materials accessible over the Web can lead to problems in relation to copyright and anonymity. Traditionally, anthropologists had a relatively clear separation between the collection of data through fieldwork and the academic analysis of that data. The Web, however, contributes to the disruption of these boundaries by making anthropological analysis accessible to a much wider audience than was hitherto possible. For some anthropologists we talked to, this was all part of the wider context of contemporary anthropology but for others it was an issue specifically relating to the development of new technology, and by implication something that could be problematic.

Using an Intranet (an internal or private network), as opposed to the Internet and treating sensitive data in such a way as to disguise the identity of individuals can alleviate many of these problems. Also, authors of web-based materials have the facility to make it impossible to download and edit certain materials, as or she sees fit. The ERA project is also using a special 'Signum fingerprint' technique by which the copyright on materials downloaded from the ERA site can be traced. Overall, concern over access to, and permission surrounding, multimedia-based primary material should be seen as a more generic problem for the social sciences. For some time the development of the U.K. Economic and Social Research Council 'Qualidata' project on the archiving of qualitative data has highlighted the specific problems which arise with video – and audio – based field-data, noting in particular issues which surround confidentiality and ethics in situations where material collected for one purpose is made available to other researchers and used for quite another. The social science research community has yet to formulate guidelines and conventions surrounding the use of primary material in multimedia environments.

Permissions are needed to use material (sometimes one's own) that has already been published. Our experience is that, as long as one is not making money from it, and not dealing with recently published material, then if you are persistent enough permission will be granted. It can take more than a year to obtain, however, and many letters need to be sent. The Royal Anthropological Institute, International Africa Institute and American Anthropological Association have been very helpful though and supportive; other publishers less so. The only real problem we encountered was with a publisher who is trying to sell electronic reprints themselves, and so asked for what we considered an impossibly high fee per page. We have contacted the author who may be able to provide an early draft to which he still owns the copyright. In some years time the publishers may be persuaded to change their mind!

Note

1. Also any of the commercial virtual learning environments, such as Blackboard or WebCT, are not needed. Whilst these offer features not available in generic HTML, equivalents are possible without locking the developer into any particular format. We were determined that ERA material would still be usable years into the future. HTML seemed the best means to achieve that goal. We also note that ICT strategies are too often technology focused at the expense of pedagogy. It is easier to write annual reports that list the number of training workshops that have been run, than to actually effect change.

References

Eisenstein, E. 1997. 'From the Printed Word to the Moving Image', *Social Research* 64(3): 1049–66.

Eisenstein, E. 1979. *The Printing Press as an Agent of Change*. Cambridge: Cambridge University Press.

Evans-Pritchard, E. 1937. *Witchcraft Oracles and Magic among the Azande*. Oxford: Oxford University Press.

Fischer, M.D. 1996. Computer-Aided Visual Anthropology. Paper presented to the *British Academy Symposium: Information Technology and Scholarly Disciplines*, British Academy. Friday 18 and Saturday 19 October 1996.

Livingston, E. 1987. *Making Sense of Ethnomethodology*. London: Routledge & Kegan Paul.

7

Ethnography, Experience and Electronic Text
A Discussion of the Potential of Hypermedia for Teaching and Representation in Anthropology

Sarah Pink

In Britain the production and use of electronic hypermedia for teaching and learning anthropology is expanding. During the 1990s anthropologists' published responses to this new form of ethnographic representation ranged from advocating caution in the application of hypermedia to anthropology (e.g., Banks 1994) to celebrating its creative potential to enhance research, representation and pedagogy intellectually and ethically (e.g., Biella 1994). The development of hypermedia learning materials has been encouraged and funded in a context where 'mass education' and 'quality control' cultures have developed in ways some anthropologists find worrying. While it is important that such issues are addressed, that is not my purpose here. Rather, acknowledging that anthropologists should be wary of how hypermedia learning is implicated in wider political agendas, I explore the positive potential of hypermedia, suggesting that hypermedia may facilitate a reflexive approach to practices of anthropological representation and pedagogy.[1]

The Medium and its Potential

Here I discuss anthropological and pedagogical hypermedia texts that use written words, sounds and visual (still and moving) images, and are published electronically on-line or using digital storage media. In particular I shall draw from my experience of designing two hypermedia texts *The Bullfighter's Braid: Unravelling Photographic Research* (Pink 1998a) and *Interweaving*

Lives, Producing Images, Creating Knowledge: Video in Ethnographic Research (Pink 1998b), both published on CD- ROM.

Interactive hypermedia publications usually consist of sets of interlinked files containing written words, still or moving images, sound, or a combination of these. The interlinkages between files, or between points (e.g., words and images, theoretical sections and ethnographic description) within files support the interactivity of hypermedia; 'the links themselves have meaning' (Biella 1996: 595). The files are usually accessed from one another by means of hypertext links embedded in their texts. These links may be represented by printed text or visual symbols.

Links between files can thus create a series of different but interconnected narratives or layers within a text. Therefore hypermedia texts may simultaneously serve as teaching and research texts. For example, these different purposes may be represented as different narratives within the text; one narrative may be intended as a representation of research, another may contain a text intended for student learning, whilst a third may contain fieldnotes, photographs or other research documents. Thus, one narrative may feature a 'finished' academic article (for example Pink 1998a), or an ethnographic film (e.g., Fruzzetti et al. [1994] laser-disc version of their ethnographic film, *Seed and Earth*), it may simultaneously contain a set of research materials, such as field-diaries, photographs, video footage, (e.g., Pink 1998b) and Biella's *Maasai Interactive* (see Biella 1997), and pedagogical narrative (see Pink 1998a, 1998b). These narratives may themselves be interlinked.

Some hypermedia projects aim to address the potential of hypermedia to link narratives of fieldwork and representation for pedagogical purposes. For example, the Experience Rich Anthropology (ERA) project at the University of Kent, is designed to 'enhance the teaching and learning of anthropology by encouraging teachers to help students explore the relationships between field data and analysis as reported in monographs and journal articles' (see <http://lucy.ukc.ac.uk/ERA/>) through electronic media.

Hypermedia as a Critical Response

Towards the end of the twentieth century the authenticity and authority of conventional ethnographic representation was questioned by calls for reflexive authorship and multivocality. Moreover, challenges to the dominance of the printed word urged ethnographers to rethink 'certain categories of anthropological knowledge in the light of understandings that may be accessible only by non-verbal means' (MacDougall 1997: 292). The capacity of electronic hypermedia to represent still and moving images, sound and written words, in a multiplicity of different but simultaneous narratives, also offers exciting possibilities for anthropologists to develop representations that incorporate visual and verbal knowledge, 'other voices' and a reflexive approach to their own 'voices'.

In the 1980s Howard pointed out that 'where connections between phenomena are as interrelated as they are in human communities, the job of orchestrating even a limited degree of interconnectivity in the written medium is a struggle at best' (1988: 305). More recently Marcus has claimed that the twentieth-century ethnographic context necessitates that anthropologists 'come to terms with multiple agencies in varying locales' and study the relationship between elements of an increasingly deterritoralised 'culture' that is 'the product of parallel diverse and simultaneous worlds operating consciously and blindly with regard to each other' (1995: 51). In this situation where, unattached to place, 'culture' travels and is produced 'in multiple, parallel and simultaneous worlds of variant connection' (1995: 51–2) he argues the conventional linear narrative of anthropological text must be rethought. Insisting on a departure from the linear description of 'models' and 'networks' that have dominated anthropological representation in the past, Marcus suggests the cinematic technique of montage as a way of representing the 'multilocale determination of the identity of subjects' who may at first appear to the ethnographer to occupy 'a situated place' but who in fact resituate themselves anew in new contexts (1995: 53). Such an ethnography acknowledges the (inter)subjectivities of the ethnographer and the 'subjects' of ethnography and implies a need for anthropological representations to accommodate the multilinearity signified by these different spatial, temporal, perspectival and discursive realities. Whilst Marcus proposes these effects should be developed in printed text, hypermedia offers (maybe more) possibilities to develop such multilinear text.

Hypermedia as Reflexive Text

Hypermedia offers interesting possibilities for developing representation that incorporates a reflexive focus on the processes by which ethnographic knowledge is created. Whilst this can also be achieved in printed (see James, Hockey and Dawson 1997) or filmic text (see MacDougall 1997), the potential of hypermedia for multilinearity and layering of information allows reflexivity to be developed in a different way. Usually this is done by creating hyperlinks between files containing information about and representations of documents and experiences from the fieldwork process with academic or report-style texts. Thus providing details of the research that informed the 'final' reports, and implying the relationship between ethnographic research and visual and written forms of representation.

Ethnographic hypermedia authors have argued that electronic representation can make the historical development of ethnographic research and interpretation explicit in ways written text or film cannot. Fisher and Zeitlyn have pointed out, 'fieldwork experience' is important for the development of an 'anthropological understanding' but is rarely reproduced in printed articles. Their *Experience Rich Anthropology* project has produced a series of excellent examples of ethnographic texts that represent both research results and fieldwork experiences upon which published articles and books are based. These include photographs, field-diaries, video-clips and other written texts. One of the most significant University of Kent Projects is '*45 years in the Turkish Village 1949–1984*' that develops Professor Paul Stirling's *Ethnographic Data Archives* as an internet resource. The resource includes Stirling's book *Turkish Village* (1965, 1994), articles, and Ph.D. thesis (*The Social Structure of Turkish Peasant Communities*) as well his field-notes, letters, photographs and database. This presentation of Stirling's work allows researchers and students to interpret the historical development of his ideas and the visual and written ethnographic research materials on which his writing was based.

Biella's hypermedia ethnography *Maasai Interactive* was developed from film, interview and photographic materials produced during a six-week period of fieldwork amongst the Maasai people in 1980. Biella shows how electronic interactive text can be used to represent and annotate the historical development of ethnographic work, thoughts, ideas and interpretations, as well as the visual, verbal and written elements of the project and to reference other ethnographers' work. A theme of *Maasai Interactive* is the 'limitations' to knowledge imposed by the brevity of Biella's fieldwork period: 'The limits to knowledge discussed in the annotations are important theoretically because the present work is designed to reflect on the nature of early fieldwork. A secondary purpose is to explore how digital technology can enhance the understanding of anthropological research in which camera and tape recorder play an important role' (Biella 1997: 60). The new technology offered advantages that neither film nor written text could facilitate; it 'permitted audio recordings, photographs and texts to be integrated on one study-screen'. It also allowed Biella to design the text in such a way that 'Through electronic footnotes, texts could instantly "call up" for review any moment of the audio, any photograph, and any text' (1997: 61).

My hypermedia projects were based on similar ideas. In *The Bullfighter's Braid* an article about my use of photography in fieldwork is published alongside other texts. An earlier version of the article had been published in Spanish (Pink 1996) but included only one photograph whereas the hypermedia article was linked to over thirty photographs and several video-clips, all original fieldwork materials. Through these hyperlinks and alternative narratives, students would be able to read my article about research methodology but also view the photographs that the visual research methods produced. *Interweaving Lives* is a similar hypermedia project that interlinks different fieldwork material and media on the same CD to indicate how, during my research in Guinea Bissau, different types of knowledge were produced and represented in field diaries and 'writing-up' on my laptop, in photography, video-recording, talking and listening.

Constructed Texts and Student Users

As I have noted elsewhere (Pink 2001) the main concerns and criticisms surrounding the use of hypermedia in anthropology refer to the wider political educational context in which it is being funded and the potential 'incoherence' of hypermedia texts. The same argument frames my discussion of student users of anthropological hypermedia. Henley criticises a 'tendency for CD-ROMs to be presented as authorless aggregates of objective information which the user can wander over at will, creating his or her own narrative threads' (Henley 1998: 55) and Biella agrees with Banks (1994) to acknowledge the possibility that 'disorientation can affect [hypermedia] users who do not follow a plan, a coherent itinerary' (1994: 6). While Henley and Banks raise significant points, nevertheless their concerns refer to issues of authorship, design and navigation, rather than highlighting a 'problem' that is essential to hypermedia itself.

The question of coherence cannot be resolved simply through a consideration of the hypermedia representations themselves, but needs to be considered in terms of the dynamic between user and text. Readers/users/viewers of ethnographic text have frequently been neglected in existing discussions of representation that have focused largely on the ethnographer, the 'subject' of the ethnography, the text and its construction. With the exception of recent work on ethnographic film audiences (see Stoller 1997, Martinez 1990, 1992, 1996) comparatively few have attended to the experience of the (maybe lone) student – who scribbles in margins, underlines 'key points', draws on photographs and is a creative collaborator in the production of ethnographic knowledge. Ethnographic knowledge does not simply exist 'in the text'; even when students 'non-reflexively' copy chunks of text from anthropology books in an attempt to directly insert knowledge found in one text into their own, the text is reframed, producing new knowledge in the context of the student's essay. Martinez has shown that students (like other viewers) appropriate ethnographic film representations, interpreting them in terms of their own experience and knowledge, on the basis of which they may develop racist ethnocentric and, for anthropologists, utterly problematic and unintended, assumptions about 'other cultures'. Especially given Howard's point that 'hypermedia has the potential for establishing an entirely new kind of relationship between authors and readers' (1988: 311), it would seem that equal attention should be paid to the ways students appropriate hypermedia productions.

However, the agency of student users is crucial since the coherence of ethnographic hypermedia texts is produced through the relationship between the creativity and intentionality of authors and readers/audiences. Howard emphasised the role of the ethnographer/author in providing theoretically informed multiple pathways constructed with 'a sense of interconnectivity that is based on a theory of multi-stranded relationships' (1988: 311). It *is* important that hypermedia learning is carefully constructed and as Biella points out, can offer coherent narratives. But, 'links incline: they do not impel' (Biella 1994: 6) and student users also construct their own narratives through hypermedia projects. By encouraging self-conscious decision-making from student users, hypermedia learning might differ from learning from ethnographic books or films; such 'new' texts might inspire 'new' strategies of learning.

However much anthropologists might tailor text for student use, without the collaboration of the individuals – the creative agents, in this case students – who participate as users of the texts, coherence is only ever implied and partial. This is because although ethnographic hypermedia representations may be constructed as multilinear texts, they will be used by individuals to create other linear narratives. As Orr Vered has pointed out, non-linearity refers to a situation where 'access to information is not dependent on serial sequencing or reflection on the order of a mirror'. Nevertheless, '…linearity is the end result of this process, despite the order in which information is acquired' (see *also* Biella 1994: 6). Therefore if the task of the student/user is to create his or her own linearity from multilinear text, the role of the tutor/author is to facilitate this.

Linearity, Non-Linearity and Self-Conscious Learning

With regard to student learning two themes are key to this discussion. First, concepts of non-linearity or multilinearity. These form significant topics in cultural theories of how individual experience and identities are constructed in relation to new technologies in a 'post' or 'late' modern context (e.g., Poster 1995); anthropological theories concerning how anthropological knowledge is produced and the narratives of ethnographic research (e.g., Hastrup 1995, Stoller 1997, Willson 1995); educational theory of student learning strategies (e.g., Jaques, Gibbs and Rust n.d.); and recent discussions of the representation of ethnographic knowledge (see above). Second, concepts of self-consciousness and individual agency, as developed primarily in recent work in anthropology (e.g., Cohen 1994, Rapport 1997a).

New communications technologies rapidly emerged as a theme in social science in the 1990s, exploring themes such as 'cybersociety', 'cybersex', 'disembodiment' and the construction of self-identity. These discussions might inform both the use of new technologies in ethnographic fieldwork and an understanding of how students learn with new technologies. To understand how individuals experience and operate in electronic 'worlds', however, an anthropological focus on self-hood and experience is important. Cohen (1994) grounds the self in the individual's sense of experience and creativity. Thus conceptualising the individual as 'self-driven' and purposeful, rather than as multiple, fragmented and unstable, as theorists of electronic 'worlds' such as Poster (1995) have suggested. Whilst an individual may perform different identities in the course of everyday life (both on- and off-line), these different representations of self are interconnected through the individual's sense of self, thus implying a coherent identity and personal narrative.

This theory combines a critical response to the modern projects of positivism, observation, objectification and scientism. It argues that the observable reality that was at the core of the 'scopic regime of modernity' (Hastrup 1995: 69) was only one version of truth; rather than being 'out there' and observable or visible, reality is experienced, sensed and subjective. However, here the arbitrary nature of reality is dealt with differently from the approach developed by Poster. Cohen's ideas of the 'self-driven' self-conscious individual, imply an interweaving of the different aspects of self (and identity) rather than their dispersal. Therefore in the case of electronic technologies it is the individual, his/her sense of self and self-conscious continuity of identity that holds the multiple narratives of the experience of new technologies together. If one applies this to the question of how knowledge is produced or authored by hypermedia users one can argue that this occurs through the individual's ability to interweave and make sense of the multilinear information represented and experienced in his/her own unique way – that is, to make the text coherent (see above). This entails an ethnographic approach to an understanding of learning and knowledge production that focuses on what Rapport has called 'the theme of *individuality*' – 'the individual's conscious and creative engagement with certain sociocultural environments' (1997a: 1).

Student Learning and Linear Narratives

The questions of 'how students learn' and 'how readers read' and use academic texts has been explored both within anthropological work on hypermedia and studies of pedagogy and student learning. Both disciplines argue that academic readers or learners tend not to approach knowledge lineally. It has been suggested that students tend not to learn in a cumulative way, building knowledge as the lecture sequence progresses on a weekly basis, but many students develop ideas 'in a more haphazard way, sometimes after a lot of mulling over and sometimes by going backwards and forward' (Jaques, Gibbs and Rust n.d.: 19), suggesting a disparity between this student strategy and 'traditionally' linear organisation of teaching. Biella makes a parallel point about scholarly reading strategies, pointing out that one of the 'conventional' requirements of scholarly work is that it 'must be inscribed in a medium which allows rapid, non-linear access to all its components' (1993: 144) and that authors should assume that their texts will be read non-lineally (1993: 145).

Howard has noted that whilst printed text may support non-linear access, its linear narrative also constrains writers by forcing them 'into linear sequential mode' where they are 'compelled to choose which aspects of a total experience are to be placed first, second, third, etc.' In this printed context, then, 'the only way to vitalise interconnections that are nonsequential, or multisequential is to refer back to previous pages' (Howard 1988: 305). Both Biella and Howard propose hypermedia as a means of resolving the restrictions imposed by the linearity of written text. Likewise, they may solve the problems of linear sequential lecturing. Clearly hypermedia can facilitate and even encourage non-linear approaches to using ethnographic representations. In doing so, Howard would argue that 'hypertext thus articulates with actual modes of thinking far better than lineally written materials' (1988: 306). Some would go further to propose that not only is readership non-linear but that the very construction and content of ethnographic texts should challenge the notion of linearity (e.g., Marcus 1995).

The concept of non-linear narrative is an important theme for anthropology. The interweaving of different strands and the multiple non-linear narratives that multimedia and hypertext enable seem especially suitable for learning about ethnography since it enables the author of the text and the user (author of his/her experience) to imagine experiences that imitate the multi-strandedness of doing ethnography. In ethnographic research the process by which knowledge is produced can involve researchers in simultaneously following multiple threads, moving between different interconnected contexts and drawing together what initially appear disparate themes. In addition to the recent emphasis in anthropology on experience and subjectivity, the non-linearity of ethnographic narratives has also been stressed, for example, by Okely's (1996: 149) notion of retrospective fieldwork whereby a previous personal experience may later be analysed as a fieldwork event. Moreover researchers produce their knowledge about local cultures through a range of different methods that may be visual, verbal or involve other senses. The challenge for ethnographers is to find appropriate ways to represent such knowledge to their audiences.

However, not only do ethnographers need to be self-conscious and reflexive over their own practices as authors, and to attempt to be aware of how the texts may be used or experienced. If we are to consider users of hypermedia as authors of *their own* ethnographic knowledge, it would also seem appropriate to encourage potential users to engage in a reflexive approach to their own practices of authorship. A similar approach is implied by Goldman-Segall's notion of 'learner as ethnographer' who 'becomes an expert on the culture of the content, decoding and recoding the meanings, and making layering interpretations of events as experiences become richer' (1998: 2). Goldman-Segall stresses the importance of 'encouraging learners to layer their knowledge and view events from various perspectives' (1998: 2) to realise how 'as readers, they construct texts as they read them' (1998: 3). The potential of electronic text for encouraging such learning practices would be to 'provide the opportunity to engage students in a more personal and collaborative experience' to realise the promise of 'emerging electronic media as cultural partners' (1998: 3). Goldman-Segall's strategy would be one that encourages students to work with montage as 'ethnographer-learners' who can 'follow paths, navigate data, and put together textured layers of knowledge within their own learning constellations' (1998: 3). These questions framed my research about user responses to my hypermedia project. To what extent did students engage reflexively with their own learning?

The Electronic Field

The CD-ROMs, *The Bullfighter's Braid* and *Interweaving Lives*, were designed to be used by undergraduate and postgraduate students to learn about photography and video in ethnographic research. The visual materials included in *The Bullfighter's Braid* were from my fieldwork in Spain (1992–4), the written texts combine a study of the visual culture of bullfighting with a semi-structured way of learning about using photography in ethnographic research. They are designed to offer choices, but remain 'coherent'. *Interweaving Lives*, based on materials from my video and photographic research with a Guinea Bissauan weaver (1997) built on my experiences of the first project. Here I focus on *The Bullfighter's Braid*. The text is intended to be reflexive in different ways. First its title page and a series of five introductory pages inform users about what they should expect to learn from the materials, making the learning process explicit. They also introduce the main characters of the research project, making the research process explicit: the researcher, the woman bullfighter, and the photograph, *The Bullfighter's Braid*. This section has hyperlinks to photographs, video clips and written texts that represent these three themes. The fifth introductory page takes the user to the main menu where he/she is presented with the following choices, each of which represents a route through the text:

Academic Article
Images as Material Culture
The Bullfighter's Braid
Meeting the Bullfighter
Learning Activities

The titles are preceded by a passage, intended to guide the user in his/her approach to the CD-ROM:

> This project contains a set of interconnected strands. You may begin to explore the text from any one of their starting points. Find the route through which you feel most comfortable learning. As you explore the different strands you will start to see how they are interlinked and draw from the same images, contexts and concepts. They are, ultimately all part of the same story.

Whilst each route can be accessed independently, the different narratives are linked through hypertext and draw from the same resource of photographic and moving image links. Thus users were intended to be able to situate their understanding of one narrative in relation to others either through their linked commentaries on the different photographs (that also imply how the same image may become meaningful in different ways in different contexts) or through the hyperlinks between the narratives themselves. Through this design I hoped to allow students of different levels to approach the project from the angle that most suited their own study skills, strategies and knowledge of ethnographic research methods. Some routes are predominantly 'documentary' and visual (e.g., *Meeting the Bullfighter*), others are predominantly written, and photography and video are accessed through hyperlinks (e.g., *Academic Article*). Here I sought to disrupt the grand narrative of 'teaching' and allow students to enter into a more interactive process of 'learning'.

Whilst *The Bullfighter's Braid* and *Interweaving Lives* allow users some freedom to choose their own linear routes, they also link specific bodies of texts and images to indicate meaningful connections and to allow users to explore the particular questions and issues they raise.

Experiencing *The Bullfighter's Braid*

In 1997 I undertook a small project to research users' responses to *The Bullfighter's Braid*. The research took two forms: first through responses to and discussion of demonstrations of *The Bullfighter's Braid*, articulated at presentations and exhibitions in the U.K., Germany, Portugal, Hungary and Sweden (1997–9); second, through detailed evaluation of the electronic text by eleven informants, entailing a questionnaire, interviews and discussions focusing on experiential aspects of the use of the CD-ROM. Informants included multimedia experts, experienced and new lecturers, information professionals and students. Inevitably each user experiences text differently and I do not hope to generalise or abstract experience. Nevertheless my informants appeared to treat the text in two distinct ways.

Half of my informants reported that they had experienced the structure in the most linear way possible. Rather than inventing their own routes they followed the order set out in the main choice pages. Their comments implied they did not self-consciously or intentionally engage with the multilinearity of the text. Whilst the introductory passage to the CD-ROM stated 'You may begin to explore the text from any one of their starting points. Find the route through which you feel most comfortable learning', they treated the structure of the options listed in the menu pages as the order in which the narratives should be approached; explaining their routes as follows, they ceded authority to 'the author' and were unwilling to actively author their own narratives through the texts:

'I suppose that the author has chosen this structure for some special reason'
'Convention'
'It seemed logical'
'It's set up that way'

Two informants, both experienced lecturers, suggested the flexibility that I assumed for multilinear representation was not obvious to students. One stressed the importance of pointing out to students that they can revisit sites and construct their own learning routes: 'students will use it in a linear fashion if they aren't told that they don't have to'. He suggested students should be more strongly encouraged to take their own personalised routes and the links and options of referring back to other narratives should be signposted at key points in the text. Two students did however explore links between the strands. One undergraduate wanted to 'see how the strands were interconnected and to see if I could understand the information adequately without following the chronological order'. Another did not follow the learning exercise narrative first because he 'wanted to do something interactive first- rather than just reading'. This has implications for theory of student learning practices and practical aspects of hypermedia learning texts design. In this research some students learned purposefully, actively, self-consciously and independently. Others sought a dominant structuring narrative in the text, rather than departing from this to structure their own experiences and engage with new types of knowledge. However, they also welcomed visual knowledge and were generally happy with the academic content and the text/image relationship, identifying learning with images as 'more interesting'. Some felt that the use of images had supported their learning in that 'we tend to learn more from seeing than reading- the visual learning stays in the mind longer: it has more impact' (student comment). However this did not necessarily encourage 'self-conscious learning' as 'the combination of visual and written texts made it more interesting: learning takes place without noticing' and 'there is less work than in the traditional approach'.

One student, reflecting on how her seminar group responded to '*The Bullfighter's Braid*' told me that from their discussions she thought some students had felt empowered by the control over their own learning that the CD-ROM offered, whilst others were overwhelmed, felt lost and did not engage with it. Biella similarly notes:

> 'users with little practice in scholarship and little knowledge of anthropology are not likely to make good use of powerful interactive tools' but will need 'the linear path of the designer's tour' (1994: 6).

Defined as an issue of agency, in order to learn from hypermedia in the way I intended, students would have to be encouraged to resituate themselves in relation to the text as creative, motivated agents: 'active learners', as the new educational discourse begs.

Hypermedia has potential for introducing new ways of engaging with knowledge and its production. For instance, hypermedia can potentially resolve problems that some have associated with a linear style of teaching that 'is traditionally planned as a succession of evolving presentations of subject matter and assumes a steadily accumulating understanding'. It has been claimed that 'it is too readily assumed that students learn in harmony with the sequence of a course and that each lecture has been "digested" fully at the time' (Jaques, Gibbs and Rust n.d: 19). If teachers and students approach course content in a linear structure whilst neither learning nor subjects taught in courses are necessarily experienced lineally, the multilinear options of hypermedia texts may be an appropriate solution. As Henley stresses, the medium itself demands an engagement with multilinearity (1998: 55), even if, in the case of some students, their own interaction with the multilinear design was kept to a minimum. Hypertext links between different narratives of hypermedia can help students to forge non-linear connections self-consciously in a way that supports the learning style identified by Jacques et al. To learn about ethnographic research methods, this style may indeed be appropriate. Ethnography itself is a process of learning through subjective experience. New ethnographic research narratives are conceptualised as multi-stranded: research itself has been defined as a multilinear process. Perhaps some aspects of ethnographic research are better learnt in contexts where experience can become the focus of student-centred knowledge production, focusing on students' personal narratives rather than the lecturer's 'grand narrative' dictated in an overcrowded lecture theatre (see Perera and Hartley 1997). However, this should not be seen as a solution to overcrowding, but as a supplement to other methods of teaching and learning.

Empowerment and Multiple Authorship

The option of exploring materials on CD-ROM was 'empowering' for some students: they gained a greater sense of control over their own learning than they experienced when dictated to in a lecture theatre. However the empowerment of students, whilst sometimes pedagogically desirable, raises ethical issues. Should students of ethnographic hypermedia be encouraged to give meanings to other people's narratives? In doing so they may make them meaningful on terms that neither the anthropologist nor the subject of the representation intended.

In some contexts hypermedia might contest 'racism and chauvinism with eminently plausible alternatives' (Biella 1994: 9). Noting Martinez's (1990) concerns about students' racist responses to ethnographic film, Biella suggests hypermedia may 'include strategies that anticipate and interrupt existing viewer-prejudices' and allow viewers to reflect more deeply about such issues, challenging racist responses by contextualising 'intimate portraits with critiques of racial stereotypes'. However, one cannot guarantee that students' approaches to hypermedia will match those anticipated by the author. Anthropologists cannot control students' (or anyone's) experiences and interpretations of hypermedia and it may be undesirable to oblige every student to receive information in the same order. Hypermedia produced for teaching and learning anthropology ought to simultaneously protect the subjects of ethnography, present a 'guiding' pedagogical narrative and encourage students to participate in the production of anthropological knowledge.

If successfully designed then hypermedia texts might invite not one learning narrative, tell one single story, nor dictate that story's narrative, but provide a series of possibilities. Hypermedia can support a lecturer/author's role as a 'facilitator' of learning, allowing students to learn from the angle they find most comfortable by following routes they find most attractive. In this sense it can engender a positive form of 'student-centred learning' that allows students to self-consciously author their own learning As my students indicated, different individuals have different learning needs and preferences. Some prefer to adhere to a structuring narrative offered by their tutor. Others will engage with the materials to author their own routes and knowledge.

Student participation in authoring their own learning might also become a technical activity whereby students actually participate in the construction of hypermedia texts. In this form of collaborative authorship students could also become makers of links and markers of connections between narratives. Here hypermedia texts would be 'open-ended', in that they are produced as 'incomplete' in the pragmatic sense. They would continue to be written by their users, who literally write their own connections by creating new hyperlinks, storing their own notes and writing new narratives into the text itself. This goes further than scribbling in the margin of an ethnographic monograph, and involves the author's recognition that text does not end as representation, but is appropriated by readers and 'learners' who make it into something else.

Hypermedia representations invite their authors and students to practise 'new' forms of engagement with texts, images, sounds and technologies. In this sense anthropological knowledge takes on new forms as it is produced and experienced through the interaction of creative individuals with electronic environments. If the aim is to encourage students to become reflexive, self-conscious learners, then I propose hypermedia, appropriately designed, has an important role to play.

Note

1. This chapter is a development of previous published work on hypermedia in anthropological representation and pedagogy (see Pink 1999, 2001).

References

Banks, M. 1994. 'Interactive Multimedia and Anthropology – a Sceptical View'. http://www.rsl.ox.ac.uk/isca/markus.banks.01.html (date of last visit: 22.11.2000).
Biella, P. 1993. 'Beyond Ethnogprahic Film'. In *Anthropological Film and Video in the 1990s*, ed. J. R, Rollwagen. Brockport NY: The Institute Inc.
Biella, P. 1994. 'Codifications of Ethnography: Linear and Nonlinear'. http://www.usc.edu/dept/elab/welcome/codifications.html (date of last visit: 22.11.2000).

Biella, P. 1996. 'Interactive Media in Anthropology: *Seed and Earth*- Promise of Rain', *American Anthropologist* 98(3): 595–616.

Biella, P. 1997. 'Mama Kone's Possession: Scene From an Interactive Ethnography', *Visual Anthropology Review* 12(2): 59–95.

Cohen, A. 1994. *Self Consciousness: an Alternative Anthropology of Identity*. London: Routledge.

Experience Rich Anthropology. http: //www.era.anthropology.ac.uk/index.html (date of last visit: 22.11.2000).

Fruzzetti, L., Guzzetti, A., Johnston, N. and Östör, Á. 1994. *Seed and Earth*. Video and Laser Disc. Middletown, USA: Wesleyan University.

Goldman-Segall, R. 1998. 'Gender and Digital Media in the Context of a Middle School Science Project', *Meridian* 1(1). http: //www2.ncsu.edu: 80/unity/lockers/project/archive_of_meridian/jan98/feat_3/gender.html (date of last visit: 22.11.2000).

Hastrup, K. 1995. *A Passage to Anthropology: Between Experience and Theory*. London: Routledge.

Henley, P. 1998. 'Filmmaking and Ethnographic Research', in *Image-based Research*, ed. J. Prosser. London: Falmer Press.

Howard, A. 1988. 'Hypermedia and the Future of Ethnography', in *Cultural Anthropology* 3(3): 387–410.

Jaques, D. Gibbs, G. and Rust, C. n.d. *Designing and Evaluating Courses*.Oxford: Oxford Brookes University Educational Methods Unit.

James, W., Hockey, J. and Dawson, A. 1997. *After Writing Culture*. London: Routledge.

MacDougall, D. 1997. 'The Visual in Anthropology', in *Rethinking Visual Anthropology*, eds M. Banks and H. Morphy. London: New Haven Press.

Marcus, G. 1995. 'The Modernist Sensibility in Recent Ethnographic Writing and the Cinematic Metaphor of Montage', in *Fields of Vision*. eds L. Devereaux and R. Hillman. Berkeley: University of California Press.

Martinez, W. 1990. 'Critical Studies and Visual Anthropology: Aberrant vs. Anticipated Readings of Ethnographic Film', *Commission on Visual Anthropology (CVA) Review*, Spring: 34–47.

Martinez, W. 1992. 'Who Constructs Anthropological Knowledge? Toward a Theory of Ethnographic Film Spectatorship', in *Film as Ethnography* eds P. I. Crawford and D. Turton. Manchester: Manchester University Press.

Martinez, W. 1996. 'Deconstructing the "Viewer": From Ethnography of the Visual to Critique of the Occult', in. *The Construction of the Viewer*, eds P.I. Crawford and S. B. Hafsteinnson. Arhuus: Intervention Press.

Okely, J. 1996. *Own or Other Culture*. London: Routledge.

Orr Vered, K. 1998. 'Plotting New Media Frontiers: Myst and Narrative Pleasure'. In *Visual Anthropology Review* 13(2): 39–47.

Perera, D. and Hartley, J. 1997. 'The Costs of Crowded Classrooms', *New Academic* 6(2): 17–18.

Pink, S. 1996. 'Una excursion fotográfica en la vida socio-visual de la gente del mundo del toreo: investigación fotográfica como proceso antropológico', in *Antropologia de los Sentidos: La Vista,* eds M. Garcia Alonso et al. Madrid: Celeste.

Pink, S. 1998a. *The Bullfighter's Braid: Unravelling Photographic Research*. CD-ROM, University of Derby.

Pink, S. 1998b. *Interweaving Lives: Producing Images, Creating Knowledge*. CD-ROM, University of Derby.

Pink, S. 1999. 'Students at the Centre: Non Lineal Narratives and Self Conscious Learning', *Journal of Computer Assisted Learning* 15: 244–54.

Pink, S. 2001. *Doing Visual Ethnography*. London: Sage.

Poster, M. 1995. *The Second Media Age*. Oxford: Polity Press.

Rapport, N. 1997a. *Transcendent Individual: Towards a Literary and Liberal Anthropology*. London: Routledge.

Rapport, N. 1997b. 'Edifying Anthropology: Culture as Conversation; Representation as Conversation', in *After Writing Culture: Epistemology and Praxis in Contemporary Anthropology*, EDS A. James, J. Hockey and A. Dawson. London: Routledge.

Stirling, P. n.d. 'Paul Stirling's Ethnographic Data Archive'. http://lucy.ukc.ac.uk/Tvillage/notes.html (date of last visit: 22.11.2000).

Stoller, P. 1997. *Sensuous Scholarship*. Philadelphia: University of Pennsylvania Press.

Willson M. 1995. 'Perspective and Difference: Sexualization, the Field and the Ethnographer', in *Taboo: Sex, Identity and Erotic Subjectivity in Anthropological Fieldwork*, eds D. Kulick and M. Willson. London: Routledge.

8

Films in the Classroom

Beate Engelbrecht and Rolf Husmann

Point of Departure

About one hundred years ago, film[1] was invented. From its very beginnings, the documentation of different cultures all over the world was one of the main topics in which the early film-makers were interested. Thus very soon, ethnographers such as Alfred Cort Haddon, Walter Baldwin Spencer, and Rudolf Pöch, to name but a few, started to carry heavy and clumsy film equipment with them into the field. As a result, film documents were published soon afterwards which amazed academic as well as public audiences alike.[2]

After these early years of enthusiasm, however, several decades elapsed, before, in the period from the 1950s to the 1980s, a special documentary film genre developed in its own right: ethnographic film.[3] In characterising this rather wide and difficult-to-define field, three points are important:

1. The main characteristic of this genre consists in its broad range of styles.
2. The films are produced by using a sophisticated and elaborate methodology.
3. The main interest of the makers of ethnographic films is an anthropological one: the aim being to understand and adequately (re-)present others and other cultures.

Almost any ethnographic film-maker must therefore come to the conclusion which David MacDougall (1998: 202) expressed thus: 'Implicit in a camera style is a theory of knowledge'.

Over the past several decades an impressive body of ethnographic films has been produced all over the world, many of them accessible from a number of commercial and non-commercial rental institutions or archives. In producing these films, the film-makers have often carried out ethnographic fieldwork of their own, or have worked in collaboration with anthropologists.[4] As a result, besides the films, and often accompanying or complementing them, a range of written material on the subjects and cultures the films deal with is published as print media. It is these combined publications which are of special value for teaching anthropology.[5]

In addition to more academic oeuvres, there exist many very well-made documentaries by non-anthropologists, which are of great interest to anthropology and may be used in teaching. Furthermore, in the last decades the genre of 'indigenous' and 'community' films has opened up new teaching opportunities, as have selected feature films and television productions.

This paper will focus on the use and value of ethnographic films, related documentaries and 'indigenous/community' films for teaching anthropology. Our main questions are practical in nature: how can film be successfully integrated with the teaching of anthropology? And how can teachers select the most appropriate films for their needs and how can such films best be located?

Which Films Can be Used for Teaching?

All films can be used! There is no single answer to the question, 'which is the right film for this topic?' For almost any given anthropological topic there is a variety of suitable films available. The choice will depend on the topic of the lesson, on the region, country or ethnic group being dealt with, but also on the didactic style and pedagogic aims of the teacher: does he/she wish to inform, provoke or shock students, does he/she wish to evoke critical statements, elicit analytic skills? As there is such a variety of teaching styles and methodological approaches, there is also no standardised answer as to the selection of films or how to teach with them.

In the following, a number of possible ideas on and methods of how to use film in teaching anthropology will be discussed. They can be applied to many different films. At the level of teaching introductory courses, both ethnographic films made for academic purposes and so-called 'indigenous/community' films[6] bear a high potential in creating basic, yet very specific knowledge for students and in stimulating their interest in these topics. Ethnographic films made for academic use offer the teacher a certain degree of methodological straightforwardness and a point of view derived from Western society, while 'indigenous/community' films are also potentially useful for teaching, because they present a different perspective derived from alternative cultures. Thus, films depicting a variety of topics can bring awareness to students that there is never any 'single truth', but that there exist different perspectives on how to perceive things, on how to judge the world and its people.

Introduction to Anthropology

Unfortunately only a small number of colleagues who actually teach anthropology use film in their introductory courses. Those who do not are missing an opportunity to make their teaching more interesting, lively and successful – but how can one devise an introductory course in anthropology that relies heavily on film? The following presents a number of concrete examples of how this is being done. The examples derive mainly from the United States, where the contents and learning aims of anthropological introductory courses are standardised and systematically designed to a higher degree than in other countries. These examples may thus provide an idea and a guiding line as to how to plan a course of one's choice.

Introduction to Ethnographic Film

Stephen C. Leavitt (1998) has designed a course focusing on ethnographic film. A closer look at the course design shows, however, that it may not only be used as an introduction to ethnographic film, but also as an introduction to ethnographic fieldwork and ethnographic writing. In his ten-week course, Leavitt treats topics such as: representing others in film, early ethnographic film, capturing culture on film, biographies and portraits, ethics in ethnographic film, etc.

According to Leavitt's course description, there are two meetings every week during term-time. In preparation for each meeting, students are given certain tasks to fulfil, such as reading texts, writing essays, watching films, searching the Web for additional information about the films and providing statements on the films shown in the classroom. The most interesting factor appears to us to be the inclusion of the Internet. Leavitt hands out research tasks to be solved with the help of the Internet. In addition, he holds a regular discussion round where students are asked and given the opportunity to comment on topics raised.

Introduction to Anthropology

A second example we would like to present is an introductory course in anthropology based on ethnographic films. The course was designed by Nancy Lutkehaus who herself is a visual anthropologist. She calls her course 'Exploring Culture through Film' and it may serve as a model of how to organise an introductory course with emphasis on the use of film. Lutkehaus taught the thirteen-week course at the University of Southern California in 1991. The main topics are similar to any other introductory seminar:

Historical Roots of Anthropology,[7] Fieldwork and Participant-Observation, Colonialism,[8] Western Fascination with the 'Other',[9] Socialisation,[10] Religion and the Supernatural[11] (e.g. Bali – Temples and Technology[12]), Shamans, Housewives and Other Restless Spirits,[13] Biographies,[14] Kinship and Gender,[15] Political Economy,[16] War and Peace,[17] Images of the 'Primitive',[18] Indigenous Media: Technology as a Weapon,[19] Old Age[20] and so forth.

This course combines the study of ethnographic literature and films in an interesting way. Films are not only watched (and discussed), they also serve as the basis for reading and writing texts. Apart from the classes based on written texts, there are others in which the students have to write film reports. They are also asked to write a term paper on the subject, 'an anthropological analysis of a life history'.

Seeing Anthropology

While many introductory courses in anthropology or written introductions very often neglect the potential of visual material to a deplorable degree, Karl Heider deserves praise for having produced probably the first comprehensive (and still most up-to-date) introduction to cultural anthropology (1997), which uses film in a very convincing and bold manner. The book is sold together with video tapes of clips taken from films used as examples throughout the course. The written publication contains seventeen chapters, each accompanied by a different video-clip, with titles such as, 'What is Cultural Anthropology?' 'Fieldwork, Exchange, Systems of Communication', and 'Social Control, Religion, Cultural Change'.

In using Heider's teaching tool, each class is carefully prepared for classroom activity. Each chapter focuses on one or two films. Heider has written an introduction to the topic of the lesson in the form of a classical lecture with photos/slides and diagrams. In addition he offers film-clips which are well-suited to the topic and provide an introduction to the culture being treated. Furthermore Heider provides information on the particulars of the film and sets up a range of questions concerning the film. Some are closely related to the different clips, others concern the whole film. As reflections on film may be new to most students, Heider also includes a general introduction for a better understanding of ethnographic films as ethnographies.

Special Courses

Apart from possibilities of using ethnographic films as a core element in introductory courses, and apart from the many opportunities to use film with almost any given anthropological topic, there are specific seminars in which a general anthropological field is combined with a focus on film. Such a course was offered by Husmann in 2000 at the University of Mainz, where he taught a course on 'The Visualised History of Anthropology' using a number of films or filmed material portraying important anthropologists whose life and work is part and parcel of every 'History of Anthropology'. The students were asked to watch, analyse and compare films from the British series 'Strangers Abroad' on Baldwin Spencer, Bronislaw Malinowski, Edward Evans-Pritchard and Margaret Mead, with other productions on Margaret

Mead, Raymond Firth and Fredrik Barth, and with some unedited interview footage with Isaac Schapera.[21]

As a result, the students not only learned how to critically view, compare and analyse such films in terms of their style, content and technical production elements, but at the same time they widened their knowledge of these central figures of the history of anthropology.

Film Guides

In the United States a number of so-called film guides have been published which can greatly help anthropology teachers in selecting films. 'Seeing Anthropology' by Karl Heider (1997) can be regarded as one of these guides. Together with Carol Hermer, Heider (1995) also published a catalogue called 'Films for Anthropological Teaching'. The authors are well aware of the difficulties of selecting film for teaching anthropology. They consulted the main anthropological journals in search of film reviews and questioned experts. The main reminder they provide for teachers is that any given lesson needs careful preparation whenever film is to be used.

The catalogue is intended to be an aid to teachers of anthropology. It is based on two major assumptions. First, nearly any film may be of some use to someone in teaching, but the instructor must be familiar with the film. Many instructors have scheduled films 'blindly' and, viewing for the first time with their students, have been unpleasantly surprised. It is just as desirable to preview a film before selecting it for classroom showing as it is to read a book before assigning it to a class; but, at the very least, the instructor should view the film earlier on the day of class screening in order to prepare students and to tell them what to look for. Secondly, no film can stand by itself as a teaching instrument. Films should be backed up by written materials that can be assigned to the class, or at least that can be read by the instructor' (Heider and Hermer 1995: 1).

In order to make the difficult task of selecting films a little easier, Jayasinhji Jhala (1998) published 'A Guide to Visual Anthropology'. The films selected can be used to teach introductory courses in cultural anthropology as well and should be used together with written material. The films are suggested as a study of cultural content and authorial intent in recognition of the fact that both reflexivity and activist agency concern more and more anthropologists in their methods of doing ethnography and anthropology.

Jhala presents the selected films in alphabetical order. He gives additional information on the team which participated in film-making, names distributors (in the U.S. only!), provides data on format, genre, and key words. A small summary is also given. A very important component is the section: 'Reasons for the Usefulness of the Film'. There are some general questions which Jhala thinks can be applied to every film: What are visual texts? How are they made? What are the techniques used? What strategy is employed, by whom, for what purpose? What is the structure? What are its components and elements? How is a visual text different from a written text? What advantages and disadvantages does its nature and use pose for teacher and student? In addition to these general points he formulates specific questions for each film. He makes a distinction between questions put before and those after the screening.

To conclude this part of the paper we would like to suggest that every teacher create his own film guide, depending on the topics in which he is specifically interested. Here are now some ideas and suggestions about how this can be done.

Selection of Films

The adequate selection of films is important for any successful use of films in teaching anthropology. Karl Heider (1997: xiv) advises us how to select films for introductory courses: they should be relatively short, relatively didactic, and should represent a wide range of culture types and world areas. They should be ethnographically accurate and have a solid written ethnographic back-up. They should be well made and fun to watch. Each film should contribute to the subject of a particular chapter/class.

The selection of suitable films is a time-consuming task. Heider (1997: 8–9) suggests that as a teacher one should review films in a systematic way. Therefore, he has developed some basic questions. For each film, the answers should be recorded on a worksheet.

1. How ethnographic is the film?
2. How much is the people's own view represented?
3. Whose voice or point of view is on the soundtrack?
4. What is the art/science balance?
5. What is the influence of the film crew?
6. Does the film create empathy or disgust?
7. Are shots given a context?
8. Does the film follow through on important acts?
9. How visual and how wordy is the film?
10. How much distortion of time and space do you see?

Having analysed the film, a summary should be made, the degree of usefulness should be defined, a personal statement/note might be helpful for future use, and questions for students should be prepared. Using the film in teaching, one's own experiences should be documented too, so that one can use the film more efficiently on the following occasion.

Methods of Teaching with Film

More and more anthropologists are using film in their classes. We now want to discuss the possibilities of what could be done with film in a class apart from and beyond merely showing them. It is important to note that working with film has a lot to do with anthropological fieldwork *per se*. The methods of teaching with film constantly reflect this. Teaching with film therefore results in teaching a subject, teaching theory and method, and teaching fieldwork at the same time, even if the films are used for teaching a given subject only. Martínez used film extensively in teaching. He comes to the conclusion that film is a valuable teaching tool, a tool that needs deeper involvement on the part of professors:

> The use of film in teaching thus demands an expanded instructional role from professors: the employment of a complex and powerful medium requires a more sophisticated 'translator' of cultures. Such an expanded role would entail understanding the language of visual representation and its rhetorical and interpellatory power, as well as knowledge and application of film criticism. Although most anthropology professors are generally not trained for assuming the task of film critique, the experimental use of films and open discussion of student interpretations in the classroom offers many possibilities for self-training in this area (Martínez 1992: 155).

Film Analysis

One of the main difficulties of using film in teaching and research is the critical evaluation of the film itself. A central question in our courses on ethnographic films is always 'Do ethnographic films show/represent/reproduce reality?' We always have long discussions about questions of objectivity and subjectivity, reality and fiction, authenticity and artificiality. There are, of course, no easy answers to these questions. Every (ethnographic) film-maker, before filming, has to define his position for him/herself with regard to these questions. Having done this, he/she will decide on the methodology to be used in the film-making process. An ethnographic film-maker with research interests trying to record and publish works of lasting value will apply the same rules for his film work as he does in written ethnography.

One of the first things students have to learn is how to read films. From early childhood onwards we are all used to and trained in reading texts critically. Amazingly enough, nowadays living in a so-called media society, the ability of similarly critical reading of films, visual reports, images, etc., has never been taught, either at school or at university. As a result, we all tend to have a very low level of competence in analysing – and understanding – films.

Film analysis is a special subject taught in all media studies departments as well as in history, language studies, and visual anthropology.[22] Some basic tools and methods can also be used in teaching anthropology. The main purpose is to achieve a higher level of competence in working with audio-visual material and therefore to be able to use this source of information in future work. It is crucial to realise that films can be analysed from quite different points of view:

1. Trying to understand the methodology used in a film.
2. Looking for ideological implications.

3. Analysing the full content of a film in detail.
4. Analysing single events shown in a film in detail.
5. Comparing a film with other available source material (other films and written material).

In order to find answers, films have to be analysed in great detail. Students should start to analyse the film on the basis of the composed sequences or single shots. Each sequence/shot has to be described in detail. It might be thought-provoking and an interesting method for the teacher to ask two students to view the same film and to let them answer the same questions, so that their (probably quite different) answers and results can be compared and discussed by the rest of the class.

Looking for the Methodology Used in the Film

Two questions are central here: Which film language has been used and how has the film process been managed? In order to answer both questions, a closer look at the film is necessary – e.g. the film has to be analysed on the basis of shots. Technical categories of analysis could be: in/out points, framing, camera angle/position, camera movements (panning/zooming/walking), original sound, small talk, interview etc., commentary, subtitles, additional textual information, music etc., duration of the shot. A rough description of the content of the shot should be given.

This range of analytic elements can be used for the whole film or for selected sequences. The results then have to be analysed against the background of general film language, e.g. the perspective of montage. On top of this, it will be necessary to think about the circumstances that allowed the film-makers to shoot the film in the way that it was shot. For instance, could it only be filmed in such a way? Did things have to be specially arranged to make the filming possible? Can the question be answered based on the material itself? Can I find material providing any information about the filming situation? Is it a scripted film? Is it an observational film with a somewhat distant camera? Is it a participatory film, where the film team was part of the event? Is it a collaborative work where the protagonists participated in the film concept? Is it a staged film? And so on!

This means one must take a closer look at the shots/scenes themselves: What are the reactions of the filmed people like? How are the shots framed, what was the position of the camera(s) and how is the film content put into context: using commentary, interviews, or additional textual information?

Looking for Ideological Implications

Very closely related to the first question is the second one: can I get an idea of the conceptual position of the film-maker based on the film material itself? What was the aim of the film-maker? What was his relationship to the people filmed? What kind of authority did the filmed people have? How was author-ship dealt with? Is the film based on an anthropological theory?

Here the images, the montage, the textual information, and the reaction of the people have to be analysed against the background of anthropological the-ory. Students should be made aware of the ideological implications of every film and the possibility to discover these in the films themselves.

Analysing the Content of a Film in Detail

Most of the time, films are selected for teaching anthropology because of their topic. Very often they are shown merely for illustration. For some films Heider (1997) offers a number of questions to be discussed with students. Additionally, students can analyse the content of a film in more detail. Here the sequence level rather than the level of the single shot would be adequate. Students have the task of defining sequences and describing the content of each one. Possible cate-gories would be: what is going on? What do I see? (image); What do I hear? (original sound/small talk/interview)? What does the commentary tell us? What could be keywords to describe the sequence? Where are the in/out points?

Film analysis simulates fieldwork in the sense that very similar skills are required and similar tasks are to be solved. The main disadvantage of film analysis is that the student cannot directly ask someone to deepen his understanding. He/she has to use additional information, e.g. other films or written material. The results of this research might be part of a term paper, providing the possibility to deepen the understanding of different cultures. Film analysis can also be used in class as team-work task for various groups. Students will learn two things straight-away: their knowledge of a culture and of a topic is growing, and everyone sees different things in the same material and interprets them differently. Comparing the results of groupwork might then even bring into relief the last point.

Analysing Events Shown in a Film in Detail

Concentrating on special topics in classes, it might be useful to go a step fur-ther and take the film as a source of detailed information. Not all the films are suitable for this, only films documenting single events and/or processes.

Again a film will be split into sequences. Each sequence is then subdivided into single shots. The content of these shots is analysed in detail. Let us take a ritual as an example: the student should try to find out the various parts of the ritual, the main actors, the interactions, the organisation and adornment of space, the adornment of people, the symbols, etc. It is important to focus on clearly defined and limited questions, as the film material may be too rich so that the student may need help by limiting the task. After observing the film and trying to understand what one has seen, the student should then try to correctly interpret the event with the help of additional literature. This exercise will strengthen abilities of observation, a skill which will be very useful for future fieldwork.

Comparing a Film with Other Source Material

It is important to note that each form of publication, film or writing, has it advantages and disadvantages. Often preference will be given to one or the other form based on what most people are more acquainted with. The important thing is to recognise the respective advantages of each form. As for film, the main disadvantage is the limited ability to include necessary or desired verbal explanations and abstract concepts. On the other side, however, the richness of any visual culture can never be adequately described in words alone. Students should therefore learn to take advantage of both sources of information. In future, the integration of both sources will be made much easier by using non-linear forms of publications such as CD-ROM, DVD or the Internet.

Film analysis can be quite a tiresome job. It takes a lot of time and the results may be difficult to communicate. Of utmost importance for a successful use of film in teaching is that teachers assign clearly defined tasks to students. In basic courses the questions must be simple and should relate to students' everyday knowledge and understanding. In advanced and special courses, the level of questions may be more abstract and complex. The analysis of a film or parts of it should be part of a written paper, where a single topic is discussed and additional sources of information are used. The presentation of the term paper provides the possibility to experiment with non-linear tools such as Powerpoint, the Internet or multimedia applications.

It seems important to us to stress that the advantage of integrating film analysis with the teaching of anthropology is a twofold one: on the one hand, students learn how to observe, something they will also have to do in their fieldwork, and on the other, they learn to critically analyse visual material, a skill which is indispensable and which will be ever more in demand in the future.

Reception Analysis

Reception analysis is an apt and very rewarding method of training students in the development of observation skills and deepening their understanding of cultures; it helps to increase their awareness of existing differences in perception, and functions as a tool for assessing their knowledge. Most students have quite a basic and general knowledge of 'other' cultures. There are two possibilities to use reception analysis in teaching: using the students as an audience themselves, or asking them to carry out reception studies with varying audiences.

Students as Audience

In a number of his investigations Wilton Martínez[23] used anthropology students as test audiences for his own films. Stressing the fact that students, as other audiences too, are biased towards other cultures, he opts for a film analysis as a way of learning to perceive other cultures in a non-biased way and, via self-reflection, learning to do anthropological research.

Students largely speak for, and are addressed by, the popular mythologies and stereotypes of the 'primitive' perpetuated and disseminated through an increasingly sophisticated 'culture industry'. As a free-floating signifier, constantly reinterpreted through the intertextual media representations, the 'primitive' is now positioned and consumed in all kinds of contexts: on other planets, in the future, in 'postmodern MTV'. Nevertheless, the popular notion of the 'primitive' retains much of its colonialist and racist signification, as subaltern 'other' to the West. While idealising the most remote 'other', students also see the more proximate 'other', such as 'Third World' people and ethnic 'minorities' in the United States as approximations to the 'primitive', emphasising their differences rather than similarities, seeing their non-mainstream lifestyles as technologically and intellectually 'inferior' and characterised by cultural 'backwardness' (Martínez 1992: 146).

As a result, merely showing films is not enough. A certain helplessness among students is to be observed whenever they are confronted with an ethnographic film without any guidance. They neither know how to read films nor do they know what to 'do' with ethnographic films. Consequently new teaching devices have to be implemented.

The most promising initiative in this field is reception analysis using students as the audience. After having defined the goal of the class and chosen and reviewed an appropriate film, the teacher should formulate questions. They might be open or closed, depending on the content and purpose of the question. Students receive the questionnaires before or after the screening of the film and are asked to answer the questions immediately after the screening, leaving them about five to fifteen minutes for the task. Depending on the subject, an open discussion might follow as well as an individual report of findings by some students. The teacher should take notes on the blackboard in order to structure the results for further discussions. Proceeding accordingly in a succession of classes, students will become acquainted with reception analysis as a research tool. They will definitely start to look at films differently and in a more intense manner, which provides good preparation for students who go on to carry out reception analysis investigations of their own later in their studies.

Testing Varying Audiences

Before starting reception analysis with other audiences, a film analysis of the content has to be made. The results will be essential for the ensuing reception analysis. But first of all the theoretical concept for research has to be defined. On the basis of the content analysis and the theoretical outline, the questions for the reception analysis should be formulated.

The audience itself will also have to be defined and analysed. Depending on the subject chosen and the research interests, one will have to decide on the composition of the audience(s). Edward T. Hall emphasises the fact that various elements determine the way an audience may perceive a film:

> The rules governing what one perceives and is blind to in the course of living are not simple; at least five sets of disparate categories of events must be taken into account. These are: the subject or activity, the situation, one's status in a social system, past experience, and culture. The patterns governing juggling these five dimensions are learned early in life and are mostly taken for granted (Hall 1981: 87).

The main object of any reception analysis is the question as to what different audiences may see and understand when viewing the films – a very good exercise for students, which we have tested among our own student groups. In the beginning the students felt rather helpless, as the content of the films was unfamiliar to them too. They needed quite a time to get an idea of what the film was about. Then they had to formulate correct questions. As it turned out, some exercises were necessary to find the right phrasing of questions. The proper mix between open and closed questions had to be found. An additional open discussion had to be recorded and analysed afterwards. These discussions were as interesting as the answers to the pre-formulated questions. Students discovered that without intending as such, research results divulged far more about the audience than about the film or the cultural differences of perception. Using situational analysis, they discovered the difficulties in communicating anthropological knowledge through ethnographic films.

Feedback Analysis

Feedback analysis is a special kind of reception analysis. The audience consists of the people being portrayed in the film. Feedback analysis is generally applied while working with film in the field. During the past two decades, modern video technology has made the use of feedback analysis much easier. Very recent digital technologies are pushing these possibilities even further so that completely new interviewing techniques can nowadays be applied.

Feedback analysis can also be used with great success in teaching anthropology. If a group of students produces a film on a local subject and analyses it afterwards together with the local protagonists, or if other films on a given local topic are screened and watched together, the taped discussions might be used for analytical purposes afterwards, too. Such exercises make particular sense for the training of students in field methods.

Conclusion

Film can be used in teaching anthropology in many ways. The integration of film with anthropological teaching is interesting and desirable for a number of good reasons: it provides an excellent opportunity to analyse anthropological content in a different and more sensually oriented way; it provides training in observational skills which are indispensable for later fieldwork; and it entails a critical review of questions of subjectivity and authorship. Working with film is closely related to doing fieldwork. Not only can the use of film in the classroom be understood as a simulation of fieldwork; more importantly, the filmmaking process itself is closely related to anthropological field research. Therefore, filming should be seen an additional tool for teaching anthropological field methods.

The possibilities of applications of film in teaching anthropology are numerous. Visual and digital technology are improving rapidly and expanding every year. As such, many new methods for adapting multimedia to teaching will have to be developed. The most hotly debated example of future developments can be clearly seen in the comprehensive incorporation of new media into teaching: CD-ROMs, DVD, the Internet. In this field we envisage great challenges for teachers of anthropology as much as for anybody else.

Notes

1. The term 'film' is used synonymously in this paper for both: film and video.
2. Jordan (1992) has published a catalogue concentrating on early films. It can be found in the Internet under: http: //www.rsl.ox.ac.uk/isca/haddon/ (Date of last visit: 30–09–2003).
3. For literature on ethnographic film see the bibliography of Husmann et al. (1992) covering almost all written publications on the topic, including film reviews, up to the date of publication.
4. The collaboration of Timothy Asch with anthropologist Napoleon Chagnon among the Yanomami has become probably the best-known example. On the topic of collaboration in filming see also Husmann (1978).
5. An excellent example is the case of the Hamar of Southern Ethiopia, about whom Jean Lydall and Ivo Strecker have not only made about ten ethnographic films (several of them award-winners), but also written and published numerous books and articles, fieldwork notes and film work. See Husmann et al. (1992) for bibliographic references. One must also mention the contentious film 'Rivers of Sand' by Robert Gardner, about which Strecker and Lydall, as collaborators in the field, are critical. Cf. Lydall and Strecker (1978).
6. Indigenous film-making has started only comparatively recently, namely with the development of video technology. Especially indigenous groups in the Americas and Australia have taken advantage of this new technology. In what is called 'indigenous film-making' they have used video for documenting their everyday life, for communicating with and informing each other, as well as for informing the rest of the world about their specific problems. Community film-making pursues similar goals, only that the groups concerned are not necessarily 'indigenous' people, but very often social minorities in their own society.
7. Film: 'Do You Take This Man?' by Elise Fried.
8. Film: 'First Contact' (1983) by Bob Conolly.
9. Film: 'Cannibal Tours' (1988) by Dennis O'Rourke.
10. Film: 'Coming of Age' by Margaret Mead.
11. Film: 'Three Worlds of Bali'.
12. Film: 'The Goddess and the Computer' by Stephen Lansing.
13. Film: 'Korean Female Shamans'.
14. Film: 'N!ai: The Story of a !Kung Woman' (1980) by John Marshall.
15. Film: 'Trobriand Cricket' by Jerry Leach and Gary Kildea.

16. Film: 'Ongka's Big Moka' published in the Granada Disappearing World Series.
17. Film: 'The Axe Fight' by Timothy Asch; 'Tapir Distribution'.
18. 'The Emerald Forest' (feature length film) by John Boorman.
19. Film: 'Out of the Forest: The Kayapo'.
20. Film: 'Number Our Days' by Barbara Myerhoff.
21. All films and footage are available from or stored at IWF Knowledge and Media, Göttingen. Catalogues or the homepage under http: //www.iwf.de.
22. Collier and Collier (1986); Maier (1995); Moore (1995).
23. Martínez (1992, 1995, 1996).

Bibliography

Collier, J. and Collier, M. 1986. *Visual Anthropology. Photography as a Research Method.* Albuquerque: University of New Mexico Press.

Engelbrecht, B. 1995. 'Film als Methode'. In *Der ethnographische Film. Einführung in Methoden und Praxis*, eds. E. Ballhaus und B. Engelbrecht. Berlin: Reimer Verlag.

Haddon 1997 – The Online Catalogue of Archival Ethnographic Film Footage 1895–1945. Accessible at: *http: //www.rsl.ox.ac.uk/isca/haddon/* (Date of last visit: 30–09–2003).

Hall, E.T. 1981 (1976). *Beyond Culture.* New York etc: Anchor Books, Doubleday.

Heider, K. 1997. *Seeing Anthropology: Cultural Anthropology Through Film,* (book and 2 video tapes). Boston: Allyn & Bacon.

Heider, K. and Hermer, C. (eds) 1995. *Films for Anthropological Teaching.* Washington: American Anthropological Association.

Husmann, R. 1978. 'Ethnographic Filming: the Scientific Approach', *Reviews in Anthropology* 5(4): 487–501.

Husmann, R., Wellinger, I., Rühl, J. and Taureg, M. 1992. *A Bibliography of Ethnographic Film.* Münster, Hamburg: LIT-Verlag.

Jhala, J. 1998 *A Guide to Visual Anthropology.* Belmont, CA: Wadsworth Publishing Company.

Jordan, P.-L. 1992. *Cinéma, Cinema, Kino.* Marseille: Musées de Marseille, Images en Manoeuvres Editions.

Leavitt, S. 1997. 'Comparing Cultures Through Film'. University Course, accessible at: *http: //www.union.edu/PUBLIC/ANTDEPT/an11syl.htm.* (Date of last visit: 30–07–2001).

Lomax, A. 1975. 'Audiovisual Tools for the Analysis of Culture Style', *Principles of Visual Anthropology*, ed. P. Hockings. The Hague, Paris.

Lutkehaus, N. 1991. 'Exploring Culture Through Film'. Los Angeles: USC.

Lydall, J. and Strecker, I. 1978. 'A Critique of Lionel Bender's Review of "Rivers of Sand"'. *American Anthropologist* 80(4).

MacDougall, D. and Taylor, L. (eds) 1998. *Transcultural Cinema.* Princeton: Princeton University Press.

Maier, B. 1995. 'Zur Methodik der Filmanalyse von ethnographischen Filmen', in *Der ethnographische Film. Einführung in Methoden und Praxis,* eds E. Ballhaus and B. Engelbrecht. Berlin: Reimer Verlag.

Martínez, W. 1992. 'Who Constructs Anthropological Knowledge? Toward a Theory of Ethnographic Film Spectatorship', in *Film as Ethnography*, eds P.I. Crawford and D. Turton. Manchester: Manchester University Press.

— — — 1995 'The Challenges of a Pioneer: Tim Asch, Otherness, and Film Reception', *Visual Anthropology Review* 11(1): 53–82.

— — — 1996. 'Deconstructing the "Viewer": From Ethnography of the Visual to Critique of the Occult', in *The Construction of the Viewer*, eds P.I. Crawford and S.B. Hafsteinsson. Proceedings from NAFA 3, Hojbjerg.

Moore, A. 1995. 'Understanding Event Analysis Using the Films of Asch', *Visual Anthropology Review* 11(1): 38–52.

Distributors

DER – Documentary Educational Resources
101 Morse Street; Watertown, Mass. 02171, U.S.A.
phone: +1/617/926–0491, fax: +1/617/926–9519, e-mail: cclose@delphi.com
Web Catalogue: http: //der.org/docued

University of California Extension Media Center
2176 Shattuck Avenue, University of California, Berkeley, CA 94720, U.S.A.
phone: +1/510/642–4124

IWF (Institut für den Wissenschaftlichen Film) – Knowledge and Media
Nonnenstieg 72, D-37075 Göttingen, Germany
phone: +49/551/5024–0; fax: +49/551/5024–400; e-mail: iwf-goe@iwf.de
Web Catalogue: http: //www.iwf.de

National Library of Australia – Film and Video Lending Service
c/o Cinemedia, 222 Park Street, South Melbourne, Victoria 3205 Australia
phone: +/3/9929–7044; fax +/3/9929–7027; e-mail: nfvlsbooking@cinemedia.net
Web Catalogue: http: //www.cinemedia.net/NLA

NAFA – Nordic Anthropological Film Association
Web Catalogue: http: //www.nafa.uib.no/nafa.htm

RAI – Royal Anthropological Institute
Film Officer, 50 Fitzroy Street, London W1P 5HS, U.K.
phone: +44/171/387–0455; fax: +44/171/383–4335; e-mail: rai@cix.compulink.ca.uk

9

Teaching Museum Anthropology in the Twenty-First Century

Mary Bouquet

Introduction

Had this essay been written even five years ago (in the mid-1990s, rather than early 2001), I would have approached it in a different manner. Many academic departments of anthropology still had a museum collection, and the issue of how to make such a resource 'relevant' for the student population as well as colleagues was still a live one. While there are certainly departments of anthropology with a museum adjunct, there are good reasons for questioning the almost automatic assumption that anthropologists should be primarily concerned with ethnographic collections in the conventional sense of that term. This observation has far-reaching implications for the task of teaching museum anthropology to contemporary students of anthropology, as I shall argue in this chapter.

There used to be a sense in which ethnographic museums seemed to belong to the past of social anthropology as it developed in many places during the twentieth century (see Bouquet 2001b). Although it would be unwise to generalise, where this tendency can be traced it seems to have been part of a broader trend towards separating the material from the social or cultural in anthropology. Starting with the fieldwork revolution in the early decades of the twentieth century and continuing right up to the 1980s, empirical fieldwork – collecting 'data', rather than making collections of artefacts, and writing it up as ethnography – became the main concern for academic anthropologists. Museum anthropologists tended to occupy the margins of academia, and were often associated with practices considered dated and irrelevant to the modern discipline (Ames 1992). This marginalisation of museum anthropology brought with it a loss of practical knowledge about collections and their uses: several generations of students passed through the system without ever really grasping what ethnographic (let alone other) collections and their museums were about. This loss of significance was often translated into the physical removal of collections from older academic departments, while for departments founded later in the twentieth century having a museum was scarcely an issue.

Despite the revival of interest in material culture and museums during the last two decades of the twentieth century (see Jones 1992), there are a number of problems with reintroducing a subject to the curriculum when it has long been neglected. While there is no lack of critical literature on museums, there may well be a problem both of finding a way through that literature, and of connecting theoretical discussions with what is happening on the ground, in the museum world (see Dias 2001, and below). How, then, is it possible to make museums 'real' for young students of anthropology, when they are or were until recently part of a system that rejected the reality of culture as found in museums? 'Real', everyday life went on in the 'field', and many anthropologists preferred to regard the decontextualised, material sediment (somehow 'artificial' by comparison) of the culture(s), for which museums were the custodians, as lying somehow outside the proper limits of their professional interest. The (mid-twentieth century and later) anthropological concept of culture, as concerning a set of characteristics connected with identity, often neglected the place of material culture in general (see, e.g., Miller 1987) and that particularly artificial form of material culture found in museums in particular. Furthermore, how is it possible to make musealised material culture 'real' again in the absence of an accessible collection? The paradox is that although there may no longer be direct access to an 'own' collection, there have never been so many museums, not only in classic metropolitan locations, but also worldwide (see Kaplan 1994, Macdonald 1996). The issue therefore becomes how to tune into this area of culture through a university course: how to become streetwise in museumland (Bouquet 2001b).

Hands-on and Hands-off: a Dilemma

This section will briefly consider the pros and cons of what might be termed hands-on and hands-off approaches to teaching museum anthropology, and suggest a third possibility as a way of getting started. The hands-on and hands-off distinction derives in part from museum discourse itself where, since the cultural revolution[1] that has taken place in many museums, there has been an emphasis on involving visitors with (certain sorts of) exhibits in more than a purely visual sense (see Macdonald 2001). Being able to touch and smell objects, for example, rather than simply looking at them involves visitors (so the argument goes) in a closer and more vivid museum experience. This sort of hands-on approach contrasts with what is often seen as an élitist bias in purely visual contemplation of aesthetically isolated objects, which involves possession of the required cultural capital that is unequally distributed across the population (Bourdieu et al. 1991).

Hands-on and hands-off approaches can also be translated into teaching methods. The hands-on approach would stress the importance of contact with collection materials: in the past, students were required to draw archaeological specimens, and to be able to describe their appearance in some detail. The same was true of ethnographic objects: classification on the basis of external characteristics was the basis of ethnographic collections, their assignment to particular sorts of museum, the research conducted on them, and their eventual display in geo-cultural terms. More recently, there have been interesting attempts to engage students in making small exhibitions (for example, in the departmental library), with the emphasis on learning through doing (see Cannizzo 2001). History students at Utrecht University made (in collaboration with the University Library) a website on the Dutch in New York in the seventeenth century, and an exhibition at the University Museum (see Mulder, Kloek and Jacobs 2000).

Another approach consists in following (part of) the process of making an exhibition that runs parallel to a lecture course, which includes input from technical specialists (photographer, designer, collections manager), and the opportunity to go behind the scenes to the work floor where the process of cultural production takes place shielded from the public gaze (see Bouquet 2001a). The advantage of this way of engaging with the museum is that it demonstrates the network of human and material actors (c.f. Latour 1993) behind the final product. Following the process of production is a very useful corrective to analysing exhibitions as finished products, and one way of connecting theoretical issues with more practical situations. However, it is difficult to imagine this being a real option outside institutions with their own collections. The focus here is thus on the relatively recent extension of ethnographic interest into various areas of musealised culture. I do not discuss teaching what might be termed conventional museum ethnography.

In the absence of a departmental or university collection, the need for an alternative to the hands-on option becomes obvious (see Bouquet 2001c). The lack of a collection, coupled with students' limited knowledge of museums (sometimes accompanied by a dated prejudice against them), as well as the cultural revolution in museumland, led me to develop a form of teaching that combines the study of theoretical literature with excursions to a variety of museums in the Netherlands.[2] The next section gives an account of how the teaching of this course has developed at Utrecht University since 1998.

Streetwise in Museumland

One of the dilemmas of teaching museum anthropology as an academic subject is the unintended but none the less adverse effect that critical museology can have in deterring inexperienced students from further engagement with the museum. This effect has been examined by Nélia Dias (2001) in her comparison of teaching ethnographic museology in two Portuguese university departments: at Coimbra University (where there is a collection), and at ISCTE (Instituto Superior de Ciências do Trabalho e da Empresa, Lisbon) where they do not have one. Critical museology was decisive in revitalising interest in museums during the last two decades of the twentieth century (see Shelton 2001). The sharp critique of earlier museum practices accompanied, and was sometimes even a prelude to, a revival of interdisciplinary interest in museums after several decades of academic neglect in many different places. Reintroducing museum anthropology into the curriculum is not, however, a straightforward matter after it has been effectively missing for a long period. Dias observed that although students in Lisbon were often exhilarated by new theoretical approaches to the museum, they sometimes felt discouraged from taking an active part in this form of cultural production due to the weight of so much critique.

Finally, the fact is that museums are one of the places where anthropology students can find not only a useful but also an exciting way of using anthropology in the world after university, which is no trivial consideration. One of the challenges of teaching museum anthropology in the twenty-first century, therefore, consists in providing students with the necessary critical understanding of museum culture, without eliminating the potential for ethnographic engagement of various sorts with the institution. In seeking this equilibrium, there are a number of factors to be taken into account, relating both to the history of anthropology and its specific connection with the ethnographic museum in the past, as well as the place of the museum in contemporary global culture.

The most significant factors with respect to teaching museum anthropology, in my view, include: (1). the former, almost automatic connection between university departments of anthropology and 'their' (sort of) museum has, in many cases, been severed; (2). the global increase in the number of museums, cultural centres, heritage sites and the like, which inevitably attract increasing attention during fieldwork, means that the museum has returned to the anthropological agenda in a rather different incarnation from its original disciplinary form; (3). the 'cultural revolution' in museums themselves has led, amongst other things, to a situation in which anthropologists are potentially well-placed to engage in the work of translation that cultural production involves.

Given these factors, the question of how exactly to reinstate the museum in the curriculum is furthermore conditioned (and to some extent hampered) by the disciplinary history of anthropology, in which the ethnographic museum played a specific role. If academic anthropology originated in the museum during the nineteenth century, this connection was gradually severed – in many places – during the twentieth century. The 'fieldwork revolution' that took place in the early decades of the twentieth century, and that is often associated with Malinowski's Trobriand island studies, was partly responsible for the gradual institutional divergence between university and museum anthropologies, although precise histories and chronologies have obviously varied (see, e.g., Segalen 2001). This meant that by the 1970s, even in cases where there was still a departmental museum (as in Cambridge), museum anthropology had become a marginal and unfashionable subject in many universities. This situation was not limited to Britain in the second half of the twentieth century: elsewhere in Europe (for example, Norway, Portugal, and the Netherlands) and beyond (see Ames 1992) the ethnographic museum had become associated with the prehistory of modern anthropology rather than its present. The majority of academic anthropologists lost touch with the collections, many of which had been acquired in anthropology's 'museum period' at the end of the nineteenth century (Sturtevant 1969).

These collections (or elements of these collections), insofar as they were used in 'modern' exhibitions designed to instruct the general public about the cultural specificity of 'other cultures' across the world, were often completely subordinated to the project of ethnographic representation, frequently in a timeless sort of present tense. This brought about a kind of crisis of representation by the 1980s, remarkably similar to that which occurred in written ethnography around the same time. Questions of authorship (who is the author of a text, or for that matter an exhibition?), for example, and of power (who has the right to represent whom?) became central issues in both universities and museums (see Shelton 2001). However, whereas the skills required to deal with a crisis of textual representation had never really been lost, there was an important sense in which academic anthropologists had lost track of events in the museum; this situation was clearly reflected in the status of teaching museum anthropology in many academic departments (see Cannizzo 2001). Furthermore, they had to learn new skills (such as working as a member of a project group) that were not traditionally associated with those of the curator.

The advantages, when starting a course from scratch, of using concrete examples from the museum world on the doorstep are numerous. Being able to 'see'/inspect in material form some aspect of a theoretical discussion is one of the didactic windfalls of teaching a subject in what has been called a 'museum culture' (Vaessen 1986). In what follows, I shall discuss how the first and the third of these three factors – collections, and the cultural revolution in museums – can be harnessed into a teaching programme, connecting theoretical discussions from the literature with examples drawn from the world on the doorstep. These remarks primarily concern situations where museum studies are being introduced or reintroduced into a curriculum, and may therefore appear rather elementary to those fully versed in what it means to undertake this step. In approaching the subject in this elementary way, I shall emphasise the importance of local factors in shaping a course. In my view, this is a sound (and a symmetrical, in Latour's [1993] sense) way of preparing students to handle the second factor, the musealisation of culture, wherever they may encounter it in the fieldwork situation.

Collections

Collections are one of the fundamental elements of museums studies, and always appear in standard definitions of the museum as an institution (see the definitions given by the International Committee of Museums [ICOM], and those by national associations such as the Museums Association [Great Britain] or the Nederlands Museum Vereniging [NMV]). Definitions in themselves are quite abstract, however, and for teaching purposes it is necessary to think of how to impart this material in a thought-provoking and vivid way.

Dias (2001), in her comparison between teaching museum ethnography at ISCTE in Lisbon (with no institutional collection) and at the Department and Museum of Anthropology in Coimbra, emphasises the difference it makes to the scope of teaching to be able to go with students from the lecture theatre into the depots. Material with which to illustrate historical and theoretical points is – literally –at hand.

The absence of a collection can, however, also form an interesting point of departure for teaching. The question of why there is no collection now, when there used to be one thirty, fifty or perhaps one hundred years ago is a way of making students think about the institutional histories of anthropology, and question what might too easily appear as a secular trend. When I started teaching museum anthropology in Utrecht in 1998, for example, I deliberately scheduled the first session in the lecture theatre (now a museum piece!) at the University Museum in Utrecht. The old benches from the Department of Anatomy form part of the exhibition about university history, centrepiece of the brand new museum building that is located in the midst of the Utrecht 'museum quarter'. This reconstructed (portion of a) lecture hall was an excellent stage setting (in 1998 we were still allowed to occupy the benches – this is no longer the case) in which to tell about the dissolution of Utrecht University's ethnographic collection at the end of the 1960s when, according to Schoonheym (1986: 68):

> The cultures of former colonies together with the study of material culture receded into the background, and it became taboo in student circles to be interested in material culture. The ethnographic collection was scarcely used any more. Since no one was interested in the collection, it was more or less abandoned as an object of curation.

The local story in Utrecht, as part of a much more general episode in the history of anthropology, was a good way to begin. Moving the location of the first lecture from the (out-of-town) university campus to the (now centrally located, new) museum premises, was a perfect way of dramatizing the changing scope of museum anthropology.

Science Collections

Although there is no ethnographic collection at the Utrecht University Museum, there is an important natural science collection including items from the eighteenth century Bleuland anatomy collection, and a significant nineteenth-century dentistry collection, in addition to the reconstruction of an early nineteenth-century cabinet of curiosities (to which I return below). What appears to be a closed chapter turns out to reflect one of the most exciting new directions for museum anthropology: an ethnographic approach to science and natural history museums. Science, as Sharon Macdonald (1998) has argued, is to a large extent 'made' in museums; and the cultural processes whereby this takes place form one of the new frontiers of ethnography (see Allison-Bunnell 1998; González, Nader and Ou 2001; Macdonald 2001). Cultural values are as deeply embedded in displays of modern technology as they are in the dioramas on display in the African Hall at the American Museum of Natural History, which Haraway has analysed as a kind of idealised vision of American manhood (Haraway 1989). Cultural values come to the surface very clearly in conflicts such as that surrounding the display, at the Smithsonian Institution in Washington, of the Enola Gay airplane, which was used to drop the first atomic bomb (see Gieryn 1998; Zolberg 1996).

Science museums in the Netherlands, such as Naturalis (the new National Museum of Natural History that opened to the public in Leiden in 1998), can be put to excellent use in teaching museum anthropology. The place of Darwinian evolutionary theory in the museum's credo is mirrored in the spectacular light-show phylogeny, which occupies a central place in the exhibitions 'Primeval Parade' and 'Nature Theatre' (on the ground and first floors respectively), and can be operated by the visitor from computers on the ground floor. Survival and extinction of all forms of life can be seen at a glance: some illuminated lines reach the ceiling (and the diversity of forms of surviving life is then shown in the display of key plant and animal specimens from the collections), other illuminated lines do not make it to the ceiling – although some of the extinct forms can be found in the fossil collection on the ground floor. Part of the ethnographic interest lies in exploring the tension between the museum's – self-legitimating – educational intentions, and the public's actual use and experience thereof, which may be very different (see Falk and Dierking 1992).

This ethnographic way of looking at science museums is a good example of how the range of museum culture that is relevant to anthropologists can be extended. All museums, of whatever sort, can be examined as particular cases of making specific cultural visions of different subjects materialise. Not only the collection itself, but also the architecture and wider setting within which that collection is re-contextualised, work to construct culturally specific values and meanings (see Duncan 1995). Apart from the physical setting of a museum object, the professional staff responsible for curating and exhibiting these materials form together what Handler (1993) refers to as a 'social arena', or what I have referred to as the actor-network (following Latour, Callon and others) that connects both humans and objects in the process of making exhibitions (Bouquet 2000).

Cabinets of Curiosity

The classifications and values involved in early collections are much easier to grasp by actually visiting a museum (re)construction than by studying the literature alone. The (re)construction of a late eighteenth- early nineteenth-century cabinet at the Utrecht University Museum brings theoretical discussions and even the best illustrations to life (see, e.g., Bennett 1995; Pomian 1990) in an immediate way for modern students, for whom such referents are often quite remote – although extremely intriguing. Other museum examples within the Netherlands include Rembrandt's cabinet of curiosities in the Rembrandt House in Amsterdam, where a reconstruction in one of the rooms adjoining the artist's atelier demonstrates both Rembrandt's professional use of these items in his work, and the personal status involved in possessing such a collection. The sixteenth-century surgeon Velius's medical and herbal cabinet also demonstrates how the practice of professional competence might be combined with making a broader collection, and hence with broader social status. Velius's cabinet in the West Fries Museum in Hoorn can be visited and analysed in conjunction with the literature on the topic, providing rich discussion material.

Museums themselves can thus be used to render the historical dimensions of collecting and collectors tangible for contemporary students. Excursions provide a way into the visceral nature of collections; they stimulate interest in the origins, historical fate (Rembrandt went bankrupt partly as a result of his extravagant life-style and collecting activities), and connections with colonialism (almost anything could be obtained in seventeenth century Amsterdam, with the VOC [Verenigde Oostindische Compagnie] transporting huge quantities of trade goods in both directions) in a direct way that facilitates discussion and understanding.

National Collections

Since the 1789 French Revolution, national collections became a way of making visible cultural distinctions between the new – basically similar – political state structures, and hence important elements in creating national identities. In allowing the general public access to these collections, which were displayed according to new classificatory principles, museums became significant instruments of government, from the nineteenth century onwards (see Bennett 1995). Such national collections were significant both for European states in the nineteenth century, and for newly independent states world-wide during the twentieth century (see Kaplan 1994; Prösler 1996).

The National Museum (Rijksmuseum) in Amsterdam, founded towards the end of the nineteenth century, illustrates the way national (Dutch) state history came to reside in a specific repertoire of objects, many of which stem from the Dutch royal collection. Visiting and analysing their local National Museum can be an instructive exercise for students of museum anthropology: they can learn to see the way in which national history is literally 'made' (in much the same way that evolutionary history is 'made' at Naturalis, the National Museum of Natural History in Leiden.) The specific combination of seventeenth-century art upstairs (with Rembrandt's *Nachtwacht* as the centrepiece) with the object-driven presentation of national and colonial history

(1500–1850) downstairs, together produce an impressive vision of the Netherlands – especially popular with tourists. The production of national cultural identity in this form provides a fascinating field for what, as Ames (1992) has observed, is in fact a form of anthropology at home. However, in the case of the modern museum world, anthropology at home is in fact only the beginning. An understanding of how the museum world is structured nationally and internationally is an essential form of preparation for undertaking further work (whether research or cultural production) anywhere in the museum world.

In this section I have deliberately used three examples of collections that might at first sight appear remote to anthropologists' former concerns. I have argued that science collections, (reconstructions of) historical cabinets of curiosity, and national collections are directly relevant to teaching museum anthropology especially, although not necessarily, in the absence of a departmental ethnographic collection. Every sort of collection, with its system of classification and professionally defined group of experts, forms the sort of social arena or actor-network that is susceptible to anthropological analysis. Furthermore, if the link between anthropologists and ethnographic collections is no longer an automatic one, then the advantages of becoming conversant with the parameters and practices associated with other kinds of collections would appear to be obvious.

The Cultural Revolution

The formation and use of collections comprise one significant area in which the resources on the doorstep can easily be harnessed to enliven the study of literature. A second area where museums themselves provide endless material for study is the cultural revolution.

Sundering of the almost automatic connection between an academic discipline such as anthropology and 'its' ethnographic museum has in part to do with what Macdonald and Silverstone (1991) refer to, with particular attention to the situation in Great Britain, as the 'cultural revolution' in museums.

The internal reorganisation of museums of all kinds that took place from the end of the 1980s had to do with a change in the relative importance attributed to collections as distinct from exhibitions. Given the limited visibility of collections (which ranges from 80 percent in storage, 20 percent on show, to 93 percent in storage and 7 percent on display in certain cases), accountability towards the public, by means of whose taxes and on behalf of whom these collections are maintained, became a major issue during the 1990s. The costs of keeping collections were one of the motives for introducing entrance fees, which in turn provoked a discussion about the quality of what was being offered to the public. If visitors now had to pay for access to what had often been free facilities, this placed museums in direct competition with other spare-time facilities. If the emphasis in the past had been on educating citizens, changing views on public responsibility suggested that entertaining consumers might be a more appropriate way of conceptualising the work of museums. Museums could no longer legitimise, it was argued, catering for the tastes of a minority élite at the expense of the general public. Furthermore, curatorial authority over collections, which had previously extended to matters of public access and exhibitions as well as knowledge and conservation, came to be modified by other considerations, such as communication, design and marketing. Providing the public with an enjoyable (as well as an educational) packet of services, which included all kinds of facilities, gave museums with a pretext for reorganisation in which curatorial authority was modified.

Whereas students wishing to carry out research or gain work experience in a museum might in the past have been almost automatically assigned to the curator of one or other ethnographic collection, a student of museum anthropology today is more likely to end up in the Public Relations or Communication departments of a natural history or art museum. Museum anthropology needs to take account of these profound changes in the museum world in its teaching programmes. This is a crucial point with regard to the observations made at the beginning of this chapter concerning critical museology. The cultural revolution that has taken place and is taking place in Dutch museums is a fact of the museum world as students will now experience it. It is, therefore, of the utmost importance that they are capable of understanding and evaluating those changes as anthropologists, and learning to see ideological positions as part of the ethnographic data.

The Dutch Open Air Museum's Cultural Revolution

One of the most interesting cases of the cultural revolution among Dutch museums is the Dutch Open Air Museum (Nederlands Openluchtmuseum, hereafter NOM). This famous national museum with its collection of regional (farm)houses and buildings was threatened with closure at the end of the 1980s, and survived only as a result of public protests and the installation of a new management structure, including privatisation (*verzelfstandiging*), and complete reorganisation (see Vaessen, 1995, 1996). The museum exhibits underwent complete revision, introducing life and action into (for example) the Zaanse bakery, which started to bake and sell bread and cakes; demonstrations of former agricultural activities – such as fence-making – in farm outbuildings provided visitors with something on which to focus and in which to take an active part. The same recipe was repeated throughout the extensive museum park. New attractions were also introduced: a tramline with working trams enabled visitors to travel all over the park, stepping out wherever they wished. Old-fashioned children's toys, such as stilts and iron hoops, together with a fairground roundabout, were placed at the disposal of young visitors. A milk factory in working order, a printing press complete with volunteer retired printer, and indeed many other – often costumed – volunteers inhabiting the farmhouses and other buildings introduced the illusion of an inhabited past at the full disposal of contemporary leisured visitors.

The most recent additions to the NOM are a new entrance complex, including a long wall showing building techniques from around the Netherlands; restaurant and shop facilities; an information desk, and (some) office space; two underground exhibition halls; and a multimedia show, the HollandRama, also reached via the underground area, based on the principles of the nineteenth-century panorama, giving a condensed version of a succession of scenes from everyday life (landscapes, townscapes and interiors), interlarded with historic film footage. This complex was built with the 'dowry' received by the NOM at the time of its privatisation, with the aim of providing the museum with a clear entrance, extra exhibition space especially for bad weather, and a further attraction likely to appeal to contemporary visitors.

If the NOM has become a more entertaining place to visit, it has scarcely become an amusement park in the derogatory sense of that term. The rationale behind the new uses of the collection is the result of both policy change and recourse to historical forms of presentation (such as the panorama) of a more popular nature than the abstract museological principles that came to dominate exhibitions from around the mid-twentieth century. However, the cultural revolution at the NOM did not take place without debate about the principles involved (see, e.g., Voskuil 2000), and these differences of opinion, combined with a visit to the institution concerned to examine what is happening on the ground, make rich teaching material.

Endnote

This account of designing and teaching an experimental course in Utrecht has underlined the advantages of its optional character. The benefits consist in trying out ways of teaching with a small group of motivated students. The need to build up practice and knowledge from the very first year did, however, become obvious after giving the course for three years. The museum visits, open to all (eighty) first-year students (who include sociologists and psychologists), can easily be slightly modified to include some elementary museological issues: for example, a visit to the Tropenmuseum in Amsterdam provides a golden opportunity to draw students' attention to the museum as a process. The regional exhibitions dating from the 1970s to the present and the principles involved make for exciting discussion – with museum staff, who are both practically involved in and at the same time reflecting upon the processes concerned. This introduces a completely different angle on museum culture: students learn that they are not 'looking at India' when they walk through the famous reconstruction of a slum, but a specific vision of 'the third world' that inspired staff at the museum during the 1970s – in the aftermath of war and Indonesian independence.

In addition to visiting the Tropenmuseum in Amsterdam, first-year students also travelled to the City Museum of The Hague (Haags Gemeentemuseum, hereafter HGM) to gain insight on and to explore the notion of museological context. Whereas the Tropenmuseum emphasises the importance of placing what are classified as 'ethnographic artefacts' in reconstructed contexts to make their meaning clear to visitors, an art museum such as the HGM seems to do the opposite. Art museums, so the argument goes, tend to show their collection to aesthetic rather than educational advantage, isolating paintings on white walls, and relying much more on what their visitors already know. However, art museums create their own kind of context, as the art historian Carol Duncan (1995) has shown using anthropological theory of ritual to make her point! Viewing Mondrian's famous unfinished painting *Victory Boogie Woogie* in the context of the HGM raises significant issues about how national identity is continually recreated according to the issues of the day. This painting was reacquired for the nation (from a private owner in the United States), for more than eighty million guilders in 1998, using national funds, to mark the end of the Dutch guilder as national currency. *Victory Boogie Woogie* occupies pride of place in the most important national collection of Mondrian's work, in the then newly restored Berlage building from the 1930s.

The museum visits were supplemented by lectures that aimed to provide the first-year students with insight on developments and issues in their immediate museum environment. This is a very important start. The next step would be to introduce a unit into the second-year programme that would provide an intermediary step – for all students majoring in anthropology – to gain further insight on musealised culture.

There is much to be said for building up a topic such as museum studies in this – very modest – way. It tests the commitment of all those involved, and can provide students with the necessary room for gaining concrete experience and exploring the labour market potential before taking a fully fledged step in this direction.

Glossary

HGM – City Museum of The Hague (Haags Gemeentemuseum)
ICOM – International Committee of Museums
ISCTE – Instituto Superior de Ciências do Trabalho e da Empresa, Lisbon
NMV – Nederlands Museum Vereniging
NOM – Dutch Open Air Museum (Nederlands Openluchtmuseum)

Notes

1. The 'cultural revolution' in museumland refers to a complete reorientation of museum work, and involved both internal reorganisation, and a revision of external relations (in terms of funding, public service, and so on). This process started in the 1980s and is still far from com-

plete. In concrete terms, it entailed a shift in the relative emphasis given to collections and exhibitions, in the balance of power between curators and communicators, and in the notion of service to the public as customers (Macdonald and Silverstone 1991).

2. The course, for seven study-points, is an option open to (occasionally enthusiastic second) third and fourth-year anthropology students, as well as interested non-anthropologists. It is taught in the first term of each academic year (September to December), and divided into three blocks, each of which is closely tied to an excursion. Since moving to University College Utrecht in 2002, I have developed a summer course ('Museum Studies: the Embarrassment of Riches) based on the same principles.

References

Allison-Bunnell, S.W., 1998. 'Making Nature 'Real' Again: Natural History Exhibits and Public Rhetorics of Science at the Smithsonian Institution in the early 1960s', in *The Politics of Display. Museums, Science, Culture*, ed. S. Macdonald. London and New York: Routledge.

Ames, M. 1992. *Cannibal Tours and Glass Boxes. The Anthropology of Museums.* Vancouver: University of British Columbia Press.

Bennett, T. 1995. *The Birth of the Museum. History, Theory, Politics.* London: Routledge.

Bouquet, M. 2000. 'Thinking and Doing Otherwise. Anthropological Theory in Exhibitionary Practice', *Ethnos* 65(2): 217–36.

— — — 2001a. 'Academic Anthropology and the Museum: Back to the Future. An Introduction', in *Academic Anthropology and the Museum: Back to the Future*, ed. M. Bouquet. Oxford: Berghahn.

— — — 2001b. 'The Art of Exhibition-Making as a Problem of Translation', in *Academic Anthropology and the Museum: Back to the Future*, ed. M. Bouquet. Oxford: Berghahn.

— — — 2001c. 'Streetwise in Museumland', *Folk-Journal of the Danish Ethnographic Society* (Special issue on Ethnographic Collections).

Bourdieu, P., Darbel, A. with Schnapper, D. 1991. *The Love of Art. European Art Museums and Their Public.* Cambridge: Polity Press.

Callon, M. 1986. 'Some Elements of a Sociology of Translation: Domestication of the Scallops and of the Fishermen of St. Brieuc Bay', in *Power, Action and Belief. A New Sociology of Knowledge?*, ed. J. Law.. London and New York: Routledge and Keagan Paul, pp. 196–229.

Cannizzo, J. 2001. 'Inside Out: Cultural Production and the Academy', in *Academic Anthropology and the Museum: Back to the Future*, ed. M. Bouquet. Oxford: Berghahn, pp. 162–76.

Dias, N. 2001. '"Does Anthropology Need Museums?" Teaching Ethnographic Museology in Portugal Thirty Years Later', in *Academic Anthropology and the Museum: Back to the Future*, ed. M. Bouquet. Oxford: Berghahn, pp. 92–105.

Duncan, C. 1995. *Civilizing Rituals. Inside Public Art Museums.* New York and London: Routledge.

Falk, J.H. and Dierking, L.D. 1992. *The Museum Experience.* Washington D.C.: Whaleback Books.

Gieryn, T.F. 1998. 'Balancing Acts: Science, *Enola Gay* and History Wars at the Smithsonian', in *The Politics of Display. Museums, Science, Culture*, ed. S. Macdonald. London and New York: Routledge.

González, R., Nader, L. and Ou, C.J. 2001. 'Towards an Ethnography of Museums: Science, Technology and Us', in *Academic Anthropology and the Museum: Back to the Future*, ed. M. Bouquet. Oxford: Berghahn, pp. 106–16.

Haraway, D. 1989. 'Teddy Bear Patriarchy; Taxidermy in the Garden of Eden, New York City, 1908–36', in *Primate Visions: Gender, Race and Nature in the World of Modern Science*. New York: Routledge.

Handler, R.. 1993. 'An Anthropological Definition of the Museum and its Purpose', *Museum Anthropology* 17(1): 33–6.

Jones, A.L. 1992. 'Exploding Canons: the Anthropology of Museums'. *Annual Review of Anthropology* 22: 201–20.

Kaplan, F.E.S. (ed.) 1994. *Museums and the Making of 'Ourselves'. The Role of Objects in National Identity*. Leicester and London: Leicester University Press.

Latour, B. 1993. *We Have Never Been Modern*. Hemel Hempstead: Harvester Wheatsheaf.

Macdonald, S. 1996, 'Introduction', in *Theorizing Museums. Representing Identity and Diversity in a Changing World*, eds M. Macdonald and G. Fyfe. Oxford: Blackwell Publishers.

——— (ed.) 1998. *The Politics of Display. Museums, Science, Culture*. London and New York: Routledge.

——— 2001. 'Behind the Scenes at the Science Museum: Knowing, Making and Using', in *Academic Anthropology and the Museum: Back to the Future*, ed. M. Bouquet. Oxford: Berghahn, pp. 117–141.

Macdonald, S. and Silverstone, R. 1991. 'Rewriting the Museums' Fictions: Taxonomies, Stories and Readers', *Cultural Studies* 4(2): 176–191.

Miller, D. 1987. *Material Culture and Mass Consumption*. Oxford: Blackwell.

Mulder, H., Kloek, E. and Jacobs, J. 2000. *Nederland aan de Hudson. Utrechters in New York in de 17de eeuw*. Utrecht: Universiteitsmuseum.

Pomian, K. 1990. *Collectors and Curiosities. Paris and Venice, 1500–1800*. Cambridge: Polity Press.

Prösler, M. 1996. 'Museums and Globalisation', in *Theorizing Museums. Representing Identity and Diversity in a Changing World*, eds M. Macdonald and G. Fyfe. Oxford: Blackwell Publishers.

Schoonheym, P. 1986. 'Culturele Antropologie. De Collectie Ethnografica van het Instituut voor Culturele Antropologie', in *Rijksuniversiteit Utrecht: 350 jaar verzamelaar*. Utrecht: Universiteitsdrukkerij Utrecht.

Segalen, M. 2001. 'Anthropology at Home and in the Museum: the Case of the Musée National des Arts et Traditions Populaires in Paris', in *Academic Anthropology and the Museum: Back to the Future*, ed. M. Bouquet. Oxford: Berghahn.

Shelton, A. 2001. 'Unsettling the Meaning: Critical Museology, Art, and Anthropological Discourses', in *Academic Anthropology and the Museum: Back to the Future*, ed. M. Bouquet. Oxford: Berghahn.

Sturtevant, W. 1969. 'Does Anthropology Need Museums?'. *Proceedings of the Biological Society of Washington* 182: 619–50.

Vaessen, J. 1986. *Musea in een Museale Cultuur. De Problematische Legitimering van het Kunstmuseum*. Zeist: Kerckebosch BV.

——— 1995. 'Een Bewogen Verbeelding van het Leven: het Nederlands Openluchtmuseum in de Jaren 90'. *Jaarboek 1995 Nederlands Openluchtmuseum*. Nijmegen: SUN.

Voskuil, J.J. 2000. Afgang. Het Bureau 6. Amsterdam: Uitgeverij G.A. van Oorschot.

Zolberg, V. 1996. 'Museums as Contested Sites of Remembrance: The Enola Gay Affair', in *Theorizing Museums. Representing Identity and Diversity in a Changing World*, eds M. Macdonald and G. Fyfe. Oxford: Blackwell Publishers.

Part 3

Experiential Learning

10

Professional Practice
in Anthropology
Course Overview, Disciplinary and Pedagogic Approaches[1]

Stella Mascarenhas-Keyes

Introduction

This chapter is based on a course entitled 'Professional Practice in Anthropology', which is a week-long, national, residential, professional practice course run by the Group for Anthropology in Policy and Practice (GAPP) since 1986. It has been developed outside mainstream university teaching in the U.K., and apart from the first one, I have directed all the courses held almost every year since 1989. In 1997, a curriculum resource manual for university teachers entitled *Professional Practice in Anthropology* was published in order to make the course's curriculum content and pedagogic approach available for use by a range of teachers and learners, as is this chapter.

This chapter opens with an overview of the course. It covers its aims and rationale, and provides a profile of participants. The development of the course's disciplinary and pedagogic approaches has been informed by the views of Boyer (1990) and Elton (1987). Boyer (1990) argues that the concept of scholarship in higher education, conventionally applied to research activities, should be extended to include teaching. Indeed, Elton suggests that teachers in higher education should 'bring to their teaching activities the same critical, doubting and creative attitudes which they bring habitually to their research activities' (1987: 56). In the GAPP course, new ideas are continually being experimented with and amended in the light of participants' and staff's critical evaluation. The preparation of the curriculum resource manual provided an opportunity to review the course more systematically. This chapter explores the key themes and issues that have emerged from this review. It demonstrates that the course is learner-centred with the following major components:

1. A curriculum whose epistemology is based on a combination of disciplinary and narrative knowledge.
2. An andragogic model of learning which values learner experience and capacity for self-directed work.
3. Collaborative learning in a vibrant learning community.
4. The development of a critical disposition.
5. Staff who have teaching, research, and research-related experience within and outside the university and play the role of facilitators.

The examination of the learning and teaching process undertaken below will enable those who use the manual to understand the rationale for the sequence of sessions in the course, the construction of the resource materials, the design of the exercises and the way in which participants' learning is assessed.

Overview of the Course

Aims

The aims of the GAPP course, which have been revised and refined over time, are to enable participants to:

1. Gain awareness of the knowledge and skills developed through studying anthropology and to increase their confidence in articulating and applying them to new research, and research-related and other employment fields.
2. Be better able to understand and relate to professionals from other disciplines.
3. Decide on a practical approach to applied research and research-related projects, assess the policy and practice implications, and make recommendations for action.
4. Develop familiarity with the strengths and weaknesses of a range of research and investigative methods in order to decide on the most appropriate method, bearing in mind time, financial, and other resource constraints.
5. Take account of ethical issues and gain a greater understanding of the organisational context in which applied work is undertaken.
6. Enhance the acquisition of a range of professional skills such as working in unidisciplinary and multidisciplinary teams; writing and defending oral and written proposals and reports to diverse professional and lay audiences.
7. Develop personal skills such as self-reliance, time and stress management.

Outline of Course Structure

The duration of the residential course is officially forty-six hours spread over five days, but because participants work on their own a good deal, they often spend a lot more time than scheduled. The director has overall responsibility for designing and running the course, and together with an assistant director, serves as a generalist resource person and facilitator. Specialist staff are recruited for particular aspects of the course.

The course is constructed around two major substantive case-studies, one U.K.-based and the other overseas-based, developed from projects undertaken by anthropologists. An active learning approach is used in which participants work on task-centred exercises related to these case-studies in teams of approximately six people. Team-working skills are regarded as being increasingly necessary for the work place (Harvey et al. 1997), as is the ability to write reports and proposals for non-academic audiences. Therefore, training and experience in communication and teamworking skills are provided. Students, particularly those who have done doctoral research, have become accustomed to perceiving research as long-term. To enable good quality applied research to be conducted within time, financial and other resource constraints, participants are shown how to use rapid research and investigative methods.[2] Data on the course is collected from secondary sources, as well as by interviewing a range of people brought in to facilitate the course. Tapes of interviews with some informants are also provided to extend the range of data available.

The sites of knowledge production and sources of funding have been changing, and increasingly researchers have become engaged in applied and strategic research outside universities (Loder 1992).[3] Anthropologists working in various institutions need an understanding of the organisational context in which they are located, and participants learn how to undertake a rapid organisational analysis as well as gain an understanding of complex ethical issues. As applied research and research-related work is rarely undertaken in unidisciplinary contexts, anthropologists have to develop the skills to work in multidisciplinary settings. Furthermore, as applied research is often used as a basis for action, the case-study related exercises help participants acquire the capacity to make informed judgements and rational recommendations for action. These recommendations form part of the proposals and reports which participants have to present to specially recruited panels. Each panel comprises around five members drawn from within and outside the universities, and from a range of disciplinary and professional backgrounds. It also includes members, or someone role playing such a person, from the community to which the research relates. Panel members are often existing or potential employers of anthropologists. Plenary sessions are held at regular intervals to draw together the work of small groups and to debate theoretical, epistemological, policy and practical issues. The pace and scheduling of sessions attempts to simulate some of the stressful conditions of applied work.

For instance, deadlines for the submission of proposals and reports are strictly enforced. The course structure, content and process attempts to integrate the explicit development of conceptual, analytical, professional and personal skills particularly appropriate for professional practice.

Profile of Participants

The GAPP course serves as initial professional education for some participants, while for others it is a form of continuing professional education. Participants (approximately twenty-five per course) come from a range of U.K. anthropology departments as well as other parts of Europe and overseas. The majority have a postgraduate qualification in anthropology although the course has also been taken by undergraduates. Alumni already in jobs, and sometimes sponsored by employers such as the Department for International Development, UNHCR, and health authorities have attended the course. A small number of professionals, from various disciplinary and professional backgrounds, have also been recruited.

The 1997 GAPP course held in Cambridge provides an example of the profile of participants. Of the twenty-one participants, there were fourteen with or studying for a higher degree in social anthropology, two midwives, one nurse tutor, two English Literature graduates, one graduate with a degree in geography and history, and one with a degree in archaeology and geography. There was thus a predominance of anthropologists, five of whom were doctoral students. Ten British universities were represented; two participants came from Denmark, one from Austria, one from the Republic of Ireland, one from Hong Kong and one from Colombia. The latter was sponsored by his employer, an international aid agency, and flew in specially for the course. There were five males and sixteen females. The participants ranged in age from twenty-one to fifty-five.

Link with Employment

The course is concerned with increasing the employability of graduates and, therefore, attempts to bridge the gap between the university and the world of applied research and research-related work. The legitimate concerns of students and alumni seeking jobs outside the university have provided compelling reasons for the development of an appropriate curriculum. The course not only takes account of disciplinary knowledge and frameworks, but incorporates educational processes intended to enhance knowledge and skills acquisition for early entry into jobs where anthropology is directly used. Indeed, the rationale for the development of an explicit emphasis on skills acquisition is based on requests contained in participants' evaluation of the course. One participant in the final stages of a doctorate said he attended the course in 1991 and again in 1997 specifically to develop teamwork skills. Although many anthropology departments in the 1990s increasingly have begun providing year-long masters' courses in applied anthropology and incorporated some components into undergraduate programmes (Mascarenhas-Keyes with Wright et al. 1995: 23–7), nevertheless, there continues to be a demand for the distinctive disciplinary and pedagogic approach of the GAPP course.

The concern with employment was also partly responsible for the selection of case-studies drawn from different sectors, one of which is U.K.-based and the other overseas-based. A justification for this approach has emerged from a study of employment patterns of alumni which revealed that individuals worked in both U.K. and overseas policy and practice contexts. This study also demonstrated that the majority had to be self-reliant, geographically and sectorally mobile, and have the flexibility to engage in a multiplicity of roles, the most common being social researcher (Mascarenhas-Keyes with Wright et al. 1995: 65–71). Indeed, anthropologists are exemplars of the 'portfolio worker', an emerging trend of the changing national and international labour market.

A related point that is addressed, but developed much more outside of formal sessions, is the relevance of anthropology to other aspects of participants' lives. In informal conversation with participants, and during the optional individual surgery sessions,[4] discussion often centres on ways to use anthropology through involvement in community activities such as membership of committees of schools and playgroups, tenants associations, appeals tribunals, etc. For these participants, using their anthropology in voluntary sector activities is a way of keeping their discipline 'on the boil' and adding to their portfolio in anticipation of future employment. This message appears to boost the self-esteem of those who are currently, or who envisage being involved in career breaks because of child-care and elder-care responsibilities, underemployed or unemployed.

The Learning and Teaching Process

The GAPP course adopts a learner-centred approach. Ramsden (1992: 4) suggests that teaching can be improved by studying how participants learn, and in preparation for writing this chapter a more systematic approach was used than before. At the course held in Cambridge in 1997, for the first time, participants were given a lecture on the educational theories underpinning the course. I felt that such an explicit exposition would help induct them to the pedagogic methods of the course and facilitate the learning process. Midway during the Cambridge course, and at the end, participants engaged in group discussions where they critically reviewed their learning against the theoretical approach. Staff also evaluated their role in the course, and theirs' and participants' views are incorporated into the sections below.

Barnett argues that 'a curriculum is an epistemological project' (1994: 46). There are two parts to this argument. First, the parameters of the curriculum determine what constitutes worthwhile knowledge. Second, the pedagogic relationship developed between educators and students itself acts as an epistemic framework. I would argue that a third dimension of the epistemic framework is the pedagogic relationship established between students. These three aspects of the GAPP course are highlighted in the examination of the learning and teaching process.

Sources of Knowledge

The GAPP course is founded on the view that there are a variety of sources of knowledge: disciplinary knowledge (deriving from formal study of anthropology and other subjects); professional knowledge (deriving from working in professional situations); and personal knowledge (deriving from the phenomenology of everyday life experiences). The personal and professional knowledge of participants constitute what Bruner calls the 'narrative construal of reality' (1996: 130) and their use in the course is elaborated in the andragogic model of learning section following this one.

Anthropology participants on the GAPP course usually have a considerable amount of disciplinary knowledge, particularly if they have studied in departments where a 'substantivist philosophy' predominates (Mascarenhas-Keyes with Wright et al. 1995: 17–18). On the GAPP course, to supplement the participants' existing disciplinary knowledge base, various anthropology books and articles pertaining to the case-studies are made available. Knowledge deriving from other disciplines is provided mainly by lectures, videos and citations in reading lists. Apart from drawing on participants' own professional knowledge, two methods are used to incorporate professional knowledge into the course. First, practising professionals from various backgrounds are brought in to facilitate particular parts of the course. Second, some of the texts participants are given, and those cited on reading lists, comprise the 'grey' literature of unpublished reports, community newsletters, etc. University lecturers and practising professionals give lectures, are available for interviews, receive and question proposals and reports produced by participants, hold individual surgeries, and provide informal careers advice.

The episteme of the GAPP course legitimates the use of various types of knowledge and the curriculum is constructed to encourage a triangulation of knowledge sources. Furthermore, some exercises are designed which specifically require students to excavate their tacit knowledge (Polanyi 1967), that is, embodied knowledge which resides in the individual's extensive and largely inarticulated private world. For instance, an exercise requiring the organisational analysis of a university is designed with this in mind. Narrative knowledge gained through idiosyncratic and multiple epistemic pathways is harnessed with propositional knowledge based on the systematic and rigorous study of social reality, and encoded in academic books and articles.

In reviewing their learning, many participants on the Cambridge course remarked that they found the use of personal and professional knowledge empowering. While there are exceptions, the use of adults' previous and present experience is only minimally used in mainstream anthropology teaching. Numerous students whom I interviewed for the survey of anthropology teaching in the U.K. (Mascarenhas-Keyes with Wright et al. 1995) remarked on this, epitomised in the words of one student who said 'I feel disempowered. I'm treated as if I am *tabula rasa*'. The GAPP approach endorses Bruner's view that participants have been led 'to recognise that they know far more than they thought they ever knew, but that they have to "think about it" to know what they know' (1996: 52). As one Cambridge participant pointed out 'when we were stuck, we encouraged each other to dig deep into our own knowledge base to see if anyone knew anything relevant to our problem... and we did'. The reflexive approach encouraged in the GAPP course mirrors the approach which I regard as valuable in fieldwork, where the 'self', in addition to the 'other', is a source of knowledge (Mascarenhas-Keyes 1987). The GAPP course also endorses Pocock's view that a participant's personal anthropology, 'formed by virtue of his being social' should be brought into a permanent relation with the 'formal anthropology of his discipline' (1971: viii–ix). Indeed, the course goes further because participants are also encouraged to develop a capacity to engage with knowledge from a number of disciplines.

Narrative knowledge is derived from subjecting participants' experiences to critical examination. The use of participants' experience in the GAPP course is in keeping with the andragogic model of learning which is discussed next.

The Andragogic Model of Learning

Knowles (1978, 1984), who consolidated and articulated ideas now associated with this approach, views andragogy as the art and science of helping adults learn. While there have been reservations about the distinction he makes between the learning process of adults and children (Hanson 1996) and the lack of clarity and specificity of his underlying assumptions (Davenport 1993), nevertheless, his emphasis on the value of learner experience and capacity for self-direction resonates with the educational philosophy underlying the GAPP course.

Knowles argues that adults derive their self-identity from experience. He contends that:

> if in an educational situation an adult's experience is ignored, not valued, not made use of, it is not just the experience that is being rejected: it is the person. Hence the great importance of using the experience of adult learners as a rich resource for learning (1984 : 11).

The use of learner experience in the GAPP course draws eclectically from a number of different traditions of adult education. Saddington (1992) identifies five traditions: liberal, progressive, humanist, technologist (behaviourist), and radical. He notes that the learner's life experience in the liberal tradition provides the capacity to engage in meaningful discussion; in the progressive tradition, it is a source of learning and inseparable from knowledge; in the humanist tradition, it is the source of knowledge and the content of the curriculum; in the technological, it determines the entry point of the learner; and in the radical, it is basic to understanding the societal context and therefore the source of knowledge. As will become evident in this chapter, all but the behaviourist tradition inform the GAPP course.

The behaviourist approach is rejected because it favours an audit of participants' knowledge and skills on entry and the determination of a step-wise training process to meet predetermined learning outcomes. The rejection of an operational competency-based approach is exemplified in the manual as none of the exercises specify learning outcomes. Rather, the course is based on the presumption that what participants bring to the course powerfully shapes and impacts on what they learn. Similarly, what each participant gains from the GAPP course will undoubtedly vary and this is testified by the range of comments made in the evaluation of the course (Mascarenhas-Keyes 1991).

The use of concrete experience – both the previous experience of participants and that obtained on the course – is encapsulated in an experiential learning cycle which underpins the course. This is based on the work of Kolb (1984) who synthesised the ideas of a number of earlier writers. Kolb argues that there is a natural learning cycle which has four stages. The first stage is based on concrete experience. The second stage involves observations and reflections on that experience. In order to make sense of these reflections, the third stage comprises the formation of abstract concepts and generalisations. Finally, the implications derived from the abstractions are tested in new situations.

The GAPP course curriculum and teaching methods are designed to follow Kolb's learning cycle by making it possible for participants to:

1. Involve themselves fully in new experiences.
2. Reflect and observe their experience from many perspectives.
3. Create concepts that integrate their observation into logically sound theories.
4. Use these theories to make decisions to solve problems.

While Kolb's learning circle provides a useful basis to structure the curriculum, in practice, individuals do not automatically follow the stages of the cycle (Dennison and Kirk 1990). In a collaborative learning situation, not all individuals in the group are at the same point in the cycle at the same time. Cambridge participants felt that there were often certain members in their teams who were more engaged at specific points of the learning cycle, a view also endorsed by Taylor (1987). The fact that teams comprised different types of learner seems to have accelerated the individual learning of some members. As one Cambridge participant who was used to learning on his own, and at a slow pace, said 'I was amazed to find I could learn so quickly'.

Self-directed learning, another component of the andragogic model, is an important feature of the GAPP course. Contrary to Knowles' view that self-directed learning is a natural way for adults to learn (1984: 42), Cambridge course participants did not, at first, find this a natural way to learn, despite an initial lecture on the andragogic process. This may well have been because their previous pedagogic experiences had developed a dependency on tutors. However, within the supportive environment of an intensive, residential course, and by working in teams, participants were able to share their anxieties and mitigate them in ways that were less threatening than if they were working individually.

Fostering self-directed learning requires considerable preparation time on the part of staff – it is not merely a case of leaving the participants to 'get on with it'. Three examples will illustrate the need for preparation:

1. To develop self-assessment and peer-assessment skills (see Boud 1995), participants have to critique each other's reports resulting from an assignment on Case-study Two . A fishbowl technique is used, in which pairs of teams are required to take turns while a third team observes the process. Staff are absent from the session to forestall any 'final arbiter's syndrome', but to ensure the session's success, the structure of the exercise and the timetable for the session has to be 'owned' by the participants. This self-managed session is later followed by a plenary session, where staff lead a discussion on the content and process of the assignment.

2. Participants are given exercises which contain a number of prompts about courses of action that they could take. This gives them the security of a sufficient basic structure to exercise control over how they will use their time, the steps they will take to complete the assignment, the methods of engaging in enquiry, and the balance between theirs' and the team's need for independence and co-operation. However, it is strongly emphasised to them that they are free to jettison the prompts. Some teams do this, and the ones that do so successfully tend to have high levels of intellectual, social and organisational skills.

3. A problem-based learning approach (Boud and Feletti 1991; Engels 1991) is used in Case-study two in which participants have greater freedom to manage their work so long as they meet the goal of providing a report by a specified deadline. Such an approach has greater potential to facilitate deep learning. As Bruner writes, 'acquired knowledge is more useful to a learner when it is discovered through the learner's own cognitive efforts, for then it is related to that used in reference to what one has known before' (1996: xi–xii).

This approach is in stark contrast to the 'banking' concept of learning (Freire 1972) where learners are seen as empty vessels whose minds have to be filled with knowledge by the teacher.

The experience of the GAPP course suggests that key features of the andragogic model – use of learner experience and self-directed learning – can be successful if adequately planned and managed by staff. The use of learner experience is well suited to multidisciplinary work because experience, and the knowledge which derives from it, is not organised in discrete disciplines. Increasing degrees of learner autonomy are phased in during the GAPP course as participants get acclimatised to the educational demands that it imposes. The friendly, competitive atmosphere that is generated as teams try to produce the best proposal or report (rewarded by a prize) promotes not only individual and group autonomy but also self reliance and interdependence. The creation and maintenance of a supportive and vibrant andragogic learning environment has implications for the role of course staff, which is taken up in detail later. It also has implications for the development of group dynamics which is discussed next.

Collaborative Learning

Applied work is often undertaken in multidisciplinary groups of heterogeneous composition. To facilitate the development and enhancement of participants' knowledge and skills to operate in such groups, collaborative learning is an integral part of the GAPP course. While there are some opportunities for participants to work individually, these are usually part of a staged process of collaborative working.

In order to foster the relational quality of learning in which the individual and the environment are mutually constitutive of the result, it is necessary to establish and sustain a vibrant learning community. In such a community, participants are more likely to be able to relate intellectually and socially to groups of various size and composition. Moreover, they need to feel relaxed to participate in plenary sessions in which staff are present. However, to ensure collaborative learning is effective from the start of the course poses considerable challenges. Participants are generally unknown to each other; most have had experience of pedagogic cultures where the individual is privileged; they come from a range of disciplinary and professional backgrounds and, in addition, there are personality and cultural differences. The complex group dynamics created by the heterogeneous composition of groups can be addressed in many ways (Collier 1983). Five techniques in the GAPP course are discussed below.

First, multiple forms of collaboration are used. Syndicate groups (teams) are set up to work over a sustained period of time on each of the two case-studies. The first syndicate team is preselected by the course director, taking account of such criteria as disciplinary and professional background, age, gender, ethnic background and institutional affiliation. The second team is self-selected by participants. At other points in the course, buzz groups, comprising pairs or threesomes, are established for specific tasks of short duration and participants are encouraged to work with those they have not worked with before. Triads run over the length of the course, and are established to provide opportunities for meta-learning, that is, learning about the way one is learning on the course, and exploring projected learning and career path-ways.[5] The outcome of discussions in syndicate groups, buzz groups and triads is fed into whole group plenary sessions with staff present.

Second, attention is paid not only to the cognitive (thinking) dimension, but also to the affective (values and feelings) and the kinaesthetic (action and doing) dimensions to accomplish a holistic appreciation of the social learning process (Boud et al. 1993: 12). In order to accelerate social interaction, a number of strategies are used. Background information about participants and staff is circulated prior to the course so that participants can identify those with whom they have a convergence of interests. Individuals display name badges and opportunities are provided for socialising immediately prior to the course, through frequent breaks during the day, by taking meals together, and by drinking in local pubs. The *esprit de corps* is further fostered by a special course dinner. The use of bright, airy rooms, and the physical layout of seating in plenary and syndicate rooms is designed to create a relaxed environment and facilitate maximum eye contact between all those present. In good weather, participants usually work outdoors. At the start of the course, various ice-breakers are used. For instance, a five-minute session of throwing a ball to each other while simultaneously calling out one's own name and that of the person to whom the ball is thrown, not only provides for the release of tension through laughter and physical movement, but also ensures that anonymity is reduced as every person is identified by name. Furthermore, this kind of kinesthetic activity creates an informal group atmosphere, which reduces tension and helps to promote active participation and listening which are essential to collaborative work.

Third, to arrive at the ideal of authentic communication, participants are asked to draw up a list of ground rules, which are reviewed periodically, to promote mutual respect, confidentiality and trust . The aim is to create a safe environment where individuals feel encouraged to take risks to explicate and revise their views in collective discourse. In plenary sessions, opportunities are provided for the sharing of emotions and ideas with the whole group, the only proviso being that such sharing is elective and does not breech rules of confidentiality. This strategy develops the professional skills of empathy, confidentiality and trust which are paramount in classical, as well as applied, anthropological fieldwork situations.

Fourth, it is recognised that while learning is more effective when it is undertaken with a co-operative spirit, conflicts are inevitable. Some degree of conflict can be healthy and stimulating, but there is a danger that it can lead to demoralising threats to the confidence and self-esteem of the individual, to the survival of the team, and the failure to accomplish designated tasks. Indeed, it was my experience, early on in directing a GAPP course, of intense conflict in one team which culminated in its dissolution and stress among participants, which led me to introduce explicit training in conflict resolution skills.

Fifth, participants require feedback from staff, in addition to that from peers, on the way they are engaging in groupwork. This strategy was used on the 1996 GAPP course and was very effective. One of the staff, adopting a 'fly on the wall' technique, circulated among teams and observed them. Feedback was given on individual, team and whole group levels. Such a strategy can help identify the barriers to authentic engagement in collaborative learning which may arise from unequal power-relations. The conscious and unconscious sources of inequalities of power generated by the legacy of patriarchy, colonialism, élitism and such like can be explicitly confronted, but not necessarily resolved, by encouraging group and individual reflection and discussion. Participants find this strategy empowering, but point out that one of the limitations of the GAPP course is its inability to provide the 'real world' situation of junior people working in teams dominated by professors, line managers, etc. whose power emanates from their senior positions in organisations.

Collaborative learning provides an ideal environment for the social construction of knowledge. Bruffee argues that unlike the transmission mode of teaching where knowledge is an entity transferred from a teacher to a student, 'collaborative learning assumes instead that knowledge is a consensus among the members of a community of knowledgeable peers – something people construct by talking together and reaching agreement' (1993: 3). It would be misleading, however, to suggest that teams in the GAPP course always reach consensus. Although this is the ideal, practical considerations, such as time constraints, sometimes result in discussions being cut short, and decisions taken on a majority view.

In the GAPP course, the outcomes of the continuous dialogue in small teams is fed into the larger group during plenary sessions. This process enables participants to see that there are many different ways in which assignments can be interpreted and different conclusions reached. In the debriefing sessions which follow all exercises, the interpretive process continues with everyone engaging in collaborative learning, and the expert panelists and other staff contribute by drawing on their own knowledge base.

While the interpretive approach is valuable in fostering understanding, participants on the GAPP course have to develop the capacity to take risks and make informed judgements leading to action. This requires the development of a critical disposition which is discussed next.

The Development of a Critical Disposition

The development of a critical disposition in the GAPP course can be analysed in terms of three areas: thinking, reflection and action. Each is discussed in turn, although in practice they are interconnected.

Thinking

Anthropology participants on the course have usually already developed the capability at theoretical levels to critique concepts, theories, research methods, etc., that derive from their own discipline. However, the course requires an extension of their critical thinking capacity in two major ways. First of all, they have to think critically about the application of disciplinary concepts and methods to an applied research- and/or research-related context. Second, they have to develop rapidly, not only a familiarity with, but a critical stance towards, other disciplinary perspectives. This is a challenging task given that, in one week, they are exposed to a range of disciplinary perspectives. In the manual there are two case-studies used as part of the course: for the HIV/AIDS in Scotland case-study, participants are presented with disciplinary perspectives from epidemiology, urban planning, finance, and social work; for the Gender and Development in Indonesia case-study, they are exposed to the approaches taken by agro-economics, geography, international relations, politics, and gender studies.

Participants working in multidisciplinary teams have to hone their critical thinking skills because they have to defend their perspective to other disciplines. In such cases, conflict can be quite intense. For instance, in Cambridge, one team had difficulty reconciling an anthropologist's qualitative and holistic approach with an economist's and a geographer's quantitative and atomistic approach. Anthropology participants said that to defend their discipline to non-anthropologists called for greater intellectual effort than when they were working with anthropologists alone, amongst whom there was a shared understanding. They felt compelled to think about the specific anthropological contributions they could make, and to find reasons to justify these. Participants on all GAPP courses generally find this a difficult task and, indeed, a senior epidemiologist who sat on one of the Cambridge course panels, specifically commented on this relative failure on the part of participants.

Reflection

Participants on the course are encouraged to engage in two types of reflection: reflection-in-action and reflection-on-action. This is derived from the work of Schon (1987) who writes about the 'reflective practitioner'. Although there have been criticisms about the validity of the distinction between the two types or reflection (Eraut 1994), nevertheless, it has been useful in structuring the course.

Schon sees reflection-in-action as reflection in the midst of action. Thus he says 'in an action-present – a period of time, variable with the context, during which we can still make a difference to the situation at hand – our thinking serves to reshape what we are doing while we are doing it' (1987: 26). While working in teams, participants are engaged in constant dialogue with each other and the comments of others helps to reshape their thinking almost instantaneously. Similarly, when undertaking interviews, reflection-in-action helps to tailor the line of questioning in response to what informants are saying rather than keeping strictly to a predetermined format.

Reflection-on-action takes places at both individual and group levels. Participants often feel they do not have sufficient time for reflection-on-action because of time constraints in an intensive course. Although structured sessions provide for reflection both on the process and on the product of action (a distinction not apparent in Schon's work), nevertheless, participants find the time too short. It may be because participants are more used to the leisured pace of university courses that they feel unable to reflect under time constraints.

While time can be one factor which can inhibit reflection in the GAPP course, another factor which needs to be guarded against is the resistance to engage in reflection. Such resistance can emanate from both participants and staff. Critical self-reflection can be painful and threatening for participants, as it requires a personal acknowledgement of weakness. Furthermore, as individual reflection in the course is part of a staged process towards group reflection, further pain may be experienced in sharing thoughts and feelings with others. This is not to say that many do not find the process ultimately emancipatory, particularly when they realise others share similar weaknesses and anxieties, and that they can work collectively towards finding solutions. The levels of personal engagement and sharing are, of course, influenced by such factors as personality and other attributes, but more importantly by the feeling of trust and mutual respect that has developed among the team. Self and group-reflection help participants to develop the capacity to work as reflective practitioners.

Action

The assignments on the GAPP course make it mandatory for participants to 'stick their necks out' and make recommendations for action, bearing in mind political and ethical issues, to improve the existing situation which each case-study addresses. This is the part of the course that participants, especially those who have had no prior professional experience, find most challenging. Not surprisingly, many of them initially resort to ideological rhetoric. Indeed, one participant on the Cambridge course, commenting on the discussions with anthropology teammates working on Case-study Two (Gender and Development in Indonesia) remarked 'They are all rabid feminists. Their recommendations will not work in Indonesian society'. Although the participant was mistaken in the perception of 'Indonesian' society in monolithic terms, nevertheless, he was pointing to the lack of contact with reality that his peers had. The situation was no different with a project closer to home. A health service practitioner working with anthropologists on Case-study One (HIV/AIDS in Edinburgh) remarked in exasperation 'They are all so idealistic. Their proposals would never be accepted by funders and by people who live in the city'.

One attempt to inject realism is made by the choice of panel members to whom proposals have to be presented and defended. Panelists are chosen to represent a range of stakeholders in a project. They are often professional people who may have some responsibility for projects anthropologists may be involved in, and to whom they will, therefore, have to be accountable. Panels also usually include someone from the lay public, or a staff member role playing the lay public, who might comprise the constituency of the project. Thus, for instance, in the Edinburgh and Hull courses, both of which included (different) case-studies on HIV/AIDS in the U.K., representatives were invited from voluntary organisations whose clientele, and sometimes staff, were living with the virus. In Hull, a middle-aged overseas African student played the role of a village elder in a case-study focusing on rural development in Africa. On the Kent course, a senior area manager for National Westminster Bank was present to comment on the financial components of proposals and reports. On another course held in Hull, the President of the local Chamber of Commerce chaired a panel.

As panelists often represent specific communities of practitioners, their involvement in the GAPP course allows participants to engage in 'legitimate peripheral participation' in their activities (Lave and Wenger 1991). These panelists represent a multiplicity of discourses and participants have to learn how to engage critically with them. While participants are usually skilled in writing academic texts, they have to learn how to write texts of different genres for different audiences. One technique used to challenge participants is to have their text read first by peers from another team, before it is read by the panel. The way peers read and assess the text is influenced by the fact that everyone has been working on the same issues, under the same constraints, and, therefore, has a shared experience.

On the other hand, the line of questioning taken by the panel is often quite different from peers. Participants have to think rapidly on their feet and articulate an oral text which is consonant with their written one, and with the views of team members. The panels, sometimes by prior design in consultation with the course directors, engage in incommensurable discourses. Thus, for instance, in Cambridge, the panel for Case-study Two comprised members who role played the in-country Minister of Agriculture, the Senior Area Desk Officer for the Department for International Development, and a representative from a women's non-governmental organisation. While the Minister asked questions relating to government control and disbursement of project funds, the Desk Officer posed a provocative question: 'Why don't you give the money to the village women themselves and let them decide how to use it to improve their lot?' This forced the teams to defend their rationale for their project. Often the panelists had earlier been interviewed in the data collection phase. In presenting their reports to these panelists, participants became acutely aware of the issues of representation (Clifford and Marcus 1984) and of writing for a 'native' audience (Mascarenhas-Keyes 1987).

Each team is usually confronted with a different set of questions, so that by the end of the session, when four to five teams have made and defended presentations, all participants have been exposed to a very wide range of action plans that have been critiqued and defended. Panelists sometimes suggest how two proposals can be combined to produce a better one. Participants are then better capable of appreciating the strengths and weaknesses of each proposal. The substantive issues raised by proposals are taken up in the subsequent debriefing sessions, when panelists who have engaged in role play resume their usual persona, and the viability of the recommendations for action are discussed at length.

The production of recommendations for action demonstrate that the thrust of the GAPP course is not to transmit a specific body of knowledge, although the participants' knowledge base is extended, but to develop a capacity to apply knowledge and skills to improve the quality of life. Indeed, Maxwell argues that the notion of enquiry should be transformed from enquiry for the enhancement of knowledge to enquiry for the enhancement of personal and social wisdom. He suggests that:

> The fundamental intellectual task of a kind of enquiry that is devoted, in a genuinely rational and rigorous way, to helping us improve the quality of human life, must be to create and make available a rich store of vividly imagined and severely criticised possible actions, so that our capacity to act intelligently and humanely in reality is thereby enhanced. (1984: 3)

Thus, by giving teams scope to draw up their own range of recommendations for action, by exposing them to criticism from multiple audiences, and by making the range available to all participants, the GAPP course helps participants to develop the capacity for making wise recommendations for action.

The capacity for making critical recommendations for action in the GAPP course could be enhanced in two ways if the course were longer. Users of the manual are encouraged to consider incorporating them in their teaching. First, the GAPP course, to some extent, is unbalanced by its focus on practice (Mascarenhas-Keyes 1996). This leaves insufficient time for extensive discussion of the dialectical relationship between theory and practice. As one participant on the Cambridge course commented: 'We have been practising development in the U.K. (Case-study One) and overseas (Case-study Two), but we have not critiqued the concept of "development"'. Other participants argued that they had done this already in university courses and that it was unnecessary as the GAPP course was supplementing university courses. However, yet another participant echoed the view of a number of peers when she said: 'at university you did that in a reified way, through already packaged case-studies written in books and articles. We have been experiencing development on this course and we should revisit concepts'.

As participants have been exposed to a range of multidisciplinary perspectives, the way in which concepts have been developed and used by different disciplines in applied work would merit greater discussion. Furthermore, the engagement in theoretical and epistemological debate, fed by issues of policy and practice, would help erode the spurious divide between 'pure' and 'applied' which is hindering the intellectual development of anthropology as a discipline (Wright 1995: 72–3).

A second shortcoming of the GAPP course is that although participants are told that there are different roles they can adopt in applied work, such as activist, broker and collaborator (van Willigen 1993), they are not given opportunities to practise these roles. It could be argued that if participants were working 'in the field' on placements, rather than in a simulated context, they could be given the opportunity to play these roles and to test out reactions to draft recommendations before committing themselves in writing. This may, of course, be an optimum way to educate participants but one which has not been feasible in the GAPP course due to time and financial constraints. The learning process elaborated so far has implications for the role of staff which is discussed next.

Role of Staff

The multidisciplinary and andragogic approaches of the GAPP course have had four major implications for the role of staff. First, the staff of different disciplines worked collaboratively; second, they took the role predominantly of facilitators of learning rather than solely transmitters of knowledge; third, they facilitated collaborative rather than individual learning; and finally, they had to develop the capacity to handle the emotions of participants which were particularly associated with the outcomes of reflexive activities. I shall elaborate on each of these in turn.

A task-centred anthropology course in a multidisciplinary context requires staff of different disciplines to work together. To some extent, this means that staff, used to a subject-centred approach, have to share their power and control of the curriculum which they might normally individually enjoy. Extensive discussion takes place so that both the specific contribution of each discipline, as well as the common intellectual ground that they share, can be brought to bear in developing the curriculum materials and assessing the outputs of assignments.

In the GAPP course, staff play the role of facilitators and have to guard against falling into the model of teacher as transmitter of knowledge. Of course, there are times on the course when the didactic mode of teaching is employed. It is used specifically to introduce new essential materials, when in the context of the time constraints in the course, it is a resource-efficient pedagogic practice.

In the GAPP course, the challenge is to 'integrate the authority of the facilitator with the autonomy of the learner' (Heron 1992: 66). Staff consciously refrain from giving answers and instead encourage participants to undertake a voyage of discovery. This is a hard thing for conventional teachers to do but it reveals interesting insights. As a senior academic who helped to facilitate the Cambridge course commented 'I did not believe that students could learn so much on their own'.

While staff have cognitive and political authority, in that they usually have a wider repository of disciplinary and professional knowledge, and power to frame the curriculum (Heron 1992), these two forms of authority are used in a facilitative manner. Staff display a willingness to take risks, and allow their cognitive knowledge to be challenged by participants, thus demonstrating that knowledge is a site for contestation.

Authority is sometimes delegated to participants, thus facilitating the blurring of boundaries between staff and participants. Thus, if a participant has particular knowledge and skills, he/she is invited to facilitate one or more sessions. For instance, in the 1996 course, a participant with expertise in international aid relations, co-facilitated one of the case-studies. In the 1993 course, a participant skilled in the presentational aspects of report writing gave a lecture on this topic. Inviting participants publicly to share their expertise not only raises self-esteem but also creates a sense of joint ownership of the course.

Staff have to be aware of the dictum that 'the medium is the message', in that participants are learning not only from the content of the course but from the social processes through which content is mediated. This means ideally that staff have to model the behaviour they want the participants to follow. Thus, good collaborative work is modelled by staff by the way in which they co-facilitate plenary sessions and publicly debate issues from their own disciplinary perspectives. For example, on the occasions when an assistant course director and I have exemplified good models of team working, participants have spontaneously and enthusiastically complimented us on this, saying that they had positive examples to emulate. In hindsight, the absence of favourable comments corresponded to the time when there was less 'chemistry' in the directors' teamwork.

In the process model of learning and teaching, staff need to be sensitive to the pulse of individuals and the group, and to the dynamics of the course as it unfolds. Staff have noticed that they need to be sensitive to the impression management of their role. For instance, some participants on the Cambridge course said they were confused about whether resistance from staff to their requests for help stemmed from the andragogic approach or whether the staff had 'no time, couldn't be bothered, did not want to be pestered'.

Taylor (1987: 191) argues that 'emotionality' is an important but underrated aspect of the self-directed learning environment. Staff, particularly in the plenary sessions of the GAPP course, need to create a supportive environment conducive to encouraging feedback from individuals and teams, in order to achieve a thorough discussion of substantive issues. To promote this, staff need to empathise with the participants to encourage the expression of various emotions ranging from anger, irritation, embarrassment, fear and confusion, all of which often obstruct constructive reflection on experience (Boud and Walker 1993). On the Cambridge course, for instance, there was an outspoken expression of conflict between some team members which required skilful handling so that there was not only a space created to allow for the expression of emotion, but also an opportunity to help resolve conflict. This allowed the individuals concerned to retain their self-esteem and for observers to learn from it. It is often easy for staff to retreat or cut short plenary sessions if they do not feel confident to cope adequately with expressions of emotionality. Indeed, on many GAPP courses, when there have been slippages of time, a common suggestion from some staff and participants has been to dispense with critical reflective activities.

Finally, to help the process of collaborative learning, staff require good facilitation skills to ensure the range of theoretical and practical issues arising from assignments are covered and all participants are drawn into critical discussion. These facilitation skills include 'structuring and organising skills, group process skills, communication skills, conflict resolution skills and often skills in counselling' (Pearson and Smith 1985: 77). There is a great danger in experiential learning that too much time is spent on 'doing' and not enough on 'reviewing'. In the GAPP course, attempts to circumvent this are made by ensuring major assignments lead to a finished 'product', such as a report, and that there is sufficient time set aside for plenary sessions to discuss the 'product'.

Conclusion

The course content, and learning and teaching process discussed above meets the stated aims of the GAPP course and goes a long way towards meeting the recommendations of the Dearing Report (1997) for the better preparation of graduates for the world of work. The involvement of potential employers on the panels increases the visibility of anthropology and promotes an image of having relevance to contemporary local and global issues. In so doing, it improves the employment prospects of alumni. The GAPP course also contributes to the personal transformation of individual participants and the course cohort as a whole. Deep, rather than surface, learning (Entwhistle 1984) is promoted because many opportunities are provided for harnessing and synthesising narrative and disciplinary knowledge. Deep learning is further enhanced through the active engagement in intellectual tasks leading to texts including recommendations for action, and the necessity to justify one's views under the critical gaze of peers and staff. The informal, but supportive pastoral environment developed through whole-group activities, teamwork, triads and surgeries creates space for the expression and creative use of emotions. The combination of the various components of the learning process leads to the intense engagement of the self and the development of a reflexive anthropology.

Finally, in the GAPP course, assessment is for formative purposes only. If summative assessment is to be adopted, techniques will need to be devised to award individual marks in group work. The summative assessment of group projects can result in problems between and within groups. To help overcome this, a number of techniques can be tried (see Brown and Knight 1994).

Notes

1. An earlier version of this chapter was published in *Professional Practice in Anthropology: A Curriculum Resource Manual for Teachers*. National Network for Teaching and Learning Anthropology. Brighton: Sussex University, 1997.
2. Over the last few years, research methods training in departments has included a broader repertoire of techniques, but often the 'hands-on' component is missing.

3. Loder's (1992) study for the Economic and Social Science Research Council showed that increasingly private companies, central and local government and charities are funding research, and their emphasis is on applied and strategic, rather than basic research.
4. Individual surgeries were introduced in 1996 in response to comments made by some participants in the evaluation of the 1995 course. They said they would welcome individual opportunities to discuss their own personal development with staff.
5. Triads were introduced for the first time in the 1997 Cambridge course. Participants were asked to form threesomes and there were specified sessions in the course when meetings were to take place. However, at one of these sessions, the triads spontaneously merged into a whole group as it appeared that overlapping themes were being discussed.

References

Ahmed, A. and Shore, C. 1995. 'Introduction', in *The Future of Anthropology: its Relevance to the Contemporary World*, eds Ahmed, A. and C. Shore. London: Athlone Press.

Barnett, R. 1994. *The Limits of Competence: Knowledge, Higher Education and Society*. Milton Keynes: Society for Research in Higher Education and Open University Press.

Boud, D., Cohen, R. and Walker, D. 1993. 'Introduction: Understanding Learning from Experience', in *Using Experience for Learning*, eds D. Boud, R. Cohen, and B. Walker. Milton Keynes: Society for Research into Higher Education and Open University Press.

Boud, D. and Walker, D. 1993. 'Barriers to reflection on experience', in *Using Experience for Learning*, eds D. Boud, R. Cohen, and B. Walker. Milton Keynes: Society for Research into Higher Education and Open University Press.

Boud, D. and Feletti, G. 1991. 'Introduction', in *The Challenge of Problem-Based Learning*, eds D. Boud, and G. Feletti. London: Kogan Page.

Boud, D. 1995. *Enhancing Learning through Self Assessment*. London: Kogan Page.

Boyer, E. 1990. *Scholarship Reconsidered: Priorities of the Professoriate*. Princeton, NJ: Carnegie Foundation for the Advancement of Teaching.

Bruffee, K. 1993. *Collaborative Learning: Higher Education, Interdependence, and the Authority of Knowledge*. London: John Hopkins University Press.

Brown, S. and Knight, P. 1994. *Assessing Learners in Higher Education*. London: Kogan Page.

Bruner, J. 1996. *The Culture of Education*. London: Harvard University Press.

Clifford, J. and Marcus, G. 1984. 'Introduction', in *Writing Culture: The Poetics and Politics of Ethnography*, eds J. Clifford, and G. Marcus. Berkeley: University of California Press.

Collier, G. (ed.) 1983. *The Management of Peer Group Learning: Syndicate Methods in Higher Education*. Guildford: Society for Research in Higher Education.

Davenport, J. 1993. 'Is there Any Way Out of The Andragogy Morass?', in *Culture and Processes of Adult Learning*, eds M. Thorpe, R. Edwards, and A. Hanson. London: Routledge.

Dearing, R. 1997. *Higher Education in the Learning Society*. Great Britain: The National Committee of Enquiry into Higher Education.

Dennison, W. and Kirk, R. 1990. *Do, Review, Learn, Apply: A Simple Guide to Experiential Learning*. Oxford: Blackwell.

Elton, L. 1987. *Teaching and Higher Education: Appraisal and Training.* London: Kogan Page.

Engels, C. 1991. 'Not Just a Method but a Way of Learning', in *A Challenge of Problem-Based Learning*, eds D. Boud, and G. Feletti. London: Kogan Page.

Entwistle, N. 1984. 'Contrasting Perspectives on Learning', in *The Experience of Learning: Implications for Teaching and Studying in Higher Education*, eds F. Marton, D. Hounsell, and N. Entwistle. Edinburgh: Scottish Academic Press. (Reprinted 1997).

Eraut, M. 1994. *Developing Professional Knowledge and Competence.* London: Falmer.

Freire, P. 1972. *Pedagogy of the Oppressed.* Harmondsworth: Penguin.

Grillo, R. 1984. *Working Party Report on Training for Applied Anthropology.* U.K.: Association of Social Anthropologists of the Commonwealth.

Hanson, A. 1996. 'The Search for a Separate Theory of Adult Learning: Does Anyone Really Need Andragogy?', in *Boundaries of Adult Learning*, eds R. Edwards, A. Hanson, and P. Raggart. London: Routledge.

Harvey, L., Moon, S. and Geall, V. 1997. *Graduates' Work: Organisational Change and Students' Attributes.* University of Central England, Birmingham: Centre for Research into Quality, and the Association of Graduate Recruiters.

Heron, J. 1992. 'The Politics of Facilitation: Balancing Facilitator Authority and Learner Autonomy', in *Empowerment through Experiential Learning: Explorations in Good Practice*, eds J. Mulligan, and C. Griffin. London: Kogan Page.

Knowles, M. 1978. *The Adult Learner: A Neglected Species.* Houston, Texas: Gulf Publishing House.

Knowles, M. 1984. *Andragogy in Action.* Houston, Texas: Gulf Publishing House.

Kolb, D. 1984. *Experiential Learning: Experience as a Source of Learning and Development.* Englewood Cliffs, NJ: Prentice Hall.

Lave, J. and Wenger, E. 1991. *Situated Learning: Legitimate Peripheral Practice.* Cambridge: Cambridge University Press.

Loder, C. 1992. *Support for Social Science Research: Setting the Scene.* Institute of Education, London University: Centre for Higher Education Studies.

Mascarenhas-Keyes, S. 1987. 'The Native Anthropologist: Constraints and Strategies in Research', in *Anthropology at Home*, ed. A. Jackson. London: Tavistock.

Mascarenhas-Keyes, S. 1991. 'Vocational Practice in Anthropology Course: An Evaluation' *BASAPP NEWS* 8 (2).

Mascarenhas-Keyes, S. with Wright, S. et al. 1995. *Report on the Teaching and Learning of Social Anthropology in the U.K..* Sussex: Anthropology in Action.

Mascarenhas-Keyes, S. 1996. 'Educational Development for Anthropology Teachers and Learners: Disciplinary and Pedagogic Issues', *Anthropology in Action* 3: 12–16

Maxwell, N. 1984. *From Knowledge to Wisdom: A Revolution in the Aims and Methods of Science.* Oxford: Blackwell.

Pearson, M. and Smith, D. 1985. In *Reflection: Turning Experience into Learning*, eds D. Boud, R. Keogh, and D. Walker. London: Kogan Page.

Pocock, D. 1971. *Social Anthropology.* London: Skeed & Ward Stagbooks. (First published 1961).

Polyani, M. 1967. *The Tacit Dimension.* New York: Doubleday.

Ramsden, P. 1992. *Learning to Teach in Higher Education.* London: Routledge.

Saddington, J. 1992. 'Learner Experience: a Rich Source for Learning', in *Empowerment through Experiential Learning: Explorations of Good Practice*, eds J. Mulligan, and C. Griffin. London: Kogan Page.

Schon, D. 1983. *The Reflective Practitioner: How Professionals Think in Action*. New York: Basic Books.

Schon, D. 1987. *Educating the Reflective Practitioner: Towards a New Design for Teaching and Learning in the Professions*. London: Jossey-Bass.

Taylor, M. 1987. 'Self-directed learning: more than meets the eye', in *Appreciating Adult Learning: from the Learners Prospective*, eds D. Boud and V. Griffin. London: Kogan Page.

Willigen, J. van 1993. *Applied Anthroplogy: An Introduction*. London: Bergin & Garvey.

Wright, S. 1995. 'Anthropology: Still the "Uncomfortable" Discipline?', in *The Future of Anthropology: Its Relevance to the Contemporary World*, eds A. Ahmed and C. Shore. London: Athlone.

11

Living Learning
Teaching as Interaction and Dialogue

Dorle Dracklé

Academic teaching is currently facing a serious crisis. Put somewhat ironically: students no longer want to learn and teachers no longer want to teach. This stalemate situation needs to be overcome by developing a novel set of teaching practices. We lack alternative means of producing knowledge; in the final analysis what is required are new strategies for sharing and for conveying knowledge. In the present article I suggest various possible solutions and present my own approach. I begin with analysis of the situation in today's universities, while directly relating the contents of our discipline – anthropology – to teaching practice. Indeed, it is no mere coincidence that our scholarly output and classroom practice are so closely interwoven.

We will certainly not be in a position to surmount the crisis as described above if a hostile atmosphere surrounding teaching continues to prevail. From anecdotal evidence it is clear, both in Germany and in other European countries, that an increasingly disparaging attitude towards teaching as opposed to research is abroad. 'Good teaching' is not seen as a quality attribute of what universities have to offer. As young academics reach the latter stages of study leading up to their final qualifications, experienced older colleagues tend to discourage them from committing themselves to a large amount of teaching in the belief that research work suffers as a result. Only recently did a Hamburg-based professor express his prejudices in this regard to a local newspaper: 'Many university teachers emphasise teaching because they are no great geniuses in the world of research. They then seek to compensate for their poor sense of self-worth by increasing their popularity – through a lowering of standards.' (Schwanitz 1999: 18).

In job applications for academic posts it is almost exclusively the quantity of published articles and other academic achievements which count, whereas the question as to whether the individual can actually teach or not is considered secondary. Young academics in the field of anthropology still continue, as in Mandelbaum's time at the beginning of the 1960s, to be exclusively trained to become researchers rather than university lecturers (Mandelbaum et al. 1963, 1967). The neglect of education in favour of research is one of the reasons for the teaching and learning crisis in today's universities.

One particular aspect of this neglect is seen in the almost exclusive concentration on verifiable learning outcome assignments in terms of quantifiable results. Viewed from such a vantage point, students are primarily regarded in terms of 'what they produce'. Criticism of the fact that today's students all manifest a far lower level of attainment than twenty to thirty years ago, that no outstanding students have emerged for years, and that students mainly pass with the equivalent of only 'C-grades' is familiar to me, both from the literature and from discussions with colleagues. The question as to whether it actually pays to provide 'good teaching' for 'the best' students remains unanswered. Who determines which students are the best? What then becomes of the large number of talented and less-talented students who remain? Is it at all worthwhile undertaking efforts on behalf of this 'mass' or ought one rather to allow them to chug through the system whilst ensuring the least possible expenditure of time and energy, enabling lecturers to dedicate themselves to their own research work in peace? These are by no means the sole considerations which creep their way into such a train of thought regarding academic performance; on top of this there is the tacit disregard for students and a certain arrogance concerning the estimation of one's own importance. This constitutes, in my interpretation of the matter, an instance of professional malpractice which often arises when lecturers come face to face with persons over a long period of time who belong to a younger age group and who have less knowledge than they do. The pedagogical satisfaction of the knowledgeable tends thus to find expression in a sense of hostility towards, and infantilisation of, students. While open hostility can be confronted, subtle disparagement is far more difficult for students to combat and fatal for their sense of fascination for anthropology and for the development of creative thinking (Roth/Prinz 1996; Roth/Wullimann 2000). There is, however, nothing condemning us to remain mired in such a situation.

Just what exactly are we able to teach? Our prime task is to help create awareness of the fact that anyone has the capacity to learn (empowerment). The most important ingredient to be mentioned is respect for students, respect for the uniqueness and autonomy of each and every student with whom we are involved – this point has in no way been taken for granted up until now. We are not in a position to teach those with whom we engage in conversation, instruct them in new skills, feed them knowledge, manipulate or force them. The only real power we possess is to offer them a means of turning their attention and gaze to what is, so as to encourage them to take a proper look at what we see (Perls 1976, 1980). We can empower students to make use of scientific tools, we can enable them to think beyond their own limitations and to develop new visions: 'teaching to transgress', as bell hooks calls it. 'I celebrate teaching that enables transgressions – a movement against and beyond boundaries. It is that movement which makes education the practice of freedom' (hooks 1994: 12).

In this regard, the origin of the verb 'to learn' is particularly instructive: both in English and in German it derives from the Germanic verb *lernen* and the Anglo-Saxon *linôn/learn*, Engl.), which signifies, 'to follow a trace, track down.' This is a wonderful image of what academic lessons are capable of achieving – namely, providing students with assistance in the pursuit of traces, in the process of searching and uncovering. From the same derivation, to learn also originally means 'to lead to know', thus to provide aid to someone in the pursuit of traces, to empower someone and to provide him/her with the means of finding something out on his/her own. 'Leading someone to know', as this image puts it, constitutes empowering students after the manner recommended in the present article – that is, passing on means of self-help, learning how to apply fundamental scientific techniques in practice, training the mind to think critically, developing independent ideas and points of view – and above all, encouraging the confidence of each individual in his/her own ability to track down such traces. There is nothing more difficult than that!

Teaching as Social and Cultural Communication

A large number of problems arising in the course of classroom activity today result from comprehension difficulties between students and teachers. This is reason enough to take a closer look at the means of communication of those involved. Firth, as far back as 1963, described teaching as personal communication. However, in his representation he restricted himself exclusively to two actors: teacher and pupil, with the one knowing and the other wanting to learn. I propose extending this representation of learning, here limited to the personal communication level, to that of the group.

Exchanges on various topics aimed at fostering learning processes do not occur in a void; rather, all those involved act within the parameters of their respective social roles. These roles and the experience ensuing from them play an equal part in moulding the given teaching situation. None of the individuals involved leaves his/her identity behind at the university cloakroom! It is no longer sufficient to assume that society at large and current political (and all other) events and theoretical developments exert no influence whatsoever – either on the elaboration of courses or on the choice of subjects and the way they are handled. In a given learning situation it is never a case of only two individuals communicating with one another; rather, communication among individuals takes place in a seminar, thus always in a group.

Strangely, this type of learning group has never been submitted to a thorough anthropological analysis, in spite of the fact that anthropology has to date primarily attached itself to the investigation of groups. The whole gamut of anthropological instruments available for the study of status, gender, age-related and other differences and their impacts on the constitution of groups is completely overlooked in the current teaching situation. These differences provide no cue for serious forms of self-analysis on the part of teachers who, nevertheless, are themselves such committed researchers – and familiar with praxis theory, etc. Let us therefore extend our self-reflection on cultural representations and our role in the construction of scientific authority in regard to texts to classroom activity!

The focal point of any given classroom lesson is constituted by this figure of anthropological authority. It is extremely doubtful whether the traditional form of transmitting knowledge, with the authoritarian teacher as centre of attention and source of knowledge/truth, will be able to be maintained in the future. It is not enough that anthropology, as a significant field of scholarly enquiry, restrict itself to a new humanism suited to our goals:

> … but we can and should seek to incorporate into our work an expanded conception of humanity appropriate to our age. Then perhaps anthropology will be a means of building bridges between the infinite particularity of individual existence and the emergent expression of human unity and social interdependence. (Grimshaw/Hart 1995: 61)

Seeing and recognising changes taking place in the world necessarily means incorporating these changes into anthropology and thus into teaching practices. In this respect, the authoritarian teacher and his power/knowledge-based interpretation of the world is an obsolescent model. The classical-hierarchical professor-student relationship needs to be dissolved; such a relationship has shown itself to be unfavourable to the creation of a positive climate of learning. It is not only in scientific research about 'others' that the interrelatedness of human society needs to be recognised, but in the classroom situation 'at home' as well. A modified self-image of teachers becomes apparent where the latter are able to perceive themselves as mentors (or as Carl Rogers 1994 puts it, as facilitators) and as advisers on the path of learning and tracking. Authority is thus relinquished in favour of emancipation, feelings of superiority transformed in terms of an interest in the ideas and work of students, and a communication channel open to social and cultural processes within the classroom established. A mentor (facilitator) sets store by developing learning processes in a group that are deemed to be intrinsically gratifying, something which has to date been neglected. The first and foremost goal of a mentor is to create favourable overall conditions for a positive working atmosphere and to provide students with constant advisory support.

Research-Based Learning

How is it possible to create a positive learning atmosphere in which knowledge is durably established? I have thus far spoken in favour of an end to the authoritarian role-perception of lecturers and of an opening up of the discipline in the sense of greater teaching practice, away from the restricted concentration on research. I propose accordingly to give 'research-based learning' the top priority in our discipline. By research-based learning I understand a process of independently organised learning in which the subject matter, the emerging goals and pace of the individual stages are collectively decided upon, simultaneously applied in a spirit of trial and error and pursued by students themselves within the group.

Research-based learning is a basic precondition to gaining meaningful learning experience geared to a specific goal. Every type of training linked to learning – qualitative fieldwork methods, for example, or courses in academic research techniques such as reading and writing, introductory courses, etc. – is perfectly well suited in this regard. Even advanced courses and basic courses in theoretical subjects can be arranged in accordance with the principles of research-based learning. Theatrical performances, role-play situations, imagework, independently organised student conferences, podium discussions and exhibitions are only a few examples of the ways in which dry and unexciting reading matter can be spiced up in order to better induce successful learning. Examples of such an inductive approach to anthropology courses are presented by the Spindlers (1990) as well as others (also see the papers by Edgar and Mascarenhas-Keyes in this volume).

Research-based learning is self-organised and active and empowers students, in accordance with the principle of 'learning by doing', to process and assimilate material and data. In order to learn something, individuals need to be constantly engaged. The old assumption that teaching consisted of telling, and learning consisted of listening, has to be rejected in line with new research results which indicate the contrary approach. Educational psychologists have proven that we only retain roughly 10 percent of what we read, and only 20 percent of what we hear. In opposition to this, we retain 90 percent of what we try out and execute ourselves (Edelmann 2000). Insofar as overloading students with indigestible intellectual fodder is not desirable: 'Repetitive, mass production is out, creative problem-solving is in. ... Students will increasingly hone their skills and abilities through co-operative problem-solving directed at real-world-problems' (Podolefsky 1997: 60).

In my own teaching practice, student self-organisation creates a teaching situation that is founded on dialogue and lively communication, while engendering awareness of the interplay amongst individuals in a learning group. It is only through such a fundamental transformation of the atmosphere of my courses that I have managed to foster satisfying experiences, both for the group and myself. In my perception, university teaching is marked by a clear dichotomy in its requirements of objectivity and humanity, between humanity and the purely cognitive transmission of knowledge. These two imperatives appear to be at loggerheads, with the common misconception that knowledge and learning have nothing to do with feeling; this in turn prevents an all-round approach to pedagogical processes being adopted. My experience shows that feelings and bodily signals need to be taken as seriously as positive knowledge, methodical rigour and original hypotheses, and indeed that the learning situation can be particularly profitable where a lively exchange is allowed to occur between these different levels. Feelings, intuition, the body, other participants within a group, the university, and the political and ambient (*Lebenswelt*) factors of classroom topics of discussion are all aspects which reflect important facets of the learning process. Learning, without incorporating these various levels, simply does not function properly. The impact of personal relationships on learning outcomes is profound, as Freud noted in a vignette on his secondary school teacher in 1914:

> I do not know what was more taxing and more significant for us: dealing with the subject matter being presented to us or with our teachers' personalities… We would either try to win them over or to turn away from them, imagined them to harbour sympathies or antipathies which were probably not there at all, studied their characters and shaped or distorted our own accordingly. They provoked our strongest protests and forced us into complete submission; we would pick out their smallest weaknesses and were proud of their small virtues, their knowledge and their justice. At bottom, we loved them dearly, if ever they gave us reason to do so; I do not know whether all of our teachers noticed as much. But it cannot be denied that we were ranged against them in a very particular way, in a way which had its discomforts for those concerned. From the very outset we were equally inclined to love and to hate, to criticism and to veneration of them. (Freud 1970: 238)

While Freud's observations reflect his own experience in the senior classes of secondary school, his depiction differs only very slightly from the situation prevailing between students and university teachers today. Interpersonal relations, even those obtaining between scholars and students, are never bereft of feelings or of history, which we constantly play out with one another. The question is whether a situation can be created in which it is possible to become aware of these attitudes and inclinations, or whether we merely experience them as bothersome and thus something to be warded off. It has become clear to me through personal observation that the more conscious one is in confronting such instances, the greater the ability to readdress the topic in question in a spirit of free enquiry. This sense of freedom expresses itself particularly in the evident reduction of student resistance to courses themselves (for example mandatory courses), to teachers, and to the world of university teaching in general. As such, participants in the teaching-learning process acquire the capacity and energy – which can otherwise be mischannelled into intense feelings of grievance, hatred, or criticism and completely wreck seminars – to clarify matters in a responsible manner.

To sum up: research-based learning fosters self-directed development in the handling of knowledge. The position of the teacher is that of facilitator, the person who encourages encounters to take place between participants within the group and accompanies rather than directs the learning process through a mixture of acceptance, respect and empathy. It is the art of non-action, of non-intervention on the part of the teacher who thereby fosters communication and the participation of students in a dialogue with a given topic (Buber 1953; Buber/Rogers 1997). Dealing with the 'third factor', the topic, is enabled via dialogue, via the conscious encounter of individuals with one another, and via their experience of interdependence (Portele 1978; 1992).

Theme-Centred Interaction

How is it possible to create a group situation in which creative problem-solving becomes feasible? Besides rejecting old-fashioned representations of authority, greater attention needs to be paid to the group situation itself. In the following I shall describe the basic didactic principles upon which I base my own teaching. Here I make reference to an approach used in humanistic psychology and pedagogics developed by Ruth Cohn:[1] Theme-Centred Interaction (TCI). The latter is not yet another easy-to-learn pedagogical technique offering a box of tricks capable of conjuring forth dazzling new ideas which also happen to be suited to taming unruly students. The TCI idea is quite different as I shall now demonstrate.

The use of TCI grew from an awareness that individual and society do not constitute an opposition, as personality and human interaction are inextricably linked. This basic assumption is compatible with new theoretical findings in anthropological theories of society according to which representations of practice and the critique of traditional abstractions such as 'individual' and 'society' can be complementary. In consequence, linking together these two levels, which were previously considered as strictly separate, leads one to the assumption that life is only conceivable in terms of interdependence amongst a variety of individuals. TCI is founded on the belief that it is important to understand and to consciously shape this interdependence; it is thus that social theory directly ends up in university seminars – as an object of course activity and as part of an understanding of the relationships which emerge in the classroom and beyond. At the same time, interdependence includes within it our potential for autonomy. Our freedom is based on the conscious shaping of our own situation and the knowledge that life consists of a constant movement between autonomy and interdependence. It is through the conscious shaping of interactions within a group that the possibility of establishing a dynamic balance between various group requirements and the ideas and needs of the individual lies. A key goal is to quest for the greatest possible level of satisfaction of all members of a group. The feeling of being able to realise one's potential within the group in a meaningful manner in turn raise one's capacity to process and assimilate what has been learnt.

In order to attain this state of dynamic balance it is necessary firstly to clarify the key features of all types of university learning groups. The latter are invariably composed of four factors:

1. the individual (I)
2. group interaction (We)

3. the topic or assignment (Theme)
4. the context in both its narrowest and broadest senses (Globe)

TCI is based on the hypothesis that the individual, group interaction and work on a common task are to be regarded as having equal value, and that at the same time the mutual influence of group and environment needs to be taken into consideration. These interconnections can be represented in terms of the diagram below:

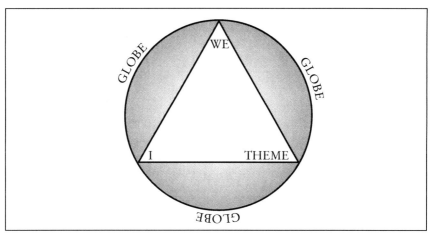

Figure 11.1: *The TCI-triangle*

In the above diagram, you will recognise a triangle in a circle. The triangle is based on the poles I, we (the group) and the theme/topic. The triangle itself is placed within a circle. The circle represents the surrounding world (university, political, social and cultural influences from without) and is termed 'globe'. The figure attempts to express that I, we, the theme/topic and globe need to be situated in a balanced and dynamic relationship with one another in order to enable a learning-oriented, open and humanly satisfying academic course to take place. Awareness of the need to foster a favourable working atmosphere and to ensure a dynamic balance between the various factors is the job of the supervisor or group leader. Having to continually re-engineer a balance requires attentiveness to the variety of possible disruptions that may intervene during interaction; this means respecting the theme (where are we in reference to the topic?), the spatial situation itself (noise, acoustics, poor ventilation), as well as motor functions, feelings and relationships. Where competition, hostility or envy predominate in a learning group[2] – which is hardly seldom in academic groups as we all know from symposia and seminars – it becomes almost impossible to learn; such group dynamics are all the more disruptive if they are not openly addressed (Portele 1995: 143).

The role of the individual lies in the responsibility that each must embrace for him or herself in order to shape group learning successfully. TCI is always geared to strengthening individual responsibility (Mann/Thomas 1988: 51). The 'I' in Figure 11.1 represents the attention of the learning group as it is directed towards the individual so as to ensure commensurateness with his or her qualities. 'Each member of a given course is cognitively, affectively and motorically different at the outset and at the end of any given educational experience' (Portele 1995: 140). Furthermore, each member of the course bears responsibility for his/her own sense of well-being. Where learning is beset by disruption, such disruption will first need to be addressed before being neutralized. In addition to the individual participants, it is necessary to ensure that a 'we' sentiment within the learning group is able to be nurtured – this is the fundamental precondition to any form of co-operative problem-solving whatsoever.

In order for individuals within a learning group to truly assume responsibility, course leaders need to be able to cede authority to participants. The leader's function is, as already stated, primarily that of a catalyst, someone who provides both the overall structure and a certain know-how. This does not mean that the leader of a learning group slips into a kind of 'laissez-faire' approach, but rather creates transparency regarding the practicalities of planning and organising seminars, ensures that participants are acquainted with one another, that confidence-building interactions are fostered, that individual particularities are respected, time schedules adhered to, that learning stages are planned and co-ordinated collectively, and that the topic is clearly formulated. The leader of the learning group can also arrange for frequent changes of working methods to replace the usual monotony of seminar work. For example, individual work can be alternated with work in pairs, small groups can be varied through discussion in the large group or 'plenum'. These forms help to intensify interaction between participants. It is thus in no way a question of group leaders attempting, through manipulation, to lead participants to a given point which they have already set their sights on in advance, but rather of accompanying participants as they endeavour to come to grips with and make use of the theme for their own purposes in a responsible and empowered manner.

In addition to individuals' preoccupation with their own respective contributions to class work and the attention paid to the interests of the group as a whole, the theme/topic itself should not be allowed to be neglected. Here, too, the rule should apply whereby all participants within a learning group (including the supervisor) assume responsibility for their learning processes and for their own well-being. Only when the theme in question is borne by all participants can an optimum working atmosphere be nurtured. A further important aspect of the theme is its contents and orientation in terms of humanistic values. In order to fully tap and develop the potential of any given theme, a number of creative and didactic ideas come to mind which can be used in addition to those practices which traditionally find favour: interactive exercises, meditation or body work. The moments of personal reflectiveness, for example in the form of guided fantasy journeys (see Edgar, this volume) are of particular significance. Equally invaluable are moments of stillness and silence, phases of deep reflection, and sentient receptivity, allowing natural pauses to intervene, for they allow participants to fully meditate upon and to find a personal means of access to the theme in question. And at intervals, everyone can then think about whether they still agree and are happy with the direction the seminar is taking regarding the theme. It goes almost without saying that extended feedback sessions need to be allowed for on a regular basis.

Just as the general human constitution does, so too the globe influences the theme. The immediate or wider social context – partners, friends, relationships, parents, timetables, external influences and further factors – all impact upon the learning situation. Research and education are not only focused on the actual seminars, but are also important as regards their social and ethical dimensions.[3] Yet the globe also has a bearing on the immediate situation surrounding a given theme and the possible outcomes. For example, it is hard to imagine holding a seminar on the various ethnic groups of the Amazon region without addressing the current situation of those who inhabit the area, and without allowing students an adequate opportunity to express their views on this situation and to confront the whole issue on a variety of levels. The same is true of all other anthropological subjects, as the outside world is always implicated in what happens in a seminar.

In this sense, the dynamics of university life are of especial consideration, because those who come together within any given learning group are individual personalities and not simply functions or roles within the institution of university ('student', 'professor', 'secretary'). Even classroom furnishings are important: flexible seating, limited use of tables, and decorating walls with items relating to course content all contribute to a sense of well-being in the immediate environment.

Rules

Two important principles supplement thoughts on learning groups based on TCI. They also double up as ground rules which need to be taken into serious consideration both in personal life and group situations. These two principles or rules ought to be addressed in the classroom at the beginning of the semester, as they constitute the mainstays of collective activity:

1. Each person is his/her own chairperson
2. Disturbances take precedence

Both of these core principles belong together, complement one another and ought not to be separated. The first rule allows one to focus attention on the fact that 'I am the chairperson of my own group', of my myriad and indeed contradictory needs. In group sessions I try to clarify and to apprehend my own sentiments. I show the same respect towards myself as towards others and take myself and my tasks seriously.

The second rule is unusual, but at least as important as the first – after all, in our everyday lives we set great store by pushing aside anything that proves disruptive. However, consciously avoiding disruptions robs us of our energies, while the attempt to suppress disruptions or to turn a blind eye inhibits the dynamism of the group. Disruptions arise in learning groups in a number of guises, whether in the form of fear, joy, sorrow, frustration or distraction. Where disruptions are not openly confronted and talked about but continually repressed, they threaten to block group activity. A university teacher describes just such a frustrating situation in retrospect in the following terms: 'For me as a university teacher, TCI is of particular interest because as a student I had to struggle with my own anger in numerous lectures and seminars, rather than dealing with the subject I should have been dealing with. I was clearly unable either to locate or to contribute my subject...' (Sielert 1994: 52). Thus in many cases it is this silent sense of unarticulated grievance which ruins the whole experience of study and learning. Where, however, each course participant is responsible for himself and for the well-being of the group as a whole and for dealing with such problems as they arise, solutions to conflicts or fruitful compromises are able to be found. Not least of all, it is the capacity for teamwork which represents such a key skill and which today's students will need in their future professional lives.

A further important dimension to the disturbance rule is its direct bearing on research. Disturbances to the research process always represent significant experiences; but before they can be positively integrated into work, rather than simply being repressed, they first need to be perceived for what they are by all those involved. By managing to pay attention to these important signals, major knowledge on research and on the area of research in question may be gained. In the same way, what happens in the classroom is not merely a case of 'let's pretend' but itself a part of an integrated research experience.

Both rules ought to be laid down as the basis for a contract negotiated collectively by participants and group supervisor at the outset of a new semester. Above all, this contract needs to be borne by all those involved, otherwise too much energy is wasted in enforcing rules. Besides the two core principles, other parts of the contract need to be negotiated. For example, I personally find a lack of commitment to group participation and poor time-keeping disruptive. In discussions on the two key principles it usually becomes clear that many participants are equally perturbed by such behaviour on the part of their classmates. In general, long discussions are needed on the remaining rules, for example on what to do if on some occasion one is unable to attend, how one can organise oneself in order to be able to arrive on time, etc.

It goes without saying that disruptions sometimes have to be factored in as inevitable and priorities laid down; the group should then draw up a ranking of possible disruptions to be addressed on a priority basis, and a list of questions and problems to be worked through. In spite of all this, one should not shy away from confronting disruption when it does occur. In teaching practice we often tend to want to insure that all necessary precautions have been taken before setting foot in the classroom. Yet in the long term, we can fool neither ourselves nor students when something is amiss. As such, I should like to call on colleagues to have the courage of their convictions and to admit gaps, while fully assuming the authenticity of the researcher and lecturer.

Large Groups

A particular concern now for European social anthropology departments is the increasing congestion experienced in so-called 'mass universities'. As deplorable as the situation may be in political terms, I am of the opinion that action is currently needed to prevent us from slipping into complete resignation. Living learning is not only possible in small groups but also in larger ones, and can be used in inter-group activities. The same system applies here too, namely that groups should not be run by charismatic personalities or in accordance with a strict set of rules, but rather through a lively process of exchange (Sielert 1994: 58). This can be achieved through a dynamic balance between the following three components: I, the small group and the large group (Cohn/Klein 1993). Large groups become more intimate when they are supplemented by smaller groups and when the discussion between the two groups is kept afoot. Both models ought to be treated as having equal value in order, on the one hand, to promote the experience of the larger group as something new and significant and, on the other, to ensure individual participants have enough time to consult one another on an active basis. Even first-year courses consisting of more than a hundred students can begin to be organised in terms of communication and exchange in line with the needs of both students and teachers (Dracklé 1999).

Living Learning

Putting the key principles of TCI into practice is not about the skilful and effective transmission of content, nor about motivating students in some superficial way. It is never a question of an objective 'subject matter', the theme, because all topics are from the very outset a form of communication and are embedded within human relationships. Considered from this perspective, TCI is of direct relevance to pedagogical as well as scientific communication (Sielert 1994: 55).[4]

As already noted, living learning is a process geared to fostering the whole individual; it embraces the whole personality, rather than exclusively intellectual capabilities. Living learning establishes a connection between rational insights and real-life social and emotional experiences as they occur. With the instructor as facilitator it becomes quite transparent that the latter's primary task is to seek to accompany the whole process: rather than handing down lessons, the instructor's main aim in any course is to enable an autonomous, inquiring spirit to take root that enables personal responsibilities to be developed within which learning can be pursued. Living learning needs to be seen as learning in the most comprehensive sense of activating both body and mind.

Thus, instead of leaving one's personality at the university cloakroom and shutting out the globe, as it were, right from the very outset, the aim is to create an open, dynamic situation in which learning is able, both to take into account and to promote the whole personality in the breadth of its social and cultural environment. It is only in this way that learning can be made to be 'living' and infuse those involved with a sense of joy and satisfaction. And it is only in such a way that students will be willing to start learning once again, and lecturers to start teaching.

Notes

1. Dr Ruth C. Cohn is a psychotherapist, educator and the founder of Theme-Centered Inter-action (TCI) and the Workshop for Living Learning (WILL). Born in Berlin of German-Jewish parents in 1912, Ruth C. Cohn fled to Switzerland in 1933, where she studied psychology, philosophy, and education at the University of Zürich and trained as a psychoanalyst at the International Association for Psychoanalysis. Finally receiving permission to emigrate to the U.S. in early 1941, she received further training at the Bankstreet School (later College) while engaged in clinical psychology work. After the Second World War she developed TCI and in 1966 founded the Workshop Institute for Living-Learning, 'WILL'. Returning to Switzerland, the institute WILL-International was established in Hasliberg-Goldern (Switzerland) in 1972. In the subsequent twenty-five years over 1,000 candidates fulfilled the requirements for a diploma in TCI (c. 750 hours) and many more participated in shorter training programmes. More information about WILL-International, TCI and Ruth Cohn can be gathered at http://www.tzi-forum.com/english/index1.html (date of last visit 09–09–2002). See also Farau and Cohn (1984).
2. Moore (1997) provides a very good account of experience with student resistance.
3. There are countless reports of course failure and attempts to provide an analytical explanation for such failure. To cite but one example among many in which the *ur*-anthropological conflict over racism almost destroyed a seminar, readers are referred to Nadia Lovell (1999). In her article, 'The Politics of Teaching and the Myth of Hybridity' the lack of understanding of student aggression, which is perceived as threatening, is palpable. It nonetheless has to be acknowledged that the latter is one of the few articles that have attempted to deal with the question of politics within anthropology and its impact on learning situations.
4. If interested in research about TCI see: Cohn (1992); Cohn/Klein (1993); Löhmer/Standhardt (1995); Portele/Heger (1995); Standhardt/Löhmer (1995).

References

Buber, M. 1953. *Reden über Erziehung*. Heidelberg: Martin Schneider Verlag.

Buber, M. and Rogers, C. 1997. *The Martin Buber-Carl Rogers Dialogue: A New Transcript With Commentary*. New York: State University of New York Press.

Cohn, R. 1984. 'Das Modell der themenzentrierten Interaktion', in *Gelebte Geschichte der Psychotherapie*, eds A. Farau and R. Cohn. Stuttgart: Klett Cotta.

Cohn, R. 1992. *Von der Psychoanalyse zur Themenzentrierten Interaktion*. Stuttgart: Klett-Cotta.

Cohn, R. and I. Klein. 1993. *Großgruppen gestalten mit Themenzentrierter Interaktion*. Mainz: Mathias-Grünewald-Verlag.

Dracklé, D. 1999. 'In andere Welten eintauchen. Erfahrungen mit einer Veranstaltung zur Einführung in die Ethnologie', *Das Hochschulwesen* 47(3): 90–6.

Edelmann, W. 2000. *Lernpsychologie*. Weinheim: Psychologische Verlagsunion.

Farau, A. and Cohn, R. 1984. *Gelebte Geschichte der Psychotherapie*. Stuttgart: Klett-Cotta.

Firth, R. 1963. 'Aims, Methods, and Concepts in the Teaching of Social Anthropology', in *The Teaching of Anthropology*, eds D. Mandelbaum et al. Berkeley: University of California Press.

Freud, S. 1970 [1914]. *Zur Psychologie des Gymnasiasten*. Studienausgabe Vol. 4, Psychologische Schriften. Frankfurt: S. Fischer Verlag.

Grimshaw, A. and Hart, K. 1995. 'The Rise and Fall of Scientific Ethnography', in *The Future of Anthropology*, eds A. Ahmed and C. Shore. London: The Athlone Press.

hooks, b. 1994. *Teaching to Transgress. Education as the Practice of Freedom*. New York: Routledge.

Löhmer, C. and Standhardt, R. 1995. *TZI. Pädagogisch-therapeutische Gruppenarbeit*. Stuttgart: Klett-Cotta.

Lovell, N. 1999. 'The Politics of Teaching and the Myth of Hybridity', *Anthropology Today* 15(3): 10–13.

Macha, H., Karczewski, M. and Schröder, K. 1988. 'TZI als hochschuldidaktische Methode', *Themenzentrierte Interaktion* 2(1): 38–45.

Mandelbaum, D., Lasker, G. and Albert, E. (eds) 1963. *Resources for the Teaching of Anthropology*. Berkeley: University of California Press.

——— 1967. *The Teaching of Anthropology*. New York: American Anthropological Association Memoir 94.

Mann, R. and Thomas, K. 1988. 'TZI an der Hochschule', *Themenzentrierte Interaktion* 2(1): 46–52.

Moore, M. 1997. 'Student Resistance to Course Content: Reactions to the Gender of the Messenger', *Teaching Sociology* 25: 128–33.

Perls, F. 1980. *Gestalt, Wachstum, Integration: Aufsätze, Vorträge, Therapiesitzungen*. Paderborn: Junfermann.

Perls, F., Hefferline, R. and Goodman, P. 1976. *Gestalt Therapy: Excitement and Growth in the Human Personality*. Harmondsworth: Penguin.

Podolofsky, A. 1997. 'Teaching and Learning Anthropology in the Twenty-first Century', in *The Teaching and Learning of Anthropology*, eds C. Kottak et al. Mountain View: Mayfield Publishing Company.

Portele, G.H. 1978. '"Lob der dritten Sache" oder: Was wir von Brecht und den Alternativlern lernen können.' Gruppendynamik im Bildungsbereich 5(3): 2–9.

——— 1992. *Der Mensch ist kein Wägelchen*. Köln: Edition Humanistische Psychologie.

——— 1995.'Gute akademische Lehre – Meine acht Grundprinzipien der Hochschuldidaktik', in *Lebendiges Lernen in toten Räumen*, eds R. Standhardt and C. Löhmer. Giessen: Focus kritische Universität.

Portele, G.H. and Heger, M. 1995. *Hochschule und lebendiges Lernen*. Weinheim: Deutscher Studienverlag.

Rogers, C. 1994 [1969]. *Freedom to Learn*. Upper Saddle River: Prentice Hall.

Roth, G. and Prinz, W. (eds) 1996. *Kopfarbeit. Kognitive Leistungen und ihre neuronalen Grundlagen*. Heidelberg: Spektrum Akademischer Verlag.

Roth, G. and Wullimann, M.F. (eds) 2000. *Brain Evolution and Cognition.* Heidelberg: Wiley-Spektrum.

Schwanitz, D. 1999. *Gespräch mit dem Hamburger Anglistik-Professor Dietrich Schwanitz.* Alster-Magazin 3: 18.

Sielert, U. 1994. 'Der wachsenden Kluft zwischen Sachlichkeit und Menschlichkeit entgegen arbeiten', *Themenzentrierte Interaktion* 8(2): 50–61.

Spindler, G. and L. 1990. 'The Inductive Case Study Approach to Teaching Anthropology', *Anthropology and Education Quarterly* 21(2): 106–12.

Standhardt, R. and Löhmer, C. 1995. Lebendiges Lernen in toten Räumen. Gießen: Focus.

12

Ethnodrama in Anthropology Education

Giuliano Tescari

Suit the action to the word, the word to the action;
with this special observance that you o'erstep not the modesty of nature.
For any thing so o'erdone is from the purpose of playing,
whose end, both at the first and now, was and is,
to hold, as 'twere, the mirror up to nature;
to show virtue her feature, scorn her own image,
and the very age and body of the time his form and pressure.

(Hamlet, Act 3, Scene 2)

In teaching cultural anthropology we face a disturbing paradox: we bring students' attention to the lives of what are often very dissimilar human beings, and to sometimes radically different ways of looking at the world, of representing it, and feeling and acting in it. Yet we, as academics, find ourselves mainly working with often very abstract mental constructs, categories and concepts, and in any case our mental formulations are very different from those used by the subjects we refer to. Real life, ultimately, is reduced to schemes, patterns and systems which monopolise all our considerations.

We suffer, first, the objective difficulty of representing and transmitting the complexity of the processes inherent in social events and cultural behaviour; but second, we have to endure the irrepressible fear of 'opening up', without preconceptions, to the whole diversity presented by our ethnographic examples. On the other hand, this process jeopardises, to some extent, our efforts: what may we really know if we keep ourselves cold and detached from the human substance of culturally different behaviours? And isn't such a detachment in marked contrast to the very methodology of the cultural anthropologist, the participant observation and the empathy s/he is supposed to fulfil in fieldwork and through living on equal terms with the studied community? It would seem therefore that simple ethnographic description, when it is not combined with some kind of experience, might leave our students indifferent to the importance of the contributions other cultures have brought or might someday bring to the common heritage of humankind.

The central position of the relationship between subjective individual and collective experience in anthropological education was fully grasped in the reconsideration of anthropological pedagogics started more than two decades ago. This reconsideration, along with ethnodramaturgy, led to the introduction of a learning approach less skewed towards pure and simple intellectual acquisition, but rather striving to combine analysis and project; action and reflection; volition, affectivity and knowledge. Its main theorist is no doubt Victor W. Turner[1] and one must necessarily refer to his guidelines in framing a teaching of anthropology approach where one can experiment, in active and subjective terms, with culturally disparate modes of interaction in the world. The guidelines of his approach are sharply phrased in these words: 'The movement from ethnography to performance is a process of pragmatic reflexivity [...], the attempt, by representatives of a generic modality of human existence – western historical experience – to understand "feeling the pulse" [...] of different modalities which up to now were barred to them by gnoseological chauvinism or cultural snobbishness' (Turner 1982).

As such, a performance-based teaching methodology aims at the re-creation of ethnographic processes – cultural configurations and culturally oriented actions – in such a way as to produce in participants a set of subjective experiences capable of summoning up culturally different experiences, hence allowing a better understanding. In other words, an ethnodramaturgical performance is the *mise-en-scène* of a specific section of socio-cultural action which may prompt some direct experience of cultural properties and social rules that characterise the context from which it comes.

During my teaching, I focus chiefly on symbolism and shamanism, largely based on the example I know best through my research, i.e., the culture of the Wirrárika – the Huichol Indians of the Western Sierra Madre of Mexico. I always felt at least three layers of possible otherness were implied here: the primary layer of general socio-cultural diversity; second, the otherness implied in shamanic arts, the key role of dream and vision viewed as concealing a truth profounder than ordinary reality; and, finally, the alteration of consciousness which, in this culture better than in many other Amerindian cultures, with its peyote[2] cult, appears as a highly valued device for individual and social reintegration. But how can one pass on, however, and make communicable domains of such radical otherness as suggested by that way of life, that ritualism and those transitions of consciousness? How can one convey their value and significance?

In co-operation with my students, I started considering a descriptive pattern of action. The ritual of the Wirrárika pilgrimage to the desert of Wirikúta, as the main phase of the whole ritual cycle, fully expresses the three levels of otherness. From the ritual we extracted a script and a role structure whose origins lie exclusively within that socio-cultural matrix. Yet the *mise-en-scène*, though artificial, needs to take place in strict obedience to the substance and solemnity of the example to which it refers: the actual pilgrimage. Everything that surrounds this ritual has an extreme importance to all Wirrárika, who invest their hopes for well-being and immediate prosperity in the pilgrimage's success.

In a figurative sense, even the pedagogical and experiential success of the performance depends on the commitment of all its participants and on their seriousness in playing their roles. By roles, I am referring not only to the specific ones held in the rite – the various ritual or authority roles which are played by students – but even more to participants' involvement in the 'ethnodramatic' role of being a member of a society (the tribe), of one of its sections (the clan) and of a specific household within which everybody holds a given status, which in turn guides their relations with everybody else. 'Assuming one's role' therefore means setting oneself up to communicate with all participants according to the 'rules of the game' in force in this context, regardless of the nature of any prior relationships held.

I started experimenting with this ethnodramaturgic method in 1991 and applied it in different pedagogical ways, from introductory courses onwards; but mainly to academic courses with sixty to eighty students. Year by year such an approach improved significantly, as did its prominence in my overall pedagogic methodology. That is why, beyond the fact that pedagogic patterns are by their nature constantly evolving, it would be misleading to present my ethnodramatic method solely in abstract terms or as a purely theoretical construct. In order to provide a synthetic and practical idea of its design, I shall thus refer mainly to the case of the academic course I ran in 1999–2000.

As previously stated, the performative component manifests at two interrelated but formally very different layers: a permanent structural layer and a 'dramaturgical' one with a more intermittent character. The structural side is quite important since it entails, in a playful way, a rearrangement of the relationships between the participants, who increasingly steer their interactions through the cultural standards of the 'other'. Also, throughout the cycle of the role play, students are assigned identities, roles and statuses, which are all modelled on the ethnographic example in question; these identities eventually begin to supplement individual social personalities with fictional, collectively worked-out biographies.

The 1999–2000 course scheduled nearly seventy hours of lectures on symbolic anthropology and the oral tradition of native peoples, complemented by optional (but universally accepted) attendance at one or more of six specialised seminars devoted to enlarging upon some of the course's more relevant subjects. All students knew from the beginning of the lectures that they would be requested to participate actively on different levels: a somewhat more intellectual one concerning the issues raised in the seminars, from which they would also submit collective reports to the entire class towards the end, and subsequently write individual papers; a second level requiring more direct involvement in the performances; and a third level of individual responsibility towards the activities of the class.

The Foundation of the Tribe

The initial step was taken two weeks after the beginning of the lectures with the first collective performance: the 'rite of the foundation of the tribe', designed to turn a generic and anomic collectivity of university students into a tribal unit horizontally structured in terms of four exogamous clans and vertically shaped as a hierarchy of politico-ceremonial statuses. The metamorphosis of a class into a tribe institutes the performative dimension of the whole pedagogic experience and serves several purposes.

The main purpose is to arouse a cumulative experience of human interactions ruled by a social logic unlike the one we are normally accustomed to, where the apparent uniformity and equality of student roles is replaced by the mark of heterogeneous affiliation to well-characterised, variously allied or mutually opposed social categories. Clan identity, stressed by the allusion to symbols specific to each individual clan, establishes a formal, referential backdrop while at the same time steering the relationships among members of different units; whereas, tribal unity appears as the context within which those identities and relationships find a certain consistency.

The second purpose, connected to the first, is to develop collective rivalry, in order to redirect spontaneous individual student competitiveness towards supporting one's clan in the contest for primacy. The third purpose is mainly organisational, both in a general and more functional way, and aimed at achieving formative targets, particularly for the execution of subsequent performances. Clan structure actually aids the self-management of the units of study, the seminars, which are accordingly inclined to set concerted work horizons and to bring about collective results. The major performance, considered further on, is made possible by the extended experience of a segmentary social dynamic backed by internal expressions of the community, whose gamut of social roles has become increasingly well defined, and whose skeletal structure has been fleshed out slowly with genealogies and biographies consistent with positions in the social and kinship structure.

From an ethnographic standpoint, the performance of the tribal foundation rite is admittedly arbitrary. Nevertheless it may be seen as a rite of passage from the state of student to member of a tribe and of one of its clan sections, which for a few students also implies the elevation to authority or ritual prestige offices. Its main purpose is to evoke the experience of ritual death followed by symbolic rebirth in a new order of social relationships.

The separation rite is introduced by the presentation of the script, which everybody must know from the start, and by appeal to the 'serious' character of the ritual work that is going to be acted out. Then the master of ceremonies (obviously played by the teacher, emulating the Wirrárika shaman's gestures) lights a candle – the token of the sacred fire marking the centre of cosmic space – and proceeds, first to the sacralisation of the ceremonial space, hailing the five directions of the world, and secondly to the ritual purification of participants through the smoke of aromatic herbs.

At this stage all students in turn cross the barrier that they have previously erected with their knapsacks and books (the 'trench of student stuff'), uttering aloud the ritual formula 'I am nothing, I am nobody'. Afterwards everybody strolls about the ceremonial ground with their eyes shut for a short time, trying to orient themselves in a condition of ritual blindness towards one of the four corners. Then the four groups, variously numbered and assembled in the four directions, receive the formal greetings of the master of ceremonies who pays homage to the new clans and recalls some elements of their distinctive symbolic sets. Following this, through a brief internal meeting, each clan must then appoint its clan chiefs and other clan offices (the shaman, the messenger, etc.) so as to structure the tribe in terms of power and prestige differences.

The reintegration ritual later consists in once again crossing the ritual threshold (the trench barrier), declaring in turn publicly and with pride one's clan identity and, as far as the tribal elders are concerned, one's position in the clan: 'I am an Eagle!' or 'I am the Snakes' chieftain!' or 'I am the shaman of the Northern Winds!' etc. The tribe then gets structured spatially as well, aligning itself according to clan directions within the ceremonial circle, facing the fire in its middle – an arrangement which will often recur in all the circumstances of the clans' work or performance. Finally, after the formal greeting of the master of ceremonies to the whole tribe, to its clans and to the dignity of the chieftains, it is time for a frugal meal, a sip of wine and a few nachos (corn tortillas), all previously offered in a ritual to the spirits of the cosmos.

This first performative experience is then reconsidered and discussed in many ways. The first step is the articulation by students of some aspects of their subjective experience of the ritual. Here participants' remarks vary a lot, yet they express a common perception of an unusual and at the same time stimulating work-frame: the discomfort of 'playing' in front of classmates, only partially offset by the awareness that 'everybody is playing' and hence 'all are actors and audience'; their curiosity aroused by a sequence of acts ruled by an almost unknown, though not impenetrable, symbolic background; the uneasiness evoked by the difficulty of guessing what practical prospects will spring from this 'transformation': what tasks or other obligations might match their new identities? Yet, urged to express some inner impression too, in contrast to the 'public' dimension at first prevailing, the students also reveal the unexpected sense of unease felt at their identity expropriation, the pain that for some came with suspending, though fictionally, their usual 'selves'. Some were amazed at the strong impact the spoken words made on their thoughts and emotions; and they recalled the peculiar and even weird moods felt in the few minutes of blind wandering and of the unusual task of perceiving the world and orienting themselves in it without the dominant sense of eyesight. On the whole, there is a common impression of living an 'event', a sensation already perceived by the end of the ritual during the calm and happy commensality, shifting from the formality of the distribution of offerings to the spirits, to the cheerful conviviality within the distinct clans.

After this experience in the lecture it becomes much easier to reconsider the conditions of ritual action, the importance and power of ritual symbols, the nature and structure of the rite of passage, the properties of the rituals' liminal phase and of liminality at large, the paradoxical state of the extra-structural person, etc. Consequently, the later teaching and discussion of symbolic anthropology allows connections and allusions to be drawn out from students' recent 'lived' experience which, although theatrical, does not lack emotions and inner echoes, thereby facilitating a reappraisal of the ritualisation of social transitions. Together with the articulation of the rules that steer intratribal relationships and the responsibilities of the chieftains of the fictitious tribe, one may tackle the subject of political dynamics in stateless societies, matrimonial rules, the importance of segmentary structures and kinship relationships, etc. One hour of theatre work gives cues, connections and food for thought across many fields of anthropology.

During the following two months, the performative dimension provides a backdrop to the mainly traditional pedagogic work that builds on some of the outstanding theoretical topics, and considers, more or less extensively, a variety of ethnographic examples. Among these, particular attention is devoted to Wirrárika ethnography, since that is the basic reference of the major performance which will take place towards the end of the course. In the meantime, new forms of relationship between the students develop and, sometimes jokingly, sometimes sticking to the rules of the game, they become acquainted with responsibilities and culturally formed stereotypes. Chieftains have the chance to make their collective decisions in the tribal council and at the same time practise a form of direct democracy, consisting in listening to 'what our people say'. On the whole, 'team spirit', which is such an important part of the ideology of corporate groups, develops. Students partially identify with the symbolic background of the clans and, through the spontaneous *bricolage* of images and representations, the distinct identities of the different clans strengthen and converge into an indefinable feeling of tribal identity. On the formal level too, the appeal of the new rules of interaction (structural and linguistic) gain a foothold among the students. The students now address or refer to one another according to tribal features and statuses, nurturing some creativity in phrases such as: 'in deference to the great wisdom of our clan-chief…', 'this Snake talks with a forked tongue…', 'we Wolves will howl till you listen to us…'. Thus the playful and creative potential of the setting, far from conflicting with the seriousness of the work, helps to build a greater understanding of the experience of cultural otherness, which is accepted as a locally and historically structured expression of potentials and valences common to all human beings.

The Pilgrimage Rite

The performative commitment intensifies during the two weeks preceding the main performance, which will take place in the hills near Turin over the space of twenty-four hours. Obviously, attendance is explicitly optional and voluntary. Since it takes place outside the confines of the University, it is reliant on the subjective interest and availability of students. Still, participation is always massive and the few students who do not join in are the ones with concurrent engagements.

The first step is reconsidering the script, which squeezes into a short span of time a ritual process that, in reality, often extends over several months: at noon the tribe will create its village – a circle of tents around the ceremonial fire which will be kindled in the centre. This will be the ceremonial space reserved for the separation rite of the pilgrims' procession, the residence of the relatives awaiting the pilgrims' home-coming and, finally, the site of the *xíkurinéyrra* (the peyote festival) that puts an end to the pilgrimage rites and engages everybody in the night vigil around the fire. Detailed consideration of the script involves role assignment, both the organisational roles relating to action and setting, and the performative ones which every participant must play, although there is a general consistency between the two kinds. For instance, the four women who co-operate in the purchase and preparation of food and beverages, one for each clan, will later also act as female household spirits and, as 'Mother Home', 'Wait', 'Patio' and 'Cleansing', will ritually manage hospitality and reception, seeing also to the ritual food distribution. Or, to give another example, the four males who are assigned to fit out an ecologically sound and relatively secluded toilet will later on be the *topíles,* the guards who keep watch and can sanction potential excesses and infringements of the rules. For every participant there is at least one ritual role and therefore also some specific task within the performance. There is plenty of preparatory work too, so that everybody comes to accept their share of responsibility and contributes to making the experience both possible and pleasant.

The intensification of preparations also entails the definition of kinship networks by which individual clans and biographies are articulated, and which will later justify the pilgrims' selection, so that in one's fictitious history and dominant relationships each pilgrim discovers their reasons for joining the pilgrimage. In scripting the biographies and social networks, however, we also insert crisis factors, life's dark episodes, illicit relationships, hidden feelings, the substance on which turn the 'confessions' that some of the participants will utter during the separation rite. A few people train in the preparation of ceremonial offerings (votive arrows and gourd bowls to be carried during the pilgrimage) which later everybody will make at the beginning of the performance. Others, trained in the ceremonial dance steps, practise dancing to the same recorded tunes which will be used for the night dances.

We meet on Saturday at midday on a mown lawn kindly put at our disposal by a local farmer. In two to three hours the campsite is set; the camp kitchen and toilet are prepared, and everybody, already 'dressed up' to a certain extent, receives Wirrárika insignia (belts, pouches, scarves, plumed sombreros, etc., from the teacher's collection), which complement the fictitious Indian identity. They also receive a variety of ritual objects, final texts relating to individual parts (including confessions, shamanic chants, vision accounts, poems, and the 'nonsense formulas' of the cognitive interferences referred to later) and lastly, instructions and suggestions for their respective tasks. At this point the transition to the actual performance has been achieved. After concluding the practical or preparatory tasks, everybody gradually mixes in with their clan, is refreshed by a light meal (now it is a pizza, whereas the evening meal is more appropriately modelled on Indian and Mexican gastronomy), and undertakes the preparation of their offerings.

Then the shaman who will lead the pilgrimage (played by the teacher) and his helpers (some students who have performed the ritual before represent the initiates) start the purification rite preceding public confession. In the ethnographic 'original' among the Wirrárika, the confession rite is a time of particular intensity. Everybody has to publicly retrace his/her own sexual sins, which means all of one's past sexual interactions with the sole exception of the current legitimate conjugal relationships. One can imagine, given the Wirrárika's restless sexuality and the dramatic nature of some of their biographies, how deeply moving these soliloquies can be in front of the silent shaman, who merely ties a knot for every mentioned 'sin' on a string which he will later burn in the fire.[3] During the performance one has to make do with an adaptation based on the 'original': first a few public confessions uttered by those who have prepared them, recalling some of the most common events of sexual tribulation (inflicted or endured rapes, a lover's abandonment, conjugal infidelity, jealousy, etc.); and then a more intimate and silent examination of conscience where everybody is supposed to mentally retrace a particularly grave episode in their own sexual biographies and then encapsulate it in the knot of their own string which the confessor shaman will burn collectively in the fire.

The exchange of formal greetings between pilgrims ready to leave the village and their kin handing them the offerings for pilgrimage stop-overs takes place in the particular atmosphere called forth by the confessions. Later on it will be revealed that the 'kin', who stay behind in the village, may feel nostalgia for the pilgrims absorbed in a feat barred to them and shrouded in mystery. Obviously the splitting of the tribe into two different performative routes (about one half projected towards a mystic journey and the other half, though involved in various other ritual activities besides the ritual wait, nevertheless bound by a feeling of absence) has the purpose not so much of diversifying collective experience, as of inducing the experience of symbolically splitting the community, followed by its recomposition at a superior level of unity and solidarity. All through the night, moreover, just as in the peyote festival model, there will be an exchange of experiences between the two components, and the community will re-elaborate these diversities as an experience belonging to its whole.

I will only mention some particularly meaningful episodes of what follows in the performance. These include: the first pilgrimage stop-over and the emotions evoked for those novices initiated by crossing the Door of the Clashing Clouds, the invisible threshold to the Wirikúta sanctuary, blind-folded and led by the initiates to the unexpected sound of a drum and a horn; the placement of offerings at the five stop-over points along the path; the euphoria of 'hunting' peyote (in this case replaced by a hundred little bottles of sangria placed head-first and half-hidden in the grass of a vast meadow, 'the desert') with all the reciprocal offerings sanctioned by a *communitas* ritual; the joyful home-coming of the pilgrims – painted with pilgrimage facial make-up – among their kin who are equally painted with clan colours, and the interchange of clan screams; the night vigil around the fire in the middle of the camp, which is held between the 'deer dances' that summon up the whole tribe on five separate occasions; the narratives through which the shamans retrace the sacred histories of the world's creation; and, criss-cross-ing all these actions, the colourful interventions of the *tsorû'rri* (pilgrimage initiates) who introduce cognitive dissonance and nonsense through their previously arranged instances of harassment, jokes, riddles and verbal para-doxes. All culminating in the sober morning ritual: a public cleansing of the face and hands with water.

Final Considerations

In the observations later exchanged in the class or formulated in the papers written by students, quite different considerations surface, both as to the sig-nificance of what has been accomplished and of applied theatrical forms, and about the ethnographic substance from which the performance takes its inspi-ration. Common to everyone is the experience of having fluctuated between 'role-playing', a result of rather discontinuous acting efforts which are never-theless somehow rewarding, and observing oneself and others 'from outside' – an experience quite similar to the one gained by the anthropologist in the field, wavering as he does between self-perception as a member of the stud-ied community and feeling the abyss of cultural difference. To most participants the assessment of the performance is very positive: acknowledg-ing a meaning to their own experience, they also come to acknowledge the meaning of cultural forms and horizons that previously might have seemed strange and, at best, fairly exotic. [4] Some also claim to have detected unex-pected sides to their classmates. They come to appreciate people, circumstances and human interactions beyond their initial expectations. At times they revel in forgetting the fictional and imitative nature of the context, and in the moral attributes of *communitas* relationships – *camaraderie*, broth-erhood, equality, human solidarity – which are posited as dominating liminal phases of social life. There are also those who report having experienced some instant of particular intensity, a transcendent intuition, some bit of magic in the twists of the flames, in the obscurity of the night, in the play of ritual phrasing or clan screams. On the whole, in spite of the manifestly artificial nature of the circumstances, there is a vague, yet broad awareness of having crossed the threshold to a genuine initiation – even if the experience begs a question with no straightforward or satisfactory answer: initiation to what?

Without wishing to mystify the importance of the experience considered in its entirety, and taking for granted that its outcomes in any case will be quite differentiated according to subjective perception and elaboration, I believe that at least on two fronts there may be some valuable results – two fronts necessarily connected to one another: namely, a much more unbiased appreciation of cultural diversity, and a more reflexive view of one's own cultural identity. Within the performance, the onion-skins of the 'roles' – Mexican Indian, clan member, chieftain or shaman, initiate or novice, etc. – involve characters endowed with a history, or even deities whose names and dignity are taken on. Such an assumption of identity contributes to shaping the bundle of statuses and roles constituting a social personality. This process enhances the most valuable characteristics of both theatre and ritual, of liminoid and liminal. As such, playing a multilayered role can allow participants to reach deeper truths about the objects and relationships represented, albeit artificially and obliquely, through symbolic forms. The sheer human substance of culturally distant behaviours (wishes, fears, affects, rivalries, intentions, ambitions, etc.) reveals itself for what it is: so common to any 'model of humanity'[5] as to make all those behaviours and processes rather familiar. The explicit regret that 'it was all a put-on' – as if, to make it a genuine transcultural experience, it lacked only a staging in the Sierra or in the Mexican desert and among true Wirrárika – illustrates the preponderance of the cultural character of the actual experience as against the ludic one, which exists as well.

Thus, such a simulation of childish reminiscence, 'let's make believe you are... and I am...', framed in the structure of the rite of passage, inspires an experience, at times truthful, of other forms of sociability which become the merciless reflection of just how stiff one's own ordinary social experience can be. Having accepted a set of arbitrary conventions and gained some familiarity with the referents of those conventions (symbolic objects, gestures, names of supernatural entities to which they refer, etc.) students gain an insight into the unmasking of conventions and rules in the forms of communication and interaction usually experienced in everyday life, forms believed to be 'natural' though they prove instead to be devices chosen and elaborated for the sake of the group's survival. These devices, though useful and perhaps vital, reveal themselves to be arbitrary, formal, and in the end perhaps oppressive, too. This raises a more or less explicit criticism of one's own society: rather than starting up a useless and wild comparison between distant and hardly similar cultures, one ends up looking 'from the outside in', from a stance of partial suspension of the current rules of the game, at one's own ordinary social experience. And so one also acknowledges the existence of certain styles of 'relating', specifically inside academia: the shabby though still prevailing typology of the 'student', and the narrow range of 'roles' one may choose and eventually shift between according to the (social) stage on which one performs; or the pettiness of academic micro-politics with its hierarchies and its cheap privileges. (A helping hand also comes via the ritual and temporary shift to the more direct '*tu*' instead of the formal '*lei*' normally used between teachers and students, at first introduced only as more practical, and then functioning as a catalyst to awareness of the relative and structural character of these relations.) Stage theatre unmasks real life theatre, ethnodramatic pretence lays bare the apparent 'naturalness' of one's social life and restores it as one of the many possible configurations of human culture.

On the whole, the work as it has been roughly depicted here seems to me, in some measure, able to achieve the goal of making students aware of certain crucial issues of the discipline. From this standpoint I would guess that the tepid reception that Turner's pedagogic proposals got in academic anthropological milieux, which privileged above all his theoretical work and regarded as naïve his pedagogic experimentation,[6] reflects the inertia of largely obsolete didactic models. Traditional pedagogy is based on a one-way communication stream, from teacher to disciple, still viewed as a 'pouring out of knowledge', above all cognitive and 'intellectualistic', in blatant contradiction to the processes of anthropological research which consist mainly of the interchange and re-elaboration of knowledge based upon human dialogue and interaction. For a discipline now well established on the Olympus of academia, such a pompous attitude evokes the aristocratic condescension of James Frazer towards 'the savages'. It would seem that with regard to our students we should say: 'God forbid we have anything to do with you!' All things considered, however, I acknowledge that, if I have refrained here from any theoretical approach to ethnodramaturgic pedagogics, it is because its practical experimentation is multifaceted and fecund enough to make any further theoretical refinement – outside Turner's guidelines – a difficult task. One which is beyond my capacities, and perhaps not all that urgent.

Notes

1. In his later works (1982, 1986a and 1986b), besides setting the theoretical foundations Turner gives extensive accounts of the didactic experiments he made after his encounter with Richard Schechner, whose co-operation greatly concurred with these developments. See 'Dramatic Ritual/Ritual Drama: Performative and Reflexive Anthropology', originally published in *Kenyon Review*, 1980, 1(3): 80–93, reprinted in Turner 1982; and 'Performing Ethnography' written with Edith Turner, originally published in *Drama Review*, 1982, 26(2): 33–50, reprinted in Turner 1986a. See also Schechner 1985, 1986 and 1990.

2. The hallucinogenic cactus (*Lophophora Williamsii*) celebrated by Wirrárika through frequent pilgrimages to the faraway area of Wirikúta. See López Carrillo and Tescari 2000.

3. See López Carrillo and Tescari (2000: 329–30). The ethnographic material on which the didactic performance is based comes mainly from this work, but also from Myerhoff 1974 and Schaefer and Furst 1996.
4. Actually Turner himself was aware of the risk of developing an emphasis on exoticism, so he recommended: 'If we attempt to perform ethnography, let us not begin with such apparently "exotic" and "bizarre" cultural phenomena as rituals and myths. Such an emphasis may only encourage prejudice, since it stresses the "otherness of the other".' (1982: 152) Yet a cumulative approach to the ethnography in question seems to meet the requisites posited to venture into performing rituals too, i.e., 'setting apart a substantial block of time to familiarize students with the culture and social system of the group whose dramas they will enact.' (ibid.).
5. '… it is perhaps in peoples' cultural peculiarities – in their oddities – that one may find some of the most instructive disclosures about what it means to be generically human'; C. Geertz, 'The Impact of the Concept of Culture on the Concept of Man', in Geertz 1973. In this regard see also the Introduction of Remotti ('Etno-antropologia. Un tentativo di messa a fuoco') to Remotti (ed.) 1997: 9–42.
6. See, for instance, De Matteis 1993: 38: '…the theatrical lexicon in Turner is only a device (letting aside the attempts of employing theatre to the purpose of ethnography teaching, whose accounts raise a smile).'

References

De Matteis, S. 1993. 'Introduzione all'edizione italiana', in *Antropologia della performance*, ed. V.W. Turner. Bologna: Il Mulino.

Geertz, C. 1973. *The Interpretation of Cultures*. New York: Basic Books.

López Carrillo, L. and Tescari, G. 2000. *Vámos a Tûríkyé. Sciamanismo e storia sacra wirrárika*. Milan: Franco Angeli.

Myerhoff, B.G. 1974. *Peyote Hunt. The Sacred Journey of the Huichol Indians*. Ithaca and London: Cornell University Press.

Remotti, F. (ed.) 1997. *Le antropologie degli altri*. Turin: Paravia.

Schaefer, S.B. and P.T. Furst (eds) 1996. *People of the Peyote. Huichol Indian History, Religion, and Survival*. Albuquerque: University of New Mexico Press.

Schechner, R. 1985. *Between Theater and Anthropology*. Philadelphia: University of Pennsylvania Press.

— — — 1986. 'Magnitudes of Performance', in *The Anthropology of Experience*, eds V.W. Turner and E.M. Bruner. Urbana and Chicago: University of Illinois Press.

Schechner, R. and Appel, W. (eds) 1990. *By Means of Performance*. Cambridge: Cambridge University Press.

Turner, V.W. 1982. *From Ritual to Theatre. The Human Seriousness of Play*. New York: Paj Publications.

— — — 1986a. *The Anthropology of Performance*. New York: Paj Publications.

— — — 1986b. 'Dewey, Dilthey, and Drama: An Essay in the Anthropology of Experience', in *The Anthropology of Experience*, eds V.W. Turner and E.M. Bruner. Urbana and Chicago: University of Illinois Press.

13

Travelling Cultures
Study Tours in the Social Anthropological Curriculum and Beyond

Andrew Russell

A person who knows only his own village will not understand it: only by seeing
what is familiar in the light of what is the norm elsewhere will we be enabled to
think afresh about what we know too well.

(quoted by Weil and McGill, 1989: 4)

Introduction

In July 1995 a colleague and I organised a Human Sciences Study Tour to India,
a three-week visit involving twenty-two students from University College,
Stockton, U.K. (now renamed University of Durham, Queen's Campus). This
tour broke new ground in the teaching and learning of U.K. anthropology, but
has not been repeated. This chapter discusses the problems and potential of
such a tour, and of fieldwork generally as experiential learning in the social
anthropological curriculum. In particular I shall look at the institutional and
cultural constraints that make organising such ventures challenging.

The reflexive turn in anthropology suggests that a person can understand
their own village through comparison with villages 'elsewhere'. The conventional 'academic' approach to anthropology is to learn what 'elsewhere' is like
from books and other materials available through academic institutions. This
is a view unnervingly akin to the 'armchair anthropology' for which nineteenth century forbears of social anthropology such as Sir James Frazer were
later criticised by Malinowski and his so-called 'fieldwork revolution'. The
central argument of this paper is that, in addition to reflexive and 'academic'
work, experience elsewhere is an important but little-considered part of good

practice in the teaching and learning of anthropology, the understanding of our own and other villages.

Fieldwork and Experiential Learning

Experiential learning is defined by Keeton as 'learning in which the learner is in direct touch with the realities being studied. It is contrasted with learning in which the learner reads, hears, talks, or writes about those referents or realities but never comes into contact with them as part of the learning process' (1982: 618). The American pragmatist philosopher John Dewey is a key figure in the theory of experiential learning, emphasising in particular experience as a cycle of 'trying' and 'undergoing', which in the best cases results in what he calls the 'reconstruction' of experience (e.g., adopting Newtonian laws or Chinese theories of the body), recodifying habits (e.g., overcoming racial bias) and ongoing, active questioning through further experimentation (and consequently a habituation to experiential learning). In addition to such reformulations of knowledge, Keeton (1982) distinguishes three other types of experiential learning: learning how to do something (e.g., surgery, new toilet habits), gaining affective and cognitive insights (particularly in the field of therapy), and action research.

It is easy to criticise Dewey's somewhat idealistic view of experience. We have to allow that some experiences are likely to be uneducative, or at least unproductive, and there is clearly a need for guidance and direction if experience is to achieve its full educational potential. Nor is experience necessarily concomitant with a rather Popperian-sounding 'active questioning' and 'further experimentation'.

Anthropology as a discipline has been markedly resistant to the idea of experiential learning in its undergraduate teaching methods, at least in the U.K.. This is in marked contrast to geography in which experiential learning, in the form of field trips, is *de rigueur*. A U.K. Department of Education and Science (DES) study of geography departments in twenty-two higher educational institutions in 1990–91 found that, for most geography departments, field trips are the major item of recurrent expenditure, averaging from between 40 and 60 percent of the budget. In terms of benefits, the DES writes that fieldwork

> provides students with first hand experience of geographical phenomena and places, and an appreciation of their characteristics, scale and complexity... Field visits play an important role in fostering good staff/student relations and in making groups of students socially cohesive. A particular feature of fieldwork in geography is that it develops personal skills of considerable vocational value, including initiative, leadership, collaboration, teamwork and organisation. Senior management often sees fieldwork as being important in marketing courses and many prospectuses contain photographs of students engaged in fieldwork. ...

Why, if they are so popular in geography, do 'field trips' remain so alien to the teaching of social anthropology, at least in the U.K.? It seems paradoxical, considering the importance of the fieldwork encounter in our disciplinary mythology, that we should slip so easily into 'armchair' modes of teaching and learning our discipline. The reservations about experiential learning permeate domains other than 'field trips'. The arguments for and against the incorporation of fieldwork in the social anthropological curriculum in the late 1980s (Sharma and Wright 1989; Ingold 1989; Shore 1990; Thorn and Wright 1990), and taken up by Watson (1995) through his work at the University of Kent, are still alive in U.K. anthropology departments. The reasons for such a debate are partly the result of the cultural dynamics of social anthropology as a discipline. These cultural factors can be analysed at three levels.

The first level concerns the central focus of anthropology compared with geography. In a nutshell, geography is based on the study of 'place', while anthropology is based on the study of 'people'. Place is resilient, people less so, or so the cultural ideology of some anthropology might have us believe. 'Place' (or, at least, significant aspects of place) can be studied in hours, days or weeks. For anthropology (in its ideal manifestation) two years amongst 'the people' is not enough. Granted, some anthropology degree programmes, particularly in the U.S.A., encourage students to ape the experience of their elders in spending up to a year somewhere doing field research. However, this is frequently poorly supervised, and is effectively denied those with financial constraints or relational commitments.

The second level concerns the still potent scientific pretensions of social anthropology. In *Social Experience and Anthropological Knowledge*, Hastrup (1994) talks of 'maps and tours' reflecting 'different poles of experience'. Tours represent 'process' rather than 'structure', and 'knowledge as a creative field rather than as a solid construction', subjective experience rather than objective knowledge. 'Social scientists', she suggests, 'are surprisingly reluctant to admit to "touring" as well as "mapping" particular worlds'. Anthropologists must share fully in this criticism. However, as Hastrup goes on to point out, the scientific, 'clinical gaze' has been largely replaced in social anthropology 'by more sensitive forms of studying and by a much wider use of the senses in ethnography'. However, for our students (at least at undergraduate level) the 'taste of ethnographic things' (Stoller 1989) remains decidedly second-hand, a diet of books, videos and recorded music or perhaps, if we are feeling really innovative, a lump of manioc, a whiff of incense, or the chance to play the *gamelan*. The serried ranks of books on subjects like 'caste' are our evidence of 'mapped' subjects. The idea of experiencing something like caste directly through a multisensory visit to a different location is more challenging.

This leads us directly to the third cultural dynamic, one common to academia as a whole, namely the relative status accorded to experiential learning as opposed to more 'traditional' forms of education. Experiential learning can be seen as a form of 'play', with all the 'fun and frolics' this word implies. Burnard makes the point that 'fun' 'is not a descriptor that is commonly used in conjunction with educational activities' (1991: 204), nor did educators using experiential learning methods cite fun or enjoyment as an outcome (Henry 1989: 35). Yet experiential learning is fun; its other benefits include the development of social and personal skills of a transferable nature which, like 'fun', are only slowly coming to be recognised within higher education as important and desirable outcomes of teaching and learning. For social anthropology, perhaps, there is a particular concern with maintaining boundaries between what we do and the frivolous pursuits of tourism or journalism.

It seems strange that a discipline interested in questions of boundary maintenance and change should not be willing to test the fluidity of its own boundaries. A study tour is neither 'anthropology' nor 'tourism' but lies somewhere on a continuum of travel experiences from groups of British tourists singing '*Viva Espana*' as their charter plane hurtles down the runway *en route* to Spain, through to the intensive fieldwork experiences that anthropologists cherish. Furthermore the individual 'gaze' can shift from 'tourist' to 'anthropologist' and back again during the course of the travelling. Transecting this continuum are the continua of other gazes, such as those stretching from 'clinical' to 'social' and from 'mapping' to 'tour'. The challenge posed by this study tour, in retrospect, was not only to encourage students to shift from 'tourist gaze' (Urry 1990) to 'anthropological gaze', but also to push them away from the 'clinical gaze', the objectifying 'mapping' of cultures, towards a more creative concept of knowledge which accepts the process, fluidity and inter-subjectivity of social experience.

First, some socio-economic context. University College Stockton (since re-named University of Durham, Queen's Campus) first opened its doors in 1992. The mission statement of the College was to serve the educational needs of Teesside, a socially and economically deprived area in the north-east of England with one of the lowest rates of progression into higher education in the country. Half our students are local, and half are mature (i.e., older than twenty-three). We feel we have risen to the challenge of teaching anthropology in such an environment with particularly innovative teaching programmes in Human Sciences and Health and Human Sciences (Simpson et al. 1995; Simpson 1995). Our educational style emphasises groupwork and hands-on, reflexive experience in the teaching and learning of anthropology, and the 'transferable skills' these processes engender.

Second, a point of nomenclature. We organise a number of 'field trips' as part of our academic curricula at Queen's Campus. For example, first-year students taking the 'Ways of Life' module spend an afternoon at a mosque, a Hindu temple or a Buddhist monastery. In their second year, students taking the 'Transitions' module visit the North of England Historical Museum, and have been to see Neolithic cave paintings in Derbyshire, while students taking 'Culture and Practical Reason' have visited Edinburgh Zoo. In their third year, students on the 'Social Constructions of the Environment' module go on a field trip to the Teesmouth Field Centre, in the shadow of Hartlepool nuclear power-station.

'Fieldwork' is also encouraged on the degree course, as part of the second-year 'Methods and Analysis' module, and in the work students do for their third-year 'dissertation' (see Coleman and Simpson, this volume). Students may conduct dissertation field research abroad under special programmes we have established with European Union ERASMUS partners in Iceland and the Czech Republic, or if they are accepted for a year abroad, in a developing country, under the auspices of the Overseas Training Programme of the U.K.'s Voluntary Service Overseas (VSO). In the case of the India study tour organised by our department (see following section), I balked at the idea of using either 'field trip' or 'fieldwork', not wishing to give students false expectations about what they would be doing. I wanted them to learn through experience, not work in the 'field', that increasingly problematic concept for social anthropology (Berger 1993).

In what follows, a short account of the tour provides the basis for a broader investigation of the concept and potential of fieldwork as a form of experiential learning in anthropology. It derives from notes, mental notes and observations, pre- and post-tour questionnaires and diaries completed by the students, and my direct experience as participant-leader of the tour. I shall look at the institutional constraints that made it particularly important to evaluate the educational value of such a tour, work which is necessary if fieldwork is to become a fully integrated and effective part of the social anthropological curriculum. More information about the logistical 'nuts and bolts' of the tour is to be found in Russell (1995).

The Human Sciences Study Tour to India

On an overnight trip to London for first-year students taking the 'Health and Society' module in April 1994, I was struck by the number of students who had little experience of London, or indeed of the world outside Teesside. Here we were, teaching anthropology – a discipline founded on the study of 'other cultures' – to people of whom many had little cross-cultural experience.

However, my ensuing dedication to the cause of fieldwork and experiential learning in anthropology can probably be traced back further than this. In a previous incarnation I worked for Project Trust, an educational charitable trust based in Scotland sending school-leavers overseas for a year. I was a volunteer myself (at Mitraniketan, a rural community-education project in Kerala State, South India that was to be the main destination point of the study tour). After returning to Britain I worked part-time for Project Trust during university vacations, and eventually became a full-time staff member of the organisation from 1984–87 when I was responsible for the welfare and education of one hundred and fifty volunteers in various parts of the world. This, I feel, equipped me to deal with the planning and implementation of a study tour and gave me the 'transferable skills' to be able to do so.

The Department of Anthropology paid for the travelling expenses of the two lecturers on the tour, but no provision could be made for the participation of students on the tour, for whom the costs came to £500 per head. This must have limited the involvement of economically disadvantaged students, but even amongst the ones that did eventually go, three had never been abroad before and of the rest only four had ever travelled outside Europe or North America. However, many of them had interesting connections with India. Several students had fathers who had worked in India during the colonial period, and one student had been born there. Another had planned to go to India overland with one of his friends in the 1960s, and had been working to save money to buy a jeep when they both met their prospective spouses and gave up the idea. For this particular student, the trip was a dream he felt he should have followed many years before. Another rewarding person to have on the tour was a student born in the U.K. of a Sikh Punjabi family. In a fascinating narrative over dinner one night in Delhi she told how, for her, to come to India 'on her own', without her family, was incredible. Had the tour not been organised through the University, her family would never have agreed to her going. For many of the students, then, the tour was exploratory at a deeper level than simply 'an interesting trip to an interesting place'.

Our route took us from Heathrow to Delhi on Uzbekistan Airways via Tashkent. After two nights in Delhi, we went by bus to Agra, and two nights later went on from there to Kerala State by train. During the tour, students were expected to keep diaries of their experiences, and to fill in pre-and post-tour questionnaires. These, and the formal and informal discussion sessions before, during and after the tour, were designed to enhance the engagement with and reflection on their experiences.

The timing of the tour, in the first three weeks of July 1995, was not climatically optimal since it coincided with the final build-up to the monsoon and the start of the rains themselves. However, the dates were dictated largely by university commitments such as graduation, and the needs of many of the students to work for the rest of the summer following the tour. There were certain financial advantages, however, to travelling 'off season'.

On our first full day in the capital, we used the services of a travel company to be taken on a sightseeing tour of Old Delhi, visiting the Gandhi Memorial at Raj Ghat (where we first became acquainted with the 'how to do it' rituals of sacred site-seeing in India), the Red Fort (where I was introduced to some of the dynamics of the Indian tourist industry in the form of two competing 'unions' of tour guides, government employees versus the generally better-educated guides employed by commercial companies), the Jama Masjid, and the Chawri Bazaar. Here, as we walked round, our guide told me about his perceptions of the differences between the nationals he leads. He did not usually like to take British groups (but had agreed to ours because they were students), finding the reaction of some of the British to the colonial past ('Well, we also did a lot of good for your country...') distasteful. His special language was German, and he had learnt how best to deal with German-speaking groups. 'It is important to be democratic with them', he said. 'If I am running out of time and we are going to have to miss one destination, I make sure to take a vote on which one it will be. Otherwise they are careful to read their brochures when they go home and are likely to say "Hey, we didn't go to that place!" and cause trouble'. Of the three types of German-speakers he guides (German, Swiss-German and Austrian) he found the Austrians the most obliging and able to deal with the contingencies of India.

Our experience of 'tourist' India (and the support offered by company guides and a tourist bus) continued on our journey to the Emperor Akbar's tomb at Sikandra, Fatehpur Sikri and, of course, the Taj Mahal and the Red Fort in Agra. The protective trappings of group tourism cosseted us during those first, culture-shocked days in India but were stripped away when we arrived at Agra Cantonment railway station to join the Kerala Express for the two day journey south. 'Although most people had a moan about the Kerala Express, including myself, I think it was a good experience' wrote one student at the end of the tour. 'As anthropologists…it seems pointless to fly or travel first class, when the majority don't do that'. Bedding arrangements for night-time travel had to be learnt, the toilets were fairly smelly, and women found the stares of some male passengers unsettling. However, the journey in each direction, across the spine of India, also offered something of a respite, a temporary objectification of life and shift from participant to observer, a chance for reflection, to catch up on sleep, or books. 'Chaos' was revised as 'organised chaos'. There was still plenty of interaction possible, much of it unwanted or awkward, with the beggars, cleaners, singers and vendors who came onto the train at every stop, but in large part, life became a series of scenes – the great crenellated fort of Gwalior towering on a rock bluff over the city at sunset, for example, or the mighty Krishna river outside Vijayawada in Andhra Pradesh. Passing such places raised questions for me concerning how much I should be telling the students about where we were passing. They had excellent guidebooks donated by Bob Bradnock, a lecturer in the geography department at the School of Oriental and African Studies (SOAS) in London, the only other British academic I know who has organised similar student trips to India. There was a limit to how much I was willing or able to go leaping about the different sections of the noisy carriage telling people what was to be seen.

Two nights in Ernakulam/Cochin introduced the students to the cultural as well as physical contrasts between North and South India – a reformulation of knowledge for those previously inclined to think of 'India' in blanket terms. We also met a British anthropologist engaged in Ph.D. research who was able to explain something of the distinctive ecology, history, society and culture of Kerala and its regions. I felt rather embarrassed to hear a few students discussing sex scenes from the British TV sit-com 'Men Behaving Badly' in front of an Indian family as we embarked on a boat tour of the harbour the following day. My colleague also caused some consternation by suggesting to some of the younger students that smiling and waving at passing fishermen was liable to misinterpretation. Appropriate codes of dress and behaviour had been mentioned in the *Travel Tips* booklet we prepared for the students prior to departure on the study tour. The issue was how much deviation into errant behaviour patterns could and should be corrected 'on the ground', since doing so was clearly demoralising and lowering in confidence. It is probably better to give as much 'information' (or, preferably, have group discussions on sensitivity and cultural awareness) as possible beforehand and then let people learn from experience and mistakes (the 'recodifying of habits', to use John Dewey's terminology).

Our journey thus far had been valuable but, in many respects, could have been done by any enterprising traveller. However, such a 'breaking-in' was perhaps a necessary prelude to the more anthropologically intense part of the tour, a week at Mitraniketan, in the hills inland from Trivandrum, south Kerala. This community development education centre had undergone major changes since my time there as a volunteer in 1976, as has Kerala state itself. In the nearest village, Vellanad, for example, the market had moved from being twice weekly to daily, there were new shops, and an overseas/STD telephone dialling booth. Auto-rickshaws and private buses lined the roads where once one would have been happy for a Kerala State Road Transport bus or an occasional taxi. Perhaps the whole of southern Kerala has become 'rurban', as one of the lecturers we heard during the week suggested.

Mitraniketan was established in 1956 by Sri K. Viswanathan, a man from the locality who, after studying at Shantiniketan, had become involved in the community college and folk high school movements of the U.S.A. and Denmark respectively. The latest development in the community, one very beneficial to our students, was a beautiful new visitors' block built using low-cost local materials.

My expectations about the nature of the educational content of the week in Mitraniketan were pleasantly revised. I had prepared a list of questions focusing on the history and contemporary life of Mitraniketan prior to our arrival, which I had envisaged the students using as a guide for their own research as they went about the community talking to people during their stay. Instead, we were surprised (and delighted) to find that the director and joint-director of the Centre for Educational Research, Innovation and Development (CERID) in Mitraniketan had developed a full programme of activities based on Indian notions of a study tour in anthropology, with morning guest lectures, afternoon visits to production units in Mitraniketan, whole-day trips outside the community, and evening 'cultural exchanges'.

Initial reactions to Mitraniketan were akin to Dewey's 'affective and cognitive insights'. At an introductory session in the CERID building, one student burst into tears saying she was overwhelmed by the atmosphere and beauty of the place. Others likened it to a 'health farm'. For me, the visit was nostalgic. The room I once occupied as an eighteen-year-old volunteer was now part of an incubator unit! Despite the transformations during its history, there were at least twelve people working in the community or living around about whom I had known in 1976–77 (some as children, now adult), and it was wonderful to renew acquaintance with them. We were taken on a number of guided walks. Classes 'in action' ended abruptly with the sudden arrival of over twenty British anthropologists. We sometimes finished up in the tea-shop.

The guest lectures, by scholars with national or international reputations, were excellent. Questions highlighted in the lectures included why Kerala, with its population density comparable with Bangladesh and West Bengal, and an average income per head of only $300, enjoys a quality of life (based on indices such as mortality and literacy) comparable with countries enjoying per capita incomes of $20,000 per year. Others looked at the relationship of the state to the so-called 'scheduled castes and tribes' of India and Kerala, and the place of Mitraniketan in Indian development, where the Tagore/Gandhian philosophies on which it is based are perhaps the only truly indigenous forms of development philosophy in India.

Our first field trip was a day in Chhatancode, a Karnikar 'tribal' village in the Western Ghats, a place where foreign anthropologists might have difficulty gaining research clearance, given the sensitive nature of 'the tribal question' in Indian politics, and tourists were unlikely to reach. We went on a dramatic walk to a nearby waterfall, which turned out to be several hours away on foot across rocks, torrential streams and narrow paths through dense forest vegetation. Several students ended up in tears, overwhelmed by the fear and challenge of it all. One, shaken by a serious fall, decided to stay put on one side of the river, although our Karnikar guides were concerned because she was sitting on a track used by wild elephants; another suffered a broken toe. At the top, one student fell into the stream and narrowly avoided being swept down a waterfall.

The other field trip was to Trivandrum, where clearance had been arranged for us as foreign students to be shown around the Ayurveda College Hospital, again something which would be denied the normal tourist and, perhaps, anthropologist. It was fascinating, particularly for the Health and Human Sciences students, to see a totally different professional medical system in operation. However, the day was rather blighted for us by the fact that one of our students had herself been admitted to an allopathic hospital that morning, suffering acute dehydration from insufficient fluid intake during a bout of gastro-enteritis, an event which had required summoning the Mitraniketan vehicle to take her to hospital, with my colleague, at 4.30 in the morning.

Such experiences indicate that such a tour was more than simply an 'academic' exercise for the students involved, and one that a university lecturer should not enter into lightly. It was necessary, as Bob Bradnock had cautioned me, to include plenty of 'unwinding' time and space for students to assimilate all they were seeing and to remain healthy. We had done this before coming to Mitraniketan, and at the end we spent two nights at Kovalam Beach before boarding the train in Trivandrum again for the fifty-four-hour journey back to Delhi, and the onward flights to Tashkent and London. The dangers and time commitment involved in such a tour, along with the cultural dynamics of anthropology outlined above, generated institutional constraints which I shall describe in the next section. These constraints necessitate clear evidence for the educational value of such a tour: not just a simple acceptance of it, and fieldwork in general, as an inherently 'good thing'. This can be provided only by an evaluation of its impact in the broadest possible terms.

Educational Outcomes and Institutional Constraints

As with most good ethnographies or accounts of social experience, one has to draw an interactive boundary around the edge marked 'political and economic factors'. These made organising the tour somewhat problematic. For example, the Anthropology Department at Durham, under pressure from the university's academic officers, had a mission to raise their grade in the research assessment exercise. This is an important determinant of higher education funding in the U.K. and my then Head of Department saw planning and running this extracurricular activity as a threat to my research output, 'a nice idea at the wrong time'. The pressure on academics to publish rather than lead study tours is a factor militating against their organisation in the current academic climate. In addition, the University of Durham was at that time dealing with a legal threat posed by a geography student who had cut her hand on barbed-wire during a local field trip and was suing the university for negligence. The university was adamant that field trips and tours should take place only as recognised parts of courses of study, and I nearly had to sign a document saying that the study tour was a venture entirely independent of the university. The students signed an indemnity document, but things can happen on any trip or tour, and the idea of running more tours without a trained health-care specialist and the full support of the university is not inspiring.

More work has to be done to establish the empirical value of study tours. Their inclusion in the curriculum, appropriately advertised in prospectuses and the like, would have great potential impact on student recruitment and the fees that come with them. However, rather than their development as a recruitment stunt, more evidence is required of their educational significance for participating students. In seeking such evidence, I followed-up students who went on the tour, comparing their grades before and after with matched pairs (based on closest average grades prior to departure) of non-tour students. Any differences observed could not be ascribed solely to the effects of the tour, since those participating on the tour were self – rather than randomly – selected, and with the numbers involved in this case, significance would be hard to prove anyway. However, no such differences were apparent. A matched-pair comparison of students on the India study tour with students who did not go on the tour indicated no difference in final grades between the six who were first-year students when they went on the tour and those who did not. The final grades of the eight second-year students who went on the tour were 2.7 percentage points higher than those who did not (57.8 percent compared with 54.1 percent), although this result, like the average for students of both years who participated in the tour, is not statistically significant.

There are also more qualitative measures of 'outcome'. The success of the tour, and the benefits to the individual participants who went on it, in all the four areas of experiential learning defined by Keeton (above), are unquestionable. Comments from the post-tour questionnaires observed (1) how the tour brought anthropology to life for participants; (2) how it related to and enhanced their understanding of particular modules, such as those concerned with development; and (3) how the continual and close interaction between lecturers and students over the three-week period, in ways and contexts impossible in the closed confines of Queen's, engendered a greater respect for the dedicated work of anthropologists (Russell 1995). In addition, the discipline and practice of keeping a diary every day will have contributed to the writing skills of all students on the tour.

One way of understanding the educational benefits of the tour is to view it as a form of 'Outward Bound' model. 'Outward Bound' is a U.K.-based organisation with international links providing courses that influence participants' personal and social development through physical challenges. This tour could be seen as a 'Cultural Outward Bound', since the primary challenge to students was cultural difference as well as physical and social environments very different from their own. It is interesting that the benefit most often mentioned by students in the post-tour questionnaires was neither intellectual nor academic but the development of self-confidence. 'At the beginning of the trip I wouldn't have ventured far without Andrew or Kate. By the end of the trip I was getting auto-rickshaws on my own', wrote one student. 'When we arrived in Delhi I wouldn't have dared go out alone without a big group. Today, however, I went out alone… I felt really confident and not at all scared. I really enjoyed it though admittedly I didn't go very far', wrote another. One might hope that this increased sense of confidence might impact on subsequent academic and extra-curricular achievements.

The effects of the tour have also been documented by two students who subsequently mentioned the tour in a reflective exercise for the third-year 'Knowledge and Practice' module that charts the subjective 'ups and downs' of a student's life diagrammatically. In another exercise for this module, providing a character sketch in the third person, one student wrote, 'going to India on her own without any of her close friends I know was a big decision for her, though I feel it made Kirsty know she can converse with anyone about anything and also build up strong friendships with new people'. Another writes 'recently we undertook a group exercise and I was able to use my experience of the tour in coming up with suggestions on the implementing of an imaginary development project. Therefore the trip has proven to be of help in transferring the experience to possibilities of development work at a later date'. Finally, the student who was shut up in hospital for thirty-six hours with my colleague in attendance wrote 'it was only after talking with

Kate Molesworth-Storer, during the three-week trip to India, that I realised that, like her, I too would like to get involved with teaching/lecturing'. One student subsequently applied successfully for a job co-ordinating student exchanges between Teesside and Germany, a job she said she would never have considered had the experience of travel in India not made the prospect of travel to and from Germany less daunting.

Another important 'Outward Bound'-type benefit from the tour, less remarked upon by students in their post-tour evaluations, was the tremendous sense of group cohesion and support it engendered. They offered each other a great deal of support, sharing experiences at the time and reflecting on them both publicly and behind closed doors afterwards, as well as caring for the unwell, homesick and 'culture-shocked'. The fact that such a mixed-age, mixed-degree and mixed-year group got on so well is attributable in no small part to the emphasis we put on group activities in our day-to-day teaching at Queen's. The network of support and friendships established on the tour persisted and developed beyond it.

There are also wider benefits to consider. 'This is so great for the college,' one student said to me at Heathrow. The announcement of a tour at the start of the academic year had a galvanising effect, not only on those who subsequently went on it. There was feedback, formal and informal, from participating students to their colleagues on return, and some students went on to appear in local news media, thus enhancing the reputation of the university and public awareness of anthropology in general.

Finally there is the question of the benefits to receiving nations from a study tour. While I did not ask people the total they reckoned to have spent on the tour, the tour contributed £7,500 to Uzbekistan Airways and their agents, and £5,000 (minimum – probably much more) to the Indian economy. Fourteen of the students thought they would return to India one day. Two students had used the trip to ascertain whether they would be prepared to work in India, and had decided that they would. Inspiring such a large number of students to want to return under their own steam (and giving them the wherewithal to be able to do it) is surely a worthwhile economic contribution to the countries from which we derive so much research material. However, it is important to consider ways in which such an exchange can be made more than simply financial, and above all less one-sided. At the moment there are few mechanisms for university exchanges equivalent to the ERASMUS programme outside the borders of the European Union.

Students in subsequent years have enquired about the possibility of the study tour being repeated, but the institutional constraints highlighted above have mitigated against such a venture. For study tours like the one described here to become a more regular part of the curriculum, and to circumvent some of the university's anxiety about litigation, they should probably become a fully accredited module. In addition to the recruitment potential of having study tours an integral part of the curriculum, a university could also organise tours like this (at a profit) for the general public, with a strong chance that some of those participating might be sufficiently inspired by their experience to go on and read for an anthropology degree.

Conclusion

The research selectivity exercise in British universities at the moment puts the onus on staff to increase time spent on research, not on extra-curricular activities such as study tours. Other institutional and cultural factors conspire to give relatively little encouragement to fieldwork generally in the social anthropological curriculum. Given the constraints outlined here, careful evaluation of the benefits (and risks) of fieldwork for students is necessary. Three weeks is a very short time for lasting, experientially-based 'transformations of knowledge' to take place, and further studies of the validity of different kinds of fieldwork are required. Without appropriate institutional support and backing, study tours such as the one described here cannot achieve their full potential for our students, universities and the world in general.

There may be interesting comparisons to be made with the situation in universities elsewhere in the world, and there is a need, in Europe at least, for such exercises to be fully integrated into social anthropology curricula. This requires financial resources if departments are to make them accessible to all students, but these are outlays accepted as normal by many geography departments. Other issues to be resolved include what selection criteria, if any, should be applied to choice of destination, and choice of participants, for such a tour. I was happy to organise such a tour to a structured environment like Mitraniketan. I would not have been willing to organise such a tour to my own field area in Nepal. We did not apply any explicit selection criteria, and took students from all three years of the degree. It is, of course, vitally important to ensure that health, safety and liability issues are adequately addressed in the planning and implementation of any fieldwork endeavour.

Finally, there are more macro-political issues to consider. The ability to organise and run such a tour is obviously completely dependent on the mass-transit technologies and organisation of late twentieth century capitalism: it would have been impossible, I would venture, to have organised a similar tour thirty years ago. However, access to global travel is most iniquitously distributed, and as anthropologists we should be concerned with ways in which tours and other forms of experiential learning can be conducted in the opposite direction, perhaps through ERASMUS-type exchange schemes between anthropology departments world-wide.

Acknowledgements

I would like to thank Tamara Kohn and our son Ben for their support, and Kate Molesworth-Storer and my student 'informants' who participated on the tour. I am grateful to Vikram Rana and Dr Narotam Singh in Delhi and Agra respectively and to K.V. Dileep for his marvellous companionship during our time in Kerala. The Director of Mitraniketan, Sri K. Viswanathan, and Drs John Mammen and Reghu Ram Das, of the Centre for Educational Research, Innovation and Development, made our stay there both stimulating and enjoyable. Fascinating lectures were provided by Dr Sonam, Mr Menon, Dr A.M. Kurup, and Dr John Mammen himself. There were many other people in the U.K. and in India, not all of whom are mentioned in the text, who helped to make the tour and its subsequent evaluation so rewarding. In particular I would like to thank Dr. Peter Craig in the Mathematics Department at Durham for his statistical advice, and Kate Melvin and Carole Hughes at Queen's for their assistance with the analysis of module grades. I am grateful to participants in the School of Oriental and African Studies, London University, seminar series 'Pedagogy and Anthropology', and particularly the organisers Stella Mascarenhas-Keyes and Stuart Thompson, for their insightful comments on a first draft of this paper presented in February 1996, and to the organisers of the session 'Teaching and Learning Social Anthropology in Europe' at the International Union of Anthropological and Ethnological Sciences Congress in Williamsburg, Virginia, U.S.A., where a second draft was presented in July 1998.

References

Berger, R. 1993. 'From Text to (Field) Work and Back Again: Theorizing a Post (Modern)-Ethnography', *Anthropological Quarterly* 66(4): 174–86.

Bradnock, R. and Bradnock, R. (eds) 1995. *India Handbook with Sri Lanka, Bhutan and The Maldives,* 4th edn. Bath: Trade and Travel Handbooks; Chicago: Passport Books.

Burnard, P. 1991. *Experiential Learning in Action.* Aldershot: Avebury.

Hastrup, K. 1994. 'Anthropological Knowledge Incorporated: Discussion', in *Social Experience and Anthropological Knowledge*, eds K. Hastrup and P. Hervik. London: Routledge.

Henry, J. 1989. 'Meaning and Practice in Experiential Learning'. In *Making Sense of Experiential Learning: Diversity in Theory and Practice*, eds S.W. Weil and I. McGill. Milton Keynes: Open University Press.

Ingold, T. 1989. 'Fieldwork in Undergraduate Anthropology: An Opposing View', *British Association of Anthropology in Policy and Practice* 3: 2–3.

Keeton, M.T. 1982. 'Experiential Education', in *Encyclopedia of Educational Research*, H.E. Mitzel, 5th edn, vol. 2. London: Collier Macmillan.

Russell, A.J. 1995. 'The Human Sciences Study Tour to India, July 1995', in *Report on Teaching and Learning Social Anthropology in the United Kingdom*, eds S. Mascarenhas-Keyes and S. Wright. London: National Network for Teaching and Learning Anthropology.

Sharma, U. and Wright, S. 1989. 'Practical Relevance of Undergraduate Courses', *British Association of Social Anthropology in Policy and Practice* 2: 7–9.

Shore, C. 1990. 'Teaching Anthropology: Projects and Placements', *Anthropology Today* 6(5): 21ff.

Simpson, B. 1995. 'Narration and Transition: The Experience of Mature Students in Higher Education', *Auto/Biography* 2/3: 1–12.

– with Hyde, S., MacLeod, D., Rostas, S. and Wemyss, G. 1995. 'Mature Students, Access and Anthropology', in *Report on Teaching and Learning Social Anthropology in the United Kingdom*, eds S. Mascarenhas-Keyes and S. Wright. London: National Network for Teaching and Learning Anthropology.

Stoller, P. 1989. *The Taste of Ethnographic Things: the Senses in Anthropology.* Philadelphia: University of Pennsylvania Press.

Thorn, R. and Wright, S. 1990. 'Projects and Placements in Undergraduate Anthropology', *British Association of Social Anthropology in Policy and Practice* 7: 4–5.

Watson, C.W. 1995. 'Case Study: Fieldwork in Undergraduate Anthropology, For and Against', *Innovations in Education and Training International* 32(2): 153–61.

Weil, S. and McGill, I. 'Introduction', in *Making Sense of Experiential Learning: Diversity in Theory and Practice*, eds S.W. Weil and I. McGill. Milton Keynes: Society for Research into Higher Education & Open University Press.

Urry, J. 1990. *The Tourist Gaze.* London: Sage.

14

Beginning with Images
An Introduction to Imagination-Based Educational Methodologies

Iain R. Edgar

The use of computer-assisted learning and the anticipated future generation of virtual ethnographic experience on-line may perhaps develop coincidentally alongside a developing interest in accessing students' imaginative potential. This chapter proposes a further development of experiential learning methods (Kolb 1984) to include a variety of imagework methods. Some humanistic groupwork methods have already been developed in education, and role-play for instance is a regular feature of current classroom activity. While psychosynthesis, Montessori and confluent educators in primary and secondary U.K. education (Whitmore 1986) regularly use imagework exercises as part of their curriculum, imagework methods have been hitherto little used in Social Science Higher Education. However, an exception is Conton (1996) who writes about her extensive classroom use of experiential methodologies, particularly the use of visualisation within a core shamanic perspective, in her teaching of shamanism. Interestingly, imagework methods are also now being developed as potential research methods, particularly in recent developments in Participatory Research Activities (PRA) (Pretty et al 1995; Stuhlmiller and Thorsen 1997; Edgar 1999).

In this chapter, I introduce the idea of imagination-based educational methodologies, notably various levels of imagework. So far, such methods, initially derived from experiential groupwork, have been little used as educational methodologies in the social sciences. I introduce a potential taxonomy of different levels of imagework and further propose that the use of imagework methods can generate more holistic, in the sense of combining rational with affective and intuitive aspects of self, expressions of implicit worldviews, than many other current educational methodologies. My argument is supported and illustrated with visual data from a recent imagework study.

What is Imagework and How Does It Work

Imagework has variously been called 'active imagination', 'visualisation' and 'guided fantasy'. Imagework is also a powerful therapeutic method, as described by Glouberman (1989) and Achterberg (1985). Imagework has developed from the active imagination technique of Jung and the theory and practice of psychosynthesis developed by Assagioli (1975). Jung's (1959: 42) concept of the 'collective unconscious' underpins imagework. The concept of the 'collective unconscious' represented Jung's perception that the human psyche contained impersonal and archaic contents that manifested themselves in the myths, dreams and images of humans. Jung's idea that all humans contain a common and universal treasury of psychic contents, which he called 'archetypes', is the core model of the unconscious that enables imagework practitioners (see Glouberman 1989: 25) to consider the spontaneous image as being potentially a creative and emergent aspect of the self. More recently, transpersonal psychotherapy has integrated the work of Assagioli and Jung to form an imaginatively based approach to therapy. Rowan's (1993: 51) definition of active imagination suggests that:

> In active imagination we fix upon a particular point, mood, picture or event, and then allow a fantasy to develop in which certain images become concrete or even personified. Thereafter the images have a life of their own and develop according to their own logic.

The imagework method is an active process in which the person 'actively imagining' lets go of the mind's normal train of thoughts and images and goes with a sequence of imagery that arises spontaneously from the unconscious. It is the quality of spontaneity and unexpectedness that are the hallmarks of this process. Imagework has creative potential because as Clandinin (1986: 17) writes:

> In this view, images are seen as the mediator between the unconscious and conscious levels of being. What is known at the unconscious level finds expression in a person's thought and actions through a person's images. Images are thus seen as the source of inspiration, ideas, insight and meaning.

Levels and Stages of Imagework

There are several different kinds of imagework or, as I term them, levels to indicate the developing depth of engagement with the imaginative resources of the mind. Imagework can be as simple as asking students individually or in a group to imagine an image in response to a question such as 'How do you picture a certain situation?', as I shall illustrate shortly. I shall call this first level *introductory imagework*. Another, second level of imagework, involves guiding participants into their memory of earlier events, such as their childhood socialization. I call this second level of imagework *memory imagework*. A third level of imagework involves the use of the Jungian active imagination technique, which facilitates a spontaneous journey into the imagination. I define this level as *spontaneous imagework*.

Imagework and dreamwork are very closely related and in certain ways they overlap in that both refer to the mind's spontaneous production of imagery that people may consider 'good to think with.' This fourth level of imagework I shall refer to as *dream imagework*.

The analytic processing of imagework into educational content can have up to *four stages*: first, the descriptive stage wherein students 'tell their story'; second, analysis by students of the personal meaning of their experience of symbols used; third, analysis of the models used to inform their imagery; and fourth, the comparative stage when students compare their imagework with that of others in the group. Each of these stages needs facilitation and is promoted through the amplification of the imagework into art, drama and so forth.

In using an experiential method such as imagework, it is also important to realise that while in itself imagework is a largely non-verbal activity it produces a verbal communication that incorporates the students' interpretations. Therefore, a student explaining the results of their imagework will typically relate a verbal account of their experience to the group.

Introductory Level Imagework

The first example of the use of imagework is at the introductory level. This 'introductory level' imagework is designed to facilitate a group in sharing and analysing how students are feeling about a certain situation. The technique simply consists of asking participants to imagine an image that reflects the situation being considered. It is as easy as that! In a recent example, the situation was a two-session study of personal and professional identity change among students on a vocational master's programme in social work at a U.K. university.

What was immediately striking about the student feedback was, first, that all of the twenty students were able to relate an image that they had pictured and, second, how 'discontented' their images were. Students particularly described 'seeing' pictures of train scenarios such as 'being in a siding', 'being derailed', 'in a tunnel' and 'I thought I was on a modern train but it's not!' Apart from the surprising amount of train imagery, other notable imagery presented was feeling 'in a fog', 'up against a brick wall' and 'climbing up a mountain without enough footholds.' I later realised that students had previously been attending a staff-student meeting about the course and that individual and group morale at that point was low.

However, the whole point about imagework is to facilitate the movement from 'seen' inner image to articulated theme through a process of 'reading' the imagery much like one might 'read' a picture in an art gallery; and indeed, further 'readings' can be obtained by asking the students to make a simple external picture of their imagery and then displaying their results on the wall for further individual and group discussion. Each student then speaks about their picture in turn before the teacher/facilitator possibly develops a group-based analysis of pertinent themes based on comparing the individual narratives that have emerged. Further amplification of meaning from such imagery can be made by doing a sculpt,[1] which in the above case would have consisted of inviting the group to first design and create a train station, railway line and so forth using chairs, tables and the like as props; then each person would have been asked to position themselves in a pose that represented their feeling state about their position on the course (i.e., 'being stuck in a tunnel' or 'derailed'). This can be jolly, is not difficult to facilitate (see Jennings 1986, for details), and as people talk from their positions and poses in the sculpt, new levels of insight and implicit knowledge can be revealed. It also enhances group cohesion and identity, and that in itself can facilitate richer levels of discussion, disclosure, group analysis and consequently the development of 'deep' rather than 'surface' learning.

So we can articulate an educational process that starts with imagework and then can move on into artwork, sculpting and possibly drama. Yet at whatever point the 'experiential' process stops, public analysis by each student needs to begin. Themes need to be drawn out and 'read' from the imagery, and as students talk about their imagery, they engage the intuitive and affective dimensions of the self in a way unlikely to be achieved solely through a cognitive engagement with an educator. Using the binary opposition model of the brain (Markham 1989), imagework connects many people to the right-hand side of their brain, the centre for creative, intuitive and lateral thinking, while the left-hand side brain hemisphere is known to control cognitive and intellectual processes. So imagework is particularly powerful as a tool for accessing the unarticulated views of individuals and groups in the educational process.

What imagework and related 'experiential' educational methods can achieve is the articulation of participants' as yet dimly perceived aspects of self and world. So, for instance, in the postgraduate Master's programme evaluation presented above, students speaking of their imagework articulated through this process their feelings about the nature, content and structure of the course, and their individual and group progress on it; further, they accessed their original hopes and fears for 'the course' and how their imagery reflected their intuited and existential predicament concerning 'the course' in their life in the 'here and now.' Not only did it reflect their immediate felt concern but through further experiential techniques, such as the use of art and sculpting, the process gave students the opportunity of 'working with' and changing their existential predicaments. When I asked students at the end of the session whose 'images' had changed during the course of the session, three participants replied affirmatively: the one who had 'thought she was on a modern train but wasn't, felt she was now on an 'express train'; another felt there was less 'fog' around her; and another felt there were more 'footholds' on the mountain.

So imagework and its amplification (artwork, sculpting and drama, updating/amplifying participants' imagery) can evoke both significant insights into psycho-social situations and even change personal and group orientation. For instance, in this last example, participants had almost no idea that fellow participants/students felt so similarly about the course experience. Using imagework, even at this most simple and introductory level, can evoke rich levels of personal and group insight and facilitate enhanced self-disclosure and group analysis. Moreover, I find groups can be easily encouraged to develop their own meta-analysis of the imagery presented; asking participants to 'identify common themes and significant differences' usually provides very useful analysis as students, if reasonably facilitated, are 'warmed up' by their personal and group encounter with the affective and intuitive aspects of themselves, something still relatively rarely encountered in contemporary Western life-styles.

Often, before doing either of the following levels of imagework, I do the introductory 'bowl of soup' exercise, to illustrate to students, the immediate, universal capacity of the mind to bring up a spontaneous and often valuable image.

Introductory Imagework Exercise: Bowl of Soup

The aim of the exercise is to show that the 'unconscious' or mind is always accessible; like a well of images awaiting our attention. The primary intention of this exercise is as a warm-up to longer imagework exercises. This exercise can be used to give a symbolic view on a person's current self-state, though I tend not to focus on this aspect.

The exercise can proceed as follows:

1. Ask students to imagine themselves drinking in silence a bowl of soup; alternatively this 'imaginary' bowl could be passed round a group (I prefer this second way).
2. Give people a couple of minutes to imagine the 'bowl of soup'; make sure people have been asked not to giggle beforehand.
3. Then ask people, or two or three people, to share:
   a. What was the soup?
   b. What was the bowl?
4. Typically, there is quite a variety of responses from:
   a. One person who 'flew' through the bottom of the bowl into a mountain range (an experienced imaginative traveller!).
   b. Others who remember a 'favourite soup' which has a particular meaning for them.

   c. Half-empty bowls which can illustrate feelings of not being fed enough. (I remember a mother who said she always focused on feeding others, hence her bowl was half empty.)

   d. Often there is a split between those who imagine their bowls with home-made (often mother's) soup which has values of family nurturance etc.; and those who have tinned soup. This contrast is 'good to work with'.

   e. the bowl itself can be of interest and is often 'special' to the person in some way; meanings and associations can be developed here.

The exercise shows how quickly the 'unconscious' throws up an image or a set of images. Moreover, these images can be read, not always easily, as being intuitively relevant picturings of some aspect of the person's life at that time, i.e., the 'exhausted' mother.

Memory Imagework

The second level type of the imagework method that I want to introduce is the memory imagework method. This method consists of leading students through their early biographical memories as a way of picturing forgotten or little-considered aspects of their childhood awareness. Remembering and (re)picturing one's first experiences of a child of another race and/or gender to oneself can be powerful triggers for recollecting the earliest experience of culturally formed and/or stereotypical thinking. A pilot session, conducted with a group of twelve anthropologists as experimental subjects, involved, after a suitable relaxation exercise, a guided journey forwards in imaginative time starting with the students' early memories/pictures of home, school and play experiences. Following the exercise, discussion and analysis took place as to how early concepts of race, gender, ability and other differences were constructed. Students' awareness came through the recollecting of others' bodily characteristics and social customs, such as table manners and joking behaviours, and their implications for the formation of self-concept and peer group formation.

Another example of memory imagework is similar in that it consisted of facilitating a group of forty participants to visualise early memories in order to assist an analysis of their implicit class awareness. So, following a relaxation exercise, they were guided to remember their early thoughts and feelings about, for example, dress, food, play, humour and significant moral advice. The material retrieved was effectively a raw psycho-ethnography that could then be subjected, through paired and small-group discussion, to an analysis of the development of personal and cultural identity, in this case with a focus towards class position and understanding. I was particularly interested in excavating their unarticulated awareness, yet embodied mastery (Bourdieu 1977) of the values and practices of a culturally specific class position.

There is probably almost no limit to the range of possible memory, and also imaginary (see next section) situations that can be 'dreamt up'. For example, recently, I have been developing and using an exercise in which students first imagine their original 'family' household (as long as this represents a 'comfortable' place for them; if not, I advise them to think of another well-known household from their childhood for this exercise) and have them as an exercise, walking around this remembered house and the actual task is for them to look for a specific piece of ritual and symbolic activity. The aim of this task is to gather data about 'household change over two generations' or even 'changing Western domestic symbolism'. I don't give examples so as not to anticipate their memory, but usually students think of mealtimes, the hearth, musical instruments or bathroom activities. Then I ask students to 'fast forward' into the present and imagine that they are in their current household (or again an equivalent example if their current situation is problematic) and consider the similarities and differences between their current and past households with regard to the symbolic value of their chosen ritual activity. Usually, time permitting, I ask participants to make a brief felt-tip picture of their imaginings and then share with the group, or in pairs, the symbols used and encountered and the preliminary explanations they have for such changes. Typically, students talk of changes in family structures; technological developments; gender and ethnic consciousness development; secularisation; changing consumption patterns; personal and public symbolism; and of developing a reflexive approach to the changing subject of experience. The group can then make a meta-analysis of the emerging themes.

The following picture (Figure 4.1) illustrates the results of a different *memory imagework* exercise. The exercise in this case was to recollect or remember one's life with respect to experiences of health and illness as a way of finding out differential models of health and well-being held by certain student populations. The session takes place in the second week of term as part of a first-year medical anthropology module, called 'Health and Society'. As part of the exercise, students also had to fill in a set of accompanying questions that related to their memory exercise. Altogether, I include three of the artwork productions to illustrate some of the conceptual understandings about health, well-being and illness that arose from this exercise.

At first sight the powerful picture in Figure 4.1 hardly seems to resemble anything much to do with health, until the respondent's explanation of their symbolic construction is read. I will report in full the answers to the following questions:

1. How did you visualise your life?
   'As a tree; with many branches and experiences, still growing and learning. The tree's roots also represent strong family roots and a stable basis upon which to grow and rely. The tree growing towards the sky is also symbolic of my ambitions and dreams for the future'.
2. What critical incidents did you remember?
   'Death'.

Figure 14.1: *Health map: tree*

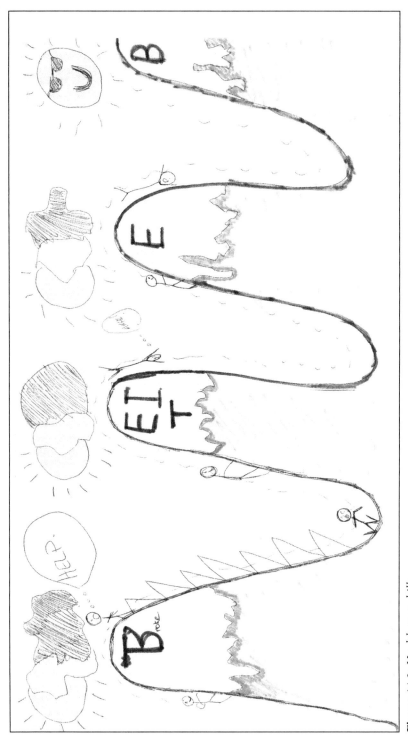

Figure 14.2: *Health map: hills*

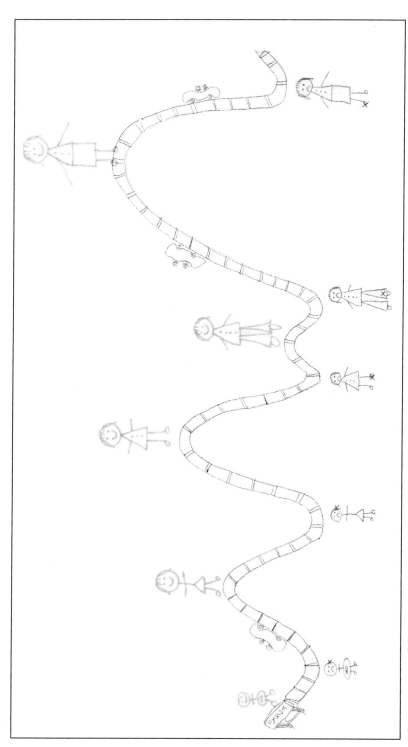

Figure 14.3: *Health map: rollercoaster*

3. What 'health' issues came up?

   'Stress, pain, headaches initially, but flowing into peace, contentment and happiness'.

4. How did you portray health-related issues? What symbols did you use to show 'healthy' and 'unhealthy' times?

   'Weather-related symbols were used because I feel they are very accurate in portraying emotions felt when going through good times (sunshine) and bad times (lightning). The sleeping bird represents the future goal of ulti-mate contentment in life'.

5. How was/is our experience of 'health' affected by the society we live in?

   'Remembering mostly the bad times rather than the good; coming from a Western society, our experience of health is more focused towards the physical being: fitness, appearance; traditionally putting much less empha-sis on the health of the spirit'.

6. As an anthropologist looking at your picture what do you see?

   'The use of symbols from Western culture – very general symbols encom-passing good and bad times with death (cross) being the only independent symbol and therefore obviously the most important issue'.

7. What ideas about health can be seen in the picture?

   'The idea that the good and the bad times are linked, one following on from another. That both are needed in order to grow and reach contentment'.

Clearly these responses represent results from a single case and without control trial experiments we cannot know if her reactions to the task, and learning/insight from it, would have been different from the results of other pedagogical methods. However, what we can deduce from an examination of this picture is perhaps the following health themes and perspectives emerging from the exercise and resulting symbolism.

This picture, in common with many of the others from the exercise, shows a marked capacity for symbolism through which to express individual per-ceptions of health 'careers'. The tree symbol itself is a powerful and cross-cultural metaphor through which to express the nature of a human being. The world tree is a well-known symbol. Other symbols evoked through the exercise are: the sleeping bird, sunshine and lightning. It is very common for participants to describe healthy times through positive meteoro-logical symbols and inversely, use of symbolic images such as rain and cloud to portray negative times. Likewise metaphors of 'ascent' and 'descent' are often used, as when the student says, referring to the tree as, 'growing towards the sky is also a symbolic image to express hope, ambitions and dreams for the future'. Other similar symbols used in the same exercise by other students were (Figure 4.2): health experiences expressed as a series of hills with ascents for 'healthy times' and descents expressing 'unhealthy times', and in Figure 4.3 we encounter a similar theme using the symbolism of a roller-coaster. The use of such symbolisation allows other participants to empathise without the stu-dent having to actually disclose possibly confidential health data.

However, what I consider valuable about the depth of the data revealed through these examples in this exercise are the many levels of understanding of health that emerge. Unlike in some of Seedhouse's (1986) four theories of health, we can 'see' an individual's metaphorical account of his/her remembered and also deeply anticipated future hopes for him/herself. Moreover, these thoughts, feelings and aspirations are couched in a visually-expressed narrative which encompasses 'stress, pain, headaches initially but flowing into peace, contentment and happiness'. Health becomes much more than pain, illness and disease episodes but includes social relationships and the thread of meaning running through his/her life and projected even into his/her future. This account is more akin to a humanistic and holistic view of health (Seedhouse 1986: 51–4) than to other Western theories of health. All the students' pictures are unique, but they often utilise common symbolism (metaphors of ascent and descent for good and bad times, for example). The pictures are open to varying levels of analysis and meta-analysis, as previously described. The data obtained is imaginatively evoked as much as thought and so the data obtained is more holistic in the sense that it can and often does draw on the affective and intuitive aspects of the self as well as the rational.

Spontaneous Imagework

The third level of imagework I call spontaneous imagework. This consists of leading a group of participants on an imaginary journey. Examples of these journeys are written up in Ernst and Goodison (1981), Glouberman (1989), and Markham (1989). Potentially, there are dozens of such exercises both available or to create.

The following example is a recent use of imagework with anthropology students. The session was in a more vocationally orientated module that aimed to relate students' applied anthropological knowledge and skills to the possibility of a career outcome in the social work field. I invited them to imagine themselves as a social worker escorting an old female client from her last home in the community to an old people's home. They silently visualised this process, with appropriate spoken directional and timing cues from myself. The imagework process lasted for about twenty minutes and involved them imaginatively talking her through the event – guiding her around her new home, through the sitting rooms, manager's office, to her bedroom and then to the leave-taking, perhaps involving a gift and/or touch. This imaginative material was discussed and provided a focus for the subsequent question as to what 'knowledge and skills' from their degree programme were relevant? Of course, as well as the feelings and identifications raised by this exercise, considerable understanding arose concerning the nature and effects of the ageing process, institutionalisation, rites of passage, residential cultures, professional relationships, personal identity and material artefacts. These understandings helped to provide a basis for anthropology students to integrate an awareness of the extensive range of understandings in relation to such a professional role with which their course had equipped them. They effectively generated their own different and similiar inner perceived case-studies. The whole session took one hour. It took place with a group of eighty students, so it can be said that the method is not solely for small groups. I conducted a similar exercise with German anthropology students 'leading them' to an imaginary refugee hostel that they were due to visit the following week.

A relatively 'quick' exercise I do in different contexts is to suggest that students consider a 'question' they have either about the educational content of the module, a possible research topic, or even a more personal one in terms of their future career orientation for example. Then, once relaxed, I suggest they imagine a 'wise person' be they a teacher, friend, parent or abstract figure and dialogue with that imaginary person about 'their question'. I usually find about 80 percent of the students have some useful experience which can range from profound and original to trivial. Here are some accounts from a short exercise in which students were invited to think of a question about the module (anthropology of mental health, illness and drug use).

1. Report from a SOCRATES exchange student:
   Dark space – a man came walking (he brought the light with him). He was very tall, big, with long grey hair. It was a man I've seen before (from student's home country) and met him once. He was a Cherokee chief. I asked him why I was here – he looked at me. I tried to ask him related questions and he just looked and told me that I knew. He turned his back to me and walked away (I was in the dark and the light went with him). He suddenly turned round and said, 'just remember (name) that this is your fieldtrip'. Now I agree with him – both the field trip to England and then the field trip within myself in England.

2. Written response from student whose question was 'what is mental health?':
   I imagined myself in the south of Spain; it was a summer's evening, balmy, bold, available. I walked onto the roof of a villa and entered a room in which there was a bath of cooled water. There was a flat wooden board across the bath upon which it would be possible to lay papers. My sage, Salvador Dali, sat in the bath, naked and drawing with a quill pen and ink. I asked, 'what and where will I find the answer to my question, what is mental health?' he spun the right frond of his moustache, looked at my forehead and said, 'I'm not eccentric, I'm concentric, your answer is everywhere'. I thanked him and withdrew walking backwards, puzzled.

3. Another write-up but without an accompanying question:
   The person within did not take the form of a male or female. I was guided into the 'hall of achievement' where I was shown all the creations of mankind. In another place were all the things that had the potential to be created but never were because the dreamer had forgotten the dream. A good state of mental health, I think, is being able to remember the dream and going after it, not letting it slip out of your grasp.

The following written reported experiences either contain a question or, as in the seventh one, describe the feeling tone of the experience:

4. I visualised my English teacher from school, Mr (name). He was a brilliant 'down to earth' teacher who helped me a lot. He answered the question I asked about our presentation topic, and it made me think about the question in a clearer way.
5. I was distracted by too many thoughts of my own and all of the noise and movement around me to do the exercise in class. I think it is an interesting idea though and I have tried it out at home. My wise person is usually my mother or a behavioural psychologist I saw a few years ago.
6. I could see my friend. He died through a form of madness. I asked him, 'what is madness'? He spoke back saying it was within us all, but only seen as madness by society, when for example his behaviour was classed as 'abnormal'. Society can change a natural drive, or individual talent, into a form of madness. This was his account of what madness was.
7. I imagined someone I knew, who I think is a wise person. He spoke to me, he listened, he reassured me. It was a relaxed atmosphere, quiet. I felt relaxed afterwards. I didn't feel like leaving that place; I felt at home. It felt like I had escaped into another world.

These written reported experiences show that from what was only a five to ten minute exercise at the beginning of a lecture on 'mental health and illness: cross-cultural paradigms', a very wide variety of experiences occurred ranging from the personally profound and insightful (numbers 1 and 3), to the bizarre and intriguing (number 2), the useful (number 4), the useless (number 5), and number 7 in which the account focuses on feeling tone rather than question outcome. Such results provide opportunities for the educator to make valuable and interesting connections between student experience and taught thematic content.

Dream Imagework

The dream presents us with the most original, often surreal and incomprehensible array of inner imagery. This fourth level of imagework I shall call dream imagework. Dream imagework refers to the occasion when the facilitator is developing in some way the reported dream imagery of the participants. Such dream reporting need not be exclusive to a dreamwork group but can happen spontaneously in discussion or can be integrated into a more general group/classroom discussion. For instance, when a student relates a dream, he/she can be facilitated to 'amplify the dream' by imagining a further development of the imaginative dream sequence: for example, the nightmarish ending of a dream can be changed to a harmonious one. The personal and group understanding of dream imagery can be enhanced through an array of experiential and artistic techniques, such as drama, artwork, dance and mask-making (Edgar, 1995).

Perhaps it is somewhat surprising to suggest that dreams can be a fruitful learning methodology for students in the social sciences, and in particular social anthropology. However, I would make the following points: first, 'dream imagery is good to think with' in a number of ways: for example I work with students' dreams to illustrate cultural paradigms of what in the West, we call the 'unconscious', but which is differently conceptualised in some other cultures as perhaps a 'world of spirits' or 'world of the ancestors'. Secondly, dreams are often viewed differently by indigenous peoples, particularly in shamanic societies, and many anthropologists have included studies of their research subjects' dreaming in their ethnographies (see Tedlock 1987 and my own summary of 'anthropology and dreaming' (Edgar 2000]). So, dreamwork is an experiential way of teaching aspects of the anthropology of consciousness, anthropology of religion, anthropology of medicine, and healing and cognitive anthropology.

Thirdly, a sensitivity to dream reports and the relevant literature is particularly useful for postgraduate students about to embark on extensive fieldwork as Kohn (1995) makes clear when writing about the value of the dreams of her principal informant during the time when this informant, Kamala, visited her in England. Coming from a remote hill village in Nepal, Kamala's awareness of cultural change seemed heightened by her experience of travel, and unusually, she shared several dreams of her homeland with Kohn. Kohn (1995: 48) relates how 'ideas about the cosmos which many hours of taped interviews had not uncovered in the field' were shared through the dialogue about her dreams in Durham, U.K. Fourthly, an awareness of the ethnographer's own dreams provide potential insight into the 'positioned standpoint' (Hastrup 1992) of the researcher, and hence emerging fieldwork themes (Hillman 1989; Levine 1981). Possible dreamwork techniques available include dream re-entry, journal keeping, and dialoguing, etc. (Williams 1984).

Ethical Issues and Conclusion

Clearly the use of the imagework method as a social science educational method requires some familiarity with its use and skill in its application, though arguably an educationalist could employ an imagework practitioner using such a method rather than using it him/herself. The concern with careful use is important as such a method can reveal latent feelings and unrealised intuitions that have often only been partially made conscious or possibly even repressed. However, specific training programmes in these hitherto 'therapeutic' methods do now exist.[2] Moreover, introductory level imagework and memory imagework are not difficult to use.

The ethics of using such an approach are important. Clearly some educationalists will feel that the imagework method is unacceptably intrusive and raises power issues that are very problematic. However, while I accept that an experiential method, such as imagework, has as its intention the development of deeper learning, I would argue that any educational method involves intrusion and can provoke problematic self-disclosure. Even a simple lecture can suddenly trigger a sensitive area for the student and leave the educationalist with ethical considerations in terms of how to handle supportively the resulting situation. The methods I have outlined will often be a catalyst for both small and large disclosure, yet the negative aspects of disclosure can be greatly prevented by making participation voluntary, by explaining sensitively beforehand the task and technique to participants, and by similar after-care. Moreover, participants can be asked again, following an imagework exercise, if they wish their contribution still to be used as part of any educational findings. I outline a set of guidelines for this work that I have developed.

Ethical/Safe Practice Guidelines

1. Explain everything beforehand: go through each part of the exercise, so that there are no surprises 'on the way'.
2. Give clear permission to people that they don't have to do this part of the session if they don't want to.
3. Ask 'any questions' after introducing the exercise and before doing it.
4. Develop trust from the beginning; open body gestures, clear quiet voice tone; reassure continually that 'they' are in control throughout the exercise and including during the sharing; it is their journey.
5. Plan the timing of the session and have enough time for each part of it; don't try and do too much. Go through each part of the session in your mind beforehand; prepare yourself.
6. Practise with friends/colleagues beforehand, if you wish.
7. If you feel really unsure about doing this exercise, as opposed to your 'normal' level of apprehension before doing a new type of exercise, then either don't do it, or choose a safer format.
8. Talk through with participants' 'self-care' issues first. Emphasise:
9. Participants are in control of all parts of the process. They can guarantee their confidentiality by what they choose to share with others; symbols have many meanings and associations, and their multivocality is a real asset for both eliciting ideas and retaining confidentiality.
10. If they are unhappy, ill, worried or preoccupied, then advise participants not to do the exercise, or particularly look after themselves.
11. Advise participants that if they become distracted in an exercise then they can gently bring their wandering attention back to the subject.
12. If someone encounters a 'difficult' memory or image then advise them that they have a choice: either to go on with the exercise or stop and imagine something more pleasant. However, remind people that their images and accompanying feelings and thoughts are their own. Also, be clear that difficult feelings can be triggered by any 'outer' event also, for

instance, the look or smell of a flower. Moreover, this subject of difficult memory/image recall can be examined in more depth, and discussion facilitated as to the possible long-term value of dealing with difficult memories that can suddenly intrude into consciousness at any time; is the 'unconscious' good at timing in all cases?

13. Be 'around' afterwards, or have a colleague around, to provide support if needed, though my experience is that such support is rarely, if ever, needed; watch carefully to see if anyone is looking upset at the end.

14. Facilitate everyone sharing their feelings and experiences that have been evoked by the exercise, at least in pairs, so that each person has had the opportunity to tell 'his' or 'her' story.

15. Pace the visualisation process by doing the visualisation yourself at the same time as the people you are facilitating. Make sure you leave plenty of time during the visualisation for peoples' imaginations to work.

16. Don't allow any interruptions: put a very clear message on the door and even an object like a chair to block late entrants! There is nothing so disturbing as a late entrant in the middle of a visualisation exercise.

It is important to be aware that the creative, emotional and cognitive influence of an image may not be completed within the time-span of the session. Parse (1995: 82), as part of her 'Human Becoming Theory,' has called this after-effect, 'lingering true presence'. The evocative power of a symbol may engage the mind in an ongoing process of self-enquiry; therefore, it may be prudent for the educationalist, as well as ensuring that their students complete the task at ease with any imaginative results, to make follow-up discussion arrangements available.

Some topics may be inappropriate for imagework, certainly in groups. However, one advantage of using imagework is that it allows participants to discuss potentially sensitive material in a coded way that allows them to retain their privacy. Students can, as we have seen, for instance, refer to 'bad times' by using stereotypical images of unhappiness such as 'bad weather' and, as a result retain their privacy and their understanding of their meaning.

Overall the article has shown the way that imagework, one of several potential experiential educational methods, offers educationalists the means to access the latent knowledge and unexpressed feelings of participants. Experiential methods can access these basic assumptions of the self and society in a way that solely cognitive methods cannot.

This chapter has not generally provided a detailed guide or manual for the beginning practitioner of the imagework method; rather, it has suggested a way forward for imagework practice as a part of the educational process, and it has outlined a basic typological framework for imagework practitioners/educationalists. Imagework educational methodologies may prove of particular interest to those educating visual sociologists and visual social anthropologists. Experiential educational methods such as imagework can be utilised in part or on their own in educational practice in such diverse fields as the social sciences, health and social care, development, and even business and marketing. The imagework method is particularly effective in accessing participants' implicit awareness of such areas as personal and cultural identity formation and change; interpersonal dynamics; organisational culture; and individual and collective vision development. Imagework is particularly useful for linking biographical experience and social structure and process to develop a 'personal anthropology' (Pocock 1975). Indeed, imagework and its consequent analytic processing may provide a portal through which any aspect of a particular experience may be analysed. The way is open for further studies using these methods, perhaps in controlled and cross-cultural studies, that would compare the value of such experiential methods against the use of more traditional educational methods.

Notes

1. Sculpting involves a group member using some of the other group members to represent physically past or present relationships in his/her current family, family of origin, or a significant group, such as a work group (see Jennings 1986: 143). The person doing the sculpt arranges the key people to display how he or she feels or would like to represent the group or family in question. So the sculpt may display the whole gamut of feelings in relationships, whether they be togetherness security, conflict, anger or hurt. Alliances and hostilities in a group can be shown easily by using 'typical' motifs such as 'the clenched fist' or 'hugging', and the spatial representation of people through closeness and distance is a powerful way to express feelings. The 'sculptor' may be very surprised by how he/she places significant people in his/her life, such as siblings or parents. The 'knowledge' that he/she represents in the sculpt may be surprising and show feelings and perceptions that have remained unacknowledged.
2. I am pioneering a training programme in imagework as a both an educational and qualitative research methodology.

References

Achterberg, J. 1985. *Imagery in Healing.* Boston: Shambhala.
Assagioli, R. 1975. *Psychosynthesis.* Wellingborough: Turnstone Press.
Bourdieu, P. 1977. *Outline of A Theory of Practice.* Cambridge, U.K.: Cambridge University Press.
Clandinin, D. 1986. *Classroom Practice: Teacher Images in Action.* London: Falmer Press.
Conton, L. 1996. 'Experiential Shamanism in the College Classroom: Rewards and Challenges', *Anthropology of Consciousness* 7(1): 39–47.
Edgar, I. 1995. *Dreamwork, Anthropology and the Caring Professions: A Cultural Approach to Dreamwork.* Aldershot: Avebury.
Edgar, I. 1999. 'The Imagework Method in Social Science and Health Research', *Qualitative Health Research,* 9(2): 198–211.
Edgar, I. 2000. 'Cultural Dreaming or Dreaming Cultures?' The Anthropologist and the Dream', *KEA: Zeitschrift für Kulturwissenschaften* 13.

Ernst, S. and Goodison, L. 1981. *In Our Own Hands: A Book of Self-Help Therapy.* London: The Women's Press.

Glouberman, D. 1989. *Life Choices and Life Changes through Imagework.* London: Unwin.

Hastrup, K. 1992. 'Writing Ethnography: State of the art', in *Anthropology and Autobiography*, eds J. Okely and H. Callaway. ASA Monographs, 29. London: Routledge, pp. 116–33.

Hillman, D. 1989. 'Dreamwork and Fieldwork: Linking Cultural Anthropology and the Current Dreamwork Movement', in *The Variety of Dream Experience*, eds M. Ullman and C. Limmer. Wellingborough: The Acquarian Press, pp. 117–41.

Jennings, S. 1986. *Creative Drama in Groupwork.* Bicester, Oxon: Speechmark Publications.

Jung, C. 1959. 'Archetypes of the Collective Unconscious', in *The Collected Works of Jung.* Eds H. Read, M. Fordham, G. Adler and W. McQuire. London: Routledge & Kegan Paul, pp. 3–41.

Kohn, T. 1995. 'She came Out of the Field and into My Home: Reflections, Dreams and a Search for Consciousness in Anthropological Method', in *Questions of Consciousness*, eds A. Cohen and N. Rapport. London: Routledge, pp. 40–59.

Kolb, D. 1984. *Experiential Learning.* Englewood Cliffs, N.J.: Prentice-Hall.

Levine, S. 1981. 'Dreams of the Informant about the Researcher: Some Difficulties Inherent in the Research Relationship, *Ethos* 9: 276–93.

Markham, U. 1989. *The Elements of Visualisation.* Shaftesbury, Dorset: Element Books.

Parse, R. 1995. 'The Human Becoming Practice Methodology', in *Illuminations: The Human Becoming Theory in Practice and Research*, ed. R. Parse. New York: National League for Nursing Press, pp. 81–86.

Pocock, D. 1975. *Understanding Social Anthropology.* London; Hodder & Stoughton.

Pretty, J., Guijt, I., Thompson, J., and Scoones, I. 1995. *A Trainer's Guide for Pparticipatory Learning and Action.* London: International Institute for Environment and Development.

Rowan, J. 1993. *The Transpersonal: Psychotherapy and Counselling.* London: Routledge.

Seedhouse, D. 1986. *Health: The Foundations for Achievement.* Chicester: John Wiley.

Stuhlmiller, C., and Thorsen, R. 1997. 'Narrative Picturing: A New Strategy for Qualitative Data Collection, *Qualitative Health Research* 7(1): 140–49.

Tedlock, B. 1987. 'Dreaming and Dream Research', in *Dreaming: Anthropological and Psychological Interpretations*, ed. B. Tedlock. Cambridge: Cambridge University Press, pp. 1–30.

Whitmore, D. 1986. *Psychosynthesis in Education.* Wellingborough: Turnstone Press.

Williams, S. 1984. *The Dreamwork Manual.* Wellingborough: Acquarian Press.

15

Performance and Experiential Learning in the Study of Ethnomusicology

Tina K. Ramnarine

In 1881, Alice C. Fletcher (1838–1923) first visited the Omaha in Nebraska. Her initial responses to their song repertoire were not favourable. She heard 'little or nothing' of this music 'beyond a screaming downward movement that was gashed and torn by the vehemently beaten drum' (1994 [1893]: 7). However, fieldwork was to be a 'transformational experience' for her. The Omaha sang for her when she fell ill and as she recovered she learnt and sang the songs too. Later on in her fieldwork, knowledge of this repertoire enabled her to participate in ceremonies. Fletcher notes, 'the whole people took up the song and I too joined, able at last to hear and comprehend the music that had through all my difficulties fascinated even while it eluded me' (1994 [1893]: 9). Such experiences motivated her to abandon the evolutionary paradigms, then fashionable, that she had hoped to apply to analysis of this music.

Fletcher's account of musical understanding resulting from experience is paralleled extensively in the ethnomusicological literature. In one influential collection of essays on fieldwork, for example, an ethnomusicological response to recent debates on the ethnographic enterprise was offered. In these essays, the focus was shifted from the 'crisis of representation' towards experience (Barz and Cooley 1997). Why do so many contemporary ethnomusicologists emphasise participation in musical performance as an integral dimension in the process of analysing musical and social structures? In terms of pedagogic as well as research strategies, performance as learning has long been a central issue to ethnomusicologists. As educators, why do ethnomusicologists encourage their students to engage in musical performance? In what follows, these two interrelated questions provide a framework for exploring the interfaces between pedagogic and research strategies in musical performance. Following a mode of reflective practice (Day 1993, Johnston and Badley 1996), illustrations will be drawn from my own experience with the ethnomusicology curriculum at Queen's University Belfast.

In the School of Anthropological Studies at Queen's University Belfast, the incorporation of performance into the ethnomusicology curriculum is used as a way into understanding different societies and systems of thought. The ethnomusicologist, Mantle Hood, noted in writing about his own involvement with performance-based pedagogic approaches that it was as recently as 1954 that the first formal training programmes in the performance of 'non-Western' musics were established. Ethnomusicologists did not unanimously welcome these early initiatives. Critics pointed to the effort required to achieve competent performance skills and suggested that time spent in musical practice would be better applied in seeking answers to research questions through dialogue with informants, in transcribing musical sounds, and in analysis. These exercises would result in speech about music that could be widely disseminated and shared with the disciplinary community rather than in an individual experience of music-making. In responding to such criticisms, Hood introduced a striking example of the mutually informative nature of speaking about and playing music in his discussion on the 'music mode of discourse'. In participating in a *rebab* (bowed lute) lesson he gained immediate insights into a point of speculation in the literature concerning performance practice:

> At the time of my first *rebab* lesson, February 1957, there were a number of references to and studies of this important instrument of the Javanese gamelan already in print. Most were based on the assumption that, since the instrument has no fingerboard but only a slender neck, it was played entirely in 'harmonics', that is, not fundamental pitches produced by stopping the string but so-called partials produced on Western stringed instruments by lightly touching the string. (Hood 1971: 231)

Hood continued in citing a significant reference which concluded that 'nothing is known with certainty concerning the essential nature of its [the *rebab*'s] tone' (Jaap Kunst cited in Hood 1971: 231), and revealed how answers were generated within a few minutes in practice, in the *rebab* lesson. For Hood, 'making music is the most direct mode of music discourse' and it can certainly develop what he regards as the ethnomusicologist's essential faculty – hearing 'without prejudice' (1971: 34–5).

In this example it may seem obvious that questions of instrumental technique and tone production can be resolved through practical examination. The benefits of the incorporation of performance into the curriculum nevertheless extend beyond such pragmatic applications and have been well rehearsed since Mantle Hood promoted the idea of bi-musicality in the 1960s. Despite the benefits, performance has sometimes been incorporated into ethnomusicological training as an optional extra. The performance study groups at the University of California at Los Angeles with which Hood was associated were run on an extra-curricular basis. These groups included Javanese *gamelan*, Balinese *gamelan*, Persian music and Japanese *nagauta*. Students were seen to be learning 'foreign music' (Hood 1960: 55) and thus developing 'bi-musical' skills. As Baily (1995) notes, the term 'bi-musical' is problematic because it implies the acquisition of skills in two different musical systems in childhood rather than basic skills learned as an adult. Hood's observations on the challenges of developing 'bi-musicality' in such groups nevertheless focused on the ultimate benefits conferred by participation and on the general development of 'musicality'. Benefits included developing the ability to hear different kinds of pitches, playing without notation and thus improving aural perception and memory, and working towards fluency in improvisation. Hood regarded basic musicianship as essential to comprehension and competent musicological analysis (Hood 1960: 58).

Recent expressions of the centrality of music's experiential qualities to knowledge about music include Titon who states: 'I would like to ground musical knowing – that is, knowledge of or about music – in musical being. …I ground musical knowledge in the practice of music, not in the practice of science, or linguistics, or introspective analysis' (Titon 1997: 94). Rice likewise writes about the importance of learning to play the *gaida* (bagpipe) in his study of Bulgarian music. For him, training as an instrumentalist led to reflection on 'the methods provided by cognitive anthropology to develop a theory of culture as mental activity'. When he fully engaged with the music he 'ran into the limits of this language-based method and its associated theory of culture' (Rice 1997: 109). Questioning some of 'the basic tenets of ethnomusicological theory and method' he sought alternative frameworks in phenomenological hermeneutics in which understanding music precedes attempts to explain it. Experience followed by explanation leads to interpretative 'new understandings of the world or culture referenced by music acting as a symbol' (Rice 1997: 115).

Many ethnomusicology programmes, including the one offered at Queen's University, use the learning and performance of diverse musical systems and styles as an experiential approach which is an essential counterpart to critical, theoretical and reflexive explorations of the kind demonstrated by the writers cited above. John Blacking, who established ethnomusicology as a special interest at Queen's, followed Hood's distinction of two modes of discourse (verbal – 'talking about music as analysts' and non-verbal – 'performing music as a way of knowing') and similarly regarded them as complementary. Their combination led to the 'most complete understanding of music' if placed in 'the context of [the music's] social uses and the cultural system of which it is a part' (Blacking 1995: 231). Rice's view that understanding can be grounded in practice leading to articulation later is a variation on the theme of the complementary nature of two modes of musical discourse.

Developing Ensembles and Performance as Learning at Queen's

Blacking was appointed Chair of Social Anthropology at Queen's University in 1970 and instituted ethnomusicology programmes, particularly with the appointment of John Baily as a lecturer in social anthropology to teach ethnomusicology in 1978. For Cameron, such an institutional location provides the right grounds for ethnomusicology to flourish:

> The field methods of participant observation, the detailed ethnographic reports and the explanation of the phenomena are part and parcel of the anthropological method. When this is coupled with primary expertise in musical materials, ethnomusicology can really take place. (Cameron 1992: 34)

While Cameron stresses participant observation, he continues to describe 'the essence of the process' in a manner which overlooks the performance aspects of the participant: 'observation, analysis and explanation. All these need to be present' (ibid).

Performance, nevertheless, has been a feature of the School's ethnomusicology programme. Baily (1995) cites from a letter which Blacking had sent him in 1972 to give some insights into the latter's ideas about performance in ethnomusicological training. Baily wanted to know if Hood's idea of bi-musicality was still relevant and if he could use this as an approach to learning Persian classical music. Blacking responded: 'Far from being out of date, learning to perform and play music is a basic field technique in ethnomusicology. We are still trying to establish it as a necessary methodological tool, because several field studies are being carried out without it even today' (Baily 1995: 334). Regarding performance as a way of knowing, John Blacking felt that some performance opportunities should be available in the School and introduced these into anthropology courses. He taught Venda songs and drumming to anthropology students who attended on a voluntary basis and Venda dance to postgraduate ethnomusicologists. At first, ensembles operated on an informal basis and were not assessed. John Baily recollects that when he arrived in Belfast in 1974 from fieldwork in Afghanistan there was a *kulintang* (gong chime of south-east Asia, for example, Philippines and Indonesia) ensemble taught by a doctoral student, Usupay Kader. The following year, Baily began teaching *dutâr* (an Afghan long-necked pyriform lute) to postgraduate ethnomusicology students, and in 1976 another doctoral student, Max Brandt, ran a Venezuelan *redondo* drumming group with the aim of helping his analysis of the music. In 1980, an Afghan band (Baily on *rubâb*, James Kippen on *tabla*, Annette Sanger on harmonium and Jonathan Molondiwa on fourteen-stringed *dutâr*) collaborated with Garry Mirsky in the making of an anthropological film called 'Bimusicality'. Cameron notes in his article on the teaching of ethnomusicology in the U.K. that by the mid-1980s, performance as a way of learning was an important new development in the Queen's University ethnomusicology curriculum (Cameron 1992: 37). Annette Sanger (who lectured in ethnomusicology during the 1980s) taught Balinese *gamelan* (1983–89) to ethnomusicology and music (but not anthropology) students. When she left the School, Kevin Dawe (at that time, a doctoral student) took over the teaching of the *gamelan* and also offered *sitar* (plucked lute-type Indian instrument) tuition.

Membership of ensembles during the late 1980s continued to operate on a voluntary basis. Some of the ensembles included staff-led groups (Annette Sanger's *gamelan* ensemble) and student-led groups (Ime Ukpanah's *uta* – African horn ensemble; Desi Wilkinson's tin whistle ensemble – Sligo style; and Jonathan Stock's *dixi* – Chinese flute ensemble). Martin Stokes, another lecturer in the School, ran a Turkish *baglama* (long-necked lute) ensemble, and workshops given by visiting groups from Turkey and from Bulgaria were also organised. In 1991, Suzel Reily, as a newly appointed lecturer (who had taken part in Ukpanah's group as a doctoral student), began running an African drumming ensemble. This was in conjunction with lectures on African music given to first-year students with the intention of adding a practical dimension to concepts like 'polyrhythm'. Reily and Stokes later offered Andean pan-pipes and Turkish *baglama*, *Arabesk* and *takht* ensembles, also in conjunction with ethnomusicology courses, and the groups performed at the School's Christmas parties as part of its festive, self-organised entertainment. The opportunity to perform at these social occasions provided a strong motivation to attend rehearsals. Preparation for and performance at an ethnomusicology concert was thus integrated into formal teaching and assessment procedures. Even though integration into formal assessment was regarded positively, questions of how ensembles should be evaluated were discussed extensively – for example, whether students should be assessed on an individual or collective basis. Various other ensembles operating during the 1990s included Algerian drumming (taught by Tony Langlois), West African drumming (Rachel Healy) and Irish traditional music (Treasa Na Earcainn). The concept of a performance ensemble could also be conceived in broad terms. Jan Fairley, for instance, ran a radio workshop which involved planning a 'radio programme'.

Case Studies of Ensemble Activity

Around five ensembles are now offered each semester. African drumming, *quenas* (run by Suzel Reily), Andalouse (Egyptian and Lebanese song, Tony Langlois) Scandinavian instrumental and English/Irish folk song (Tina Ramnarine), are examples of ensembles which ran in the second semester of 1998. Reflection on performance and the linking of performance experience to ethnomusicological theory form part of current assessment procedures (and have done so since the mid-1990s), providing evidence of the importance attached to these teaching and learning methods. Student reflections are submitted for assessment in the form of ensemble reports. The guidelines with which they are issued ask them to consider how musical style becomes evident through the experience of performance, what the teaching and learning procedures are and how they relate to the musical style, and how the ensemble experience relates to theoretical or regional issues raised during lectures. Thus the experiential qualities of music practice are regarded as essential to an understanding of music and in developing knowledge of ethnomusicological theory, but students are also asked to reflect on what kinds of understandings have been generated by the ensemble experience. The report can also be seen, then, as a reflective commentary on experiential learning.

Student reports indicate that the practical dimensions of ensemble work do contribute to their understandings of conceptual and theoretical issues. This kind of experiential learning seems to enrich the learning process considerably. Performance is learning, and this is learning by doing. First-year reports on African drumming included the following observations:

> I am a drummer and I assumed that participation would be relatively easy. It was not! (Armstrong, ensemble report 1998).

> Although our drumming sessions are only one hour long, traditional African drum music can go on all night. Before participating in this ensemble the prospect of this sounded incredibly boring, but now I think that it would be a very memorable experience. The boredom should be embraced because once you break through it the polyrhythmic structures and repetition seem to defeat all time. I feel that without this hands-on experience, full appreciation of this music would not be possible.' (Graham, ensemble report 1998)

> It was through the experience of group participation that the importance of social interaction was appreciated. ...Taking part in the ensemble also helped me with my outside activities. I attend an African dance class where the idea of polyrhythms is incorporated in the dancing, where we are clapping and dancing different rhythms at the same time.' (Hall, ensemble report 1998)

Ensemble participation should provide a forum for both understanding and articulating the experience in which a critical stance can be developed to the musical traditions studied and even, as in Rice's case, to ethnomusicological theory. The following discussion will focus on a number of overlapping themes broadly relating, first, to the interfaces between performance in pedagogic and in research contexts, and second, to the problematics of music as 'foreign' or as 'familiar'. This reflexive exploration of performance-oriented activities will raise questions about 'authenticity', pedagogic methods and musical transmission. These kinds of question are often intimately related to those posed in studies of the musical traditions themselves and will be illustrated here through examination of the ensembles which were amongst the first that I ran – Scandinavian instrumental and English/Irish folk song. Both of these ensembles were part of a regional module, 'Music of Europe'. One aim of the module was to explore the notion of 'ethnomusicology at home'.

This notion raises obvious possibilities for reflecting on the status of music as 'familiar' or as 'foreign' (an issue raised in Hood's UCLA groups). For some participants, the repertoires rehearsed in these ensembles were 'foreign'. Others had grown up with these kinds of repertoire. These ensembles offered perspectives on ideas about 'foreign' musics and ethnomusicology as a discipline preoccupied with them, on 'bi-musicality', and on the problematics of 'distance' between musics. As Baily asks, is the term 'bi musical' applicable to the musician 'who combines competence in European art music and rock music? Baroque music and minimalism? North and South Indian art musics?' (1995: 332). Moreover, although I was not concerned with the history of ensembles at Queen's at the time, running the English/Irish folk song group could also be regarded in relation to this history as a continuation of former School interests in a local music scene and in Irish traditional music. In addition to ensembles on Irish traditional music, Queen's was the home of the Irish Folk Music Society during the early 1970s and, at that time, Blacking and Baily were planning a cross-cultural project focusing on Herati *dutâr* and Irish fiddle (which did not, however, materialise: Baily 1991).

Through rehearsing a repertoire in the Scandinavian instrumental ensemble which included Finnish *schottishes*, Swedish *polskas* and Norwegian *rheinlendars* in preparation for a performance event, and through the writing of a report as evidence of critical reflection on the process, it was hoped that insights into Scandinavian fiddle-based folk dance music would be gained. Formal folk music education programmes in Scandinavian contexts, particularly the modes of folk music transmission in the Finnish higher education sector (at the Sibelius Academy), provided models for the running of this ensemble. Thus the emphasis was on 're-creating tradition', using practical, theoretical and historical knowledge to reinterpret tradition, and using notated examples in teaching as well as learning through processes of oral transmission. These teaching methods reflect changing patterns in the transmission and performance of folk music and challenge models of folk music which emphasise orally transmitted traditions of an illiterate European peasantry (see Ramnarine 1996 for a discussion of initiatives in Finnish folk music education). The institutionalisation of folk music in educational contexts like the Sibelius Academy, Finland's foremost centre for music performance, has led to a recontextualisation of traditional repertoires and to the emergence of 'professional folk musicians'. Thus 'authenticity' has been debated by those who encourage creative innovations and by those who adopt a more purist view of folk music.

The theme of authenticity is replicated in critical examination of ensembles at Queen's University. The Scandinavian instrumental ensemble operated within a formalised institutional context similar to that at the Sibelius Academy, and participation in it likewise contributed to a degree programme. Differences lay in the traditions rehearsed not being of a 'national' significance and in the musical backgrounds of the group's members. While the performance groups offered at Mantle Hood's institutional base, UCLA, were taught by visiting musicians – 'professional performers' in the traditions being taught – current ensemble leaders at Queen's have studied various musical practices as part of their own research programmes. The ensembles are not run to simulate a field-learning experience and long-term tuition is therefore not provided. There are, nevertheless, some qualifications to add to these comments which complicate the question of musical authenticity. The Scandinavian instrumental ensemble incorporated and presented performance and transmission strategies which had been explored as part of a research project. Yet, in the Finnish example itself, the institutionalisation of folk music was partly motivated by research-led groups. The members of a group that played an influential role in the folk revival movement, *Nelipolviset*, were folk-lorists who began performing because they wanted to recreate the practice of the folk traditions they researched. Moreover, if in the case of folk music, 'authenticity' can be determined on the basis of intensive, long-term involvement with a musical tradition, and transmitting repertoire from one generation to another, there was evidence of this in the ensemble. One student in the Queen's group did come from a Finnish folk fiddling background and others were Irish folk fiddlers whose extensive performing experience was easily applied to the Scandinavian repertoire. As proficient players, the group could work at an advanced level focusing on issues about articulation and different bowing styles, comparing musical structures and the presentation of melodic material and exploring interpretative possibilities. The players' skills presented an explicit pedagogical opportunity to draw on and incorporate existing musical knowledge and experience into the ensemble. Despite familiarity with the performance style, ensemble members were challenged in relation to forging individual roles and adapting instrumental techniques to their own particular instrument. A flautist in the ensemble wrote:

> The teaching and learning procedures which we adopted are the same as those which are currently used in Scandinavia, a mixture of oral transmission and use of transcriptions. I tried as far as possible to learn orally, listening to the melodies and playing them back... Being the only flute player in the ensemble, there were many aspects of the style of playing which were challenging. The first problem was the bowing style characteristic of Scandinavia... In order to master this technique I listened to the sound of the bowing and tried to blow in a similar way to the style. This required experimentation and practice at home and although I was able to produce the same accentuation, the effect was not the same as that of the fiddles. (Stanex, ensemble report 1998)

The keyboard player, who took on the role of 'harmonium' player in a traditional fiddle group by using an electric keyboard, also reported on the difficulties of adapting instrumental techniques and on the insights generated by the attempt:

> My participation in the Scandinavian instrumental ensemble seemed in the beginning to be a little ambitious, given that I had never held nor attempted to play a

fiddle in my life. Not to be deterred, however, I found myself in the role of the keyboard accompaniment which I initially found particularly agreeable due to ample piano lessons since an early age. I soon discovered that adapting my own experience to the necessities required of my position was going to be quite a challenge.

...An added complication was the keyboard itself. The difference between a piano and an electric keyboard is dramatic. The unfamiliar sensation of plastic beneath my fingertips and the lack of pedals to sustain chords was a little unnerving at first, but thanks to a friend and fellow pianist who recognised the advance of technology and on this premise bought himself an electronic keyboard which he willingly lent to me so that I could practise, I soon became accustomed to the change. The folk musician's role in society necessitates this kind of adaptation to contexts in which s/he finds her/himself. Apart from the sheer impracticality of transporting a piano from one venue to another, the electronic keyboard also symbolises modernisation processes in terms of musical sound and performance techniques. In this day and age, almost everything can be plugged into a socket and often to great effect. The electronic keyboard allows the pianist to explore sound in an innovative and improvisational manner.

...All in all, the ensemble experience provided me with access to some of the music I have been studying throughout the term and allowed me to adapt my own skills born of one tradition to another, with the goal of both a deeper understanding of Scandinavia from a musical perspective and a further exploration of my own musicality. (Scullion, ensemble report 1998)

The benefits of musical practice and insights given into conceptual issues were not dependent on radical challenges to musical perceptions. This was a point further accentuated in the folksong ensemble.

In terms of looking at 'national' folk repertoires, the English/Irish folk song ensemble offered at the School paralleled the teaching of Finnish folk traditions at the Sibelius Academy. In this sense it added a further practical dimension to the notion of 'ethnomusicology at home'. The focus of this ensemble was English folk song with the Irish versions of shared repertoires introduced for comparative purposes. Examples of ballads and sea shanties that have been collected over the last one hundred years were rehearsed. In one session, a carol was rehearsed so that the group members could compare two performances of the same material and experience how different transmission processes affect musical performance (transcription used – first verse – for the carol, 'On Christmas Day', in Hamer 1967). The group was divided into two subgroups. One subgroup (group A) consisted of members who read music notation, the other (group B) of those who did not. The groups worked in different rooms and I divided my time between both of them, acting as a facilitator to the groups' experiential learning. The aim of group A was to interpret the musical notation provided for the carol and to arrange an accompaniment as directed by the harmonic outline provided in the score. Group B was to learn the song through listening to a recording. In lectures, we had been discussing the ways in which folk material becomes transformed in different contexts, and indeed, transmitting the carol following these two methods led to two very different performances of the 'same' carol. Towards

Figure 15.1 *Folk song ensemble*

the end of the session the groups were reunited. They performed to each other and told each other about their rehearsal processes. The information that had been given to each subgroup was disclosed to the whole group. For example, group A heard the recording from which group B had learnt the song, and group B explained what kinds of group decisions concerning interpretation had been made.

How did the participants respond to these practical methods? Two examples from student ensemble reports can be compared. The first example was written by a student who was very familiar with the kinds of folk traditions explored in the folk song ensemble. In fact, with a lifelong involvement with these kinds of songs, he was 'fluent' in folk song performance. His report indicates a reflexive exploration of the ensemble and an engagement with notions explored in formal lectures (for example, the 'tradition bearer', 'ethnomusicology at home', and patterns of transmission) in relation to his own practice:

> Blacking said, 'there are so many different perceptions and conceptualisations of music, it is necessary to approach the music-making of any in relation to several different "worlds of music"'. These 'worlds of music' include culture, tradition, the individual, the environment, the style, the ensemble members, the audience and much more. What I was looking for in this ensemble was to in some way touch these 'worlds' in a context outside of my normal performance setting. As an individual, I hoped to contextualise the idea of 'ethnomusicology at home'. By becoming more aware of my own position as a singer and musician and possible tradition bearer... I looked not at the 'Other' but at the 'Self', within the context of a comparative folk style, in order to find the answers. As a group member, I

hoped to see 'the multitude of meanings, responses, and attachments each individual is bringing to the experience'. Both intentions were realised...

For me folk singing has been an oral tradition, transmitted to me by my father and others. In our ensemble, the words and music were written down and presented to us for all the songs except my solo performance; though I did have to transcribe the words for supervision purposes. For me, having the words to a song made learning easier, but as I do not read music, learning the tune was done through oral transmission or listening to recorded material. (O'Sullivan, ensemble report 1998)

The second ensemble report was written by a student for whom the folk songs were 'foreign'. She is an ethnomusicology student whose own performance experience has been largely in Western art music (singing in choirs). I quote an extract in which she comments on the comparison exercise described above:

I found this ensemble particularly interesting because it soon became obvious that folk song can be a great leveller of musical ability, consequently all members were able to participate equally... The freedom of folksong singing (as contrasted against typical art music performance style) ostensibly precludes the obsessive approach which can cripple renditions. 'Natural' instincts, such as spontaneous ornamentation and harmonisation, and the use of glissandos to join notes were indulged by these songs, allowing for an unfettered and often highly personalised performance, irrespective of prior training or level of 'classical' talent.

...Whilst the ideal mode of transmission is traditionally restricted to the oral domain, lengthy and somewhat involved texts complicated such techniques, and we therefore employed written scores and lyric sheets to accommodate the brevity of our learning period. An interesting lesson was learnt with regard to this disparity between oral and written transmission in a mid-semester exercise initiated by Ramnarine. This involved dividing the group into those who could/could not read music, and placing each sub-group in a separate room. The musically literate members were given scores and lyrics and had to produce the song from their sense of relative pitch/sight-singing abilities alone. The non-readers were provided with an audio-cassette featuring a live performance of this same piece which, through a repeated sequence of listen, imitate, rewind tape, listen, would guide them to a final rendition of the piece. Re-united after some twenty minutes, each group performed. The marked variation between the two versions brought to life certain ethnomusicological debates of current lectures, underlining the consequences of declining oral traditions, and reinforcing the importance of the role played by 'tradition bearers' – not only for the cultures involved, *but for the music itself*. I found that practical experience within this ensemble brought me to a more tangible appreciation of the fact that considerable variation can be introduced to musical material merely through different modes of learning.' (Cummings, ensemble report 1998)

Performance, Research and Local Public Visibility: The World Music in the Community Project

Learning to perform in ensembles is also preparation for learning performance in field research (Hood 1960, Herndon and McCleod 1983, Baily

1995). This learning is, as Myers succinctly puts it, 'good fun and good method' (Myers 1992: 31). The impact of ethnomusicology performance activities resonates within the wider social anthropology programme offered by the School. At an immediate level this is apparent in terms of the School's social activities and ethos. Participation in the ensembles is obligatory for those following ethnomusicology modules but membership is open to all students in the School and ethnomusicology concerts are attended by anthropology students as well as by those from other university departments.

With regard to disciplinary developments, ethnomusicologists have become more insistent in their discussions of music practice as entries into a truly participant field experience. As Barz and Cooley state, 'because of the potential for truly participatory participant-observation through actively joining in a society's "music-culture", ... we believe ethnomusicologists are well positioned to offer unique perspectives on postmodern fieldwork processes for all ethnographic disciplines' (1997: 4). Indeed, for Barz, field research is performance (1997: 45).

The ethnomusicological ethos and emphasis on practical experience of music-making is certainly paralleled throughout the School by viewing field experience as an important component of anthropology programmes. Practical work is offered through such modules as 'Anthropology in Practice' and project or field-based work for dissertations. Undertaking fieldwork for undergraduate projects is an option available to anthropology as well as ethnomusicology students. This is usually pursued during vacation periods. As an integral feature of the School's programmes, the factor of cost is taken into

Figure 15.2 Gamelan *ensemble*

account: 'the scheduling of "fieldwork" in the vacation enables state-funded students to get additional grants' (Mascarenhas-Keyes and Wright 1995: 35).

What is learnt within the School in ethnomusicology ensembles is also taken outside the institutional context, for example to public performance events. During the 1980s, Sanger ran *gamelan* groups in the context of the wider community to physically challenged adults and children (reported in Sanger and Kippen 1987). The use of the *gamelan* in music therapy contexts is an on-going practice. Ime Ukpanah's drumming ensemble was very active in performing in the community and played at venues all around Belfast and on the radio. Students continue to use the skills learnt at ensembles in public performance contexts, especially in organising and performing at charity events.

To build on this tradition of ethnomusicology ensemble involvement with various community performances and to highlight performance work as an integral part of the ethnomusicology programme, I set up the 'World Music in the Community Project' in January 2000. The project aims to encourage and develop performances of musics from around the world in community contexts, adding another dimension to 'cross-cultural'/'cross-community' dialogue in Northern Ireland. In its first year, ensembles performed at hospitals, museums, festivals and schools as part of the project. Performance as a public event raises and offers further possibilities for local visibility and introduces ethnomusicological concerns to a variety of audiences. Almost as soon as the project was launched, Ulster Television visited the School of Anthropological Studies to spend a day filming for a feature on ethnomusicology (broadcast in March 2000). Performance in the ethnomusicology curriculum brings exposure to the public gaze so that the observer also explicitly becomes the observed – axiomatic to refining the notion of 'ethnomusicology at home'. For students, public musical performance is an evident 'real-life application' of their ethnomusicology studies. It is perhaps because of performance that ethnomusicologists, as Kisliuk observes, 'are especially aware that there is much one can only learn by doing' (Kisliuk 1997: 33). The demands for developing technical and aesthetic musical skills and taking part in performance are great, but so too are the rewards.

Note

1. Information provided in this section, for which I am grateful, has been communicated to me by Hastings Donnan, Peter Cooke, John Baily, James Kippen, Suzel Reily and Martin Stokes.

References

Baily, J. 1991. 'John Blacking: Dialogue with the Ancestors'. The John Blacking memorial lecture, European Seminar in Ethnomusicology, Geneva 1991.

——— 1995. 'Learning to Perform as a Research Technique in Ethnomusicology', in *'Lux Oriente': Begegnungen der Kulturen in der Musikforschung*. Festschrift for Robert Günther. Kassel: Gustav Bosse Verlag, pp. 331–47.

Barz, G. and Cooley, T. (eds) 1997. *Shadows in the Field: New Perspectives for Fieldwork in Ethnomusicology*. Oxford and New York: Oxford University Press.

Blacking, J. 1995. 'Music, Culture, and Experience: Selected Papers of John Blacking', in *Music, Culture, and Experience: Selected Papers of John Blacking*, ed. R. Byron. Chicago and London: University of Chicago Press.

Cameron, F. 1992. 'The Teaching of Ethnomusicology in United Kingdom Universities', in *European Studies in Ethnomusicology: Historical Developments and Recent Trends (Intercultural Music Studies 4)*, eds M. P. Baumann, A. Simon and U. Wegner. Wilhelmshaven: Florian Noetzel Verlag.

Day, C. 1993. 'Reflection: A Necessary but Not Sufficient Condition for Professional Development', *British Educational Research Journal* 19(1): 83–93.

Fletcher, A.C. 1994. *A Study of Omaha Indian Music*, ed. H. Myers. Lincoln and London: University of Nebraska Press.

Hamer, F. 1967. *'Garners Gay': English Folk Songs Collected by Fred Hamer*. London: EFDSS Publications Ltd.

Herndon, M. and McCleod, N. 1983. *Field Manual for Ethnomusicology*. Pennsylvania: Norwood Editions.

Hood, M. 1960. 'The challenge of "bi-musicality"', *Ethnomusicology* 4(2): 55–9.

——— 1971. *The Ethnomusicologist*. Kent: Kent State University Press.

Johnston, R. and Badley, G. 1996. 'The Competent Reflective Practitioner', *Innovation and Learning in Education: The International Journal for the Reflective Practitioner* 2(1): 4–10.

Kisliuk, M. 1997. '(Un)doing Fieldwork: Sharing Songs, Sharing Lives', in *Shadows in the Field: New Perspectives for Fieldwork in Ethnomusicology*, eds G. Barz and T. Cooley. Oxford and New York: Oxford University Press, pp. 23–44.

Mascarenhas-Keyes, S. and Wright, S. 1995. *Report of Teaching and Learning Social Anthropology in the United Kingdom*. London: National Network for Teaching and Learning Anthropology.

Myers, H. 1992. *Ethnomusicology: An Introduction*. London: Macmillan Press.

Ramnarine, T. 1996. 'Folk Music Education: Initiatives in Finland', *Folk Music Journal* 7(2): 136–54.

Rice, T. 1997. 'Toward a Mediation of Field Methods and Field Experience in Ethnomusicology', in *Shadows in the Field: New Perspectives for Fieldwork in Ethnomusicology*, eds G. Barz and T. Cooley. Oxford and New York: Oxford University Press, pp. 101–20.

Sanger, A. and Kippen, J. 1987. 'Applied Ethnomusicology: the Use of Balinese Gamelan in Recreational and Educational Music Therapy', *British Journal of Music Education* 4(1): 5–16.

Titon, J. 1997. 'Knowing fieldwork', in *Shadows in the Field: New Perspectives for Fieldwork in Ethnomusicology*, eds G. Barz and T. Cooley. Oxford and New York: Oxford University Press, pp. 87–100.

Epilogue

Epilogue

Keith Hart

I divide my comments into two parts. In the first, I draw briefly on five individual papers when presenting a historical analysis of the crisis faced by university teachers of social anthropology today; this is focused on Britain in particular, as are the majority of papers here. In the second, I consider the remaining nine papers collectively to show how concerns with specific techniques and media of learning point to the possibility of an anthropology which would stand the twentieth century academic discipline on its head. The inspiration for this speculative exercise is Kant who after all invented the modern term 'anthropology' (Kant 1978); but the dialectic of actual and possible worlds employed here is, of course, Hegelian.

In my report on the Frankfurt conference where I met many of the contributors to this volume and its companion (Hart 1998), I likened the contemporary discipline to a driverless bus whose passengers were looking out of the back window. I was particularly scathing about a failure of collective reproduction which now sees a few established academics enjoying much improved privileges, while the majority of young anthropologists languish in casual labour and unemployment. This is a reflection of what has been happening in world society for the last two decades. If we are to take heart from the teaching manifestos on offer here, we must also ask why now is an appropriate moment in history to imagine a more positive future for anthropology.

The Crisis of the Universities

Universities seem to have been with us a long time. The earliest of them are almost a thousand years old; but the modern university is very much a by-product of twentieth century society. A hundred years ago, if the British middle classes wanted some higher education, they were more likely to go to a theological seminary; and the universities themselves were still very much tied up with the reproduction of established religion. The design of the syllabuses with which we are now familiar with belongs to the period after the First World War and universities only began mass enrolments after the Second World War. In many cases, the 1960s and 1970s saw a considerable expansion of the role of universities in national society, while the 1980s and 1990s were characterised by a sense of crisis and decline. Each country has its own trajectory within this general picture.

Nowhere can emulate the U.S.A. for the sheer quantity, range and quality of its universities, nor for its unique mix of public and private funding. Most Western European countries decided after 1945 that access to higher education should be a democratic right. They have since had to cope with mass numbers and the exigencies of state funding and control. In Britain, a high quality university education was maintained for about one in eight of the population, until in the last decade the number of institutions labelled 'university' was doubled and the proportion entering them was increased to around one in three. State control of this process has been expressed through a number of intrusive bureaucratic measures; the university teachers struggle to maintain standards while being underfunded and overwhelmed. It is no wonder that many of them are demoralised.

It is important to recognise how short-lived modern universities are. Academics are among the most conservative people I know. We typically demand a great deal of control over the reproduction of our ideas, which we imagine to be based on timeless principles. This leads us to cling to outmoded practices as if they were not radically undermined by developments taking place right under our noses. Elsewhere (Hart 2001) I have tried to outline the history of the twentieth century's dominant social form, which I take to be 'state capitalism', the attempt to manage markets and accumulation through centralised national bureaucracies. The last quarter-century has seen a shift to 'virtual capitalism', a condition where information services have overtaken the place of material goods in the economy and the money circuit has become increasingly detached from real production and exchange. This has been speeded up by the convergence during the 1990s of telephones, television and computers into a single digital technology of communications. World society has consequently become more connected and unequal than ever before; and nation-states are losing their grip over the social monopolies they exercised for less than a century.

This is the context for the highly contradictory developments now transforming British universities and similar institutions everywhere. Having once turned their backs on modern mass higher education, the British universities are now enduring a paroxysm of dirigiste modernisation, featuring some of the most atavistic forms of the twentieth century academic division of labour, all of this administered with a passion for market rhetoric and coercive bureaucracy which has become the hallmark of the 'neo-liberal' consensus. It is hard to resist the conclusion that we are witnessing the death throes of an institution which failed to adapt. No doubt the names and the buildings of many universities will persist in some form; but what goes on in them will be unrecognisable within two or three decades.

British social anthropology's relationship to all this has been and remains anomalous. The leaders of the profession after the second world war (Radcliffe-Brown, Fortes, Evans-Pritchard, Firth, Forde, Gluckman) formed a trade union (the Association of Social Anthropologists of the U.K., later the Commonwealth) to which they admitted only their own Ph.D.s, after a vetting process. A decision was taken to keep social anthropology not just out of the schools and other institutions of further education, but even out of twothirds of the universities licensed as such at the time. Social anthropology was thus taught to undergraduate and graduate students exclusively in the top fifteen or so universities. When several of the founders were approached by UNESCO to take part in its 1950 survey of race, they declined on the grounds that they did not want to be mixed up with anything that smacked of public controversy.[1] For these anthropologists were set on establishing their discipline as a social science capable of meeting the needs of a national bureaucracy of which the universities were now such an integral part. Links with archaeology and biological anthropology were retained in only three social anthropology departments. More often, these were associated with sociology, which itself enjoyed only a belated expansion in Britain during the 1960s, after decades of having been held back by a reactionary alliance of classicists, engineers and their ilk.

Once the links with folklore, ethnology, archaeology and similar 'amateur' Victorian pursuits had been broken by Malinowski's functionalist revolution, social anthropology in Britain settled into being 'the sociology of primitive societies' (Evans-Pritchard 1951). When sociology itself exploded as an academic discipline in the 1960s, many of the founding chairs were occupied by social anthropologists, since there were not enough experienced sociologists to fill them. An uneasy truce has been observed between the two disciplines in subsequent decades, but the distinctive position held by social anthropology as a social science remains vulnerable and moot. Some take refuge in the notion that we join the people as part of our research method ('fieldwork'); others maintain that we study the exotic parts of the world that the others cannot reach. While this particular demarcation dispute is monitored anxiously, it largely passes without comment that the experiment known as 'social sciences' is fast running out of credibility.

The social sciences, branches of applied impersonal knowledge formed at the turn of the last century on a loose analogy with the natural sciences, arose to meet the needs of middle classes released from commerce to staff the national bureaucracies erected by state capitalism. They had a corporate structure which organised teaching and learning as a rigid hierarchy of specialisation. At one level, post-war social anthropology conformed to this model and generations of students have been forced to endure turgid syllabuses dominated by the positivist ghost of Radcliffe-Brown (1952), but, as most insiders know, ours is also an anti-discipline which allows its individual practitioners to embark on free-spirited intellectual journeys where we do anything we like and call it social anthropology. There has long existed a ten-

sion between this romantic quest of lone rangers and our obligation to reproduce a collective discipline within the academy. Appealing to a small minority
of students, we have attracted our fair share of bright mavericks, as well as
some looking for an undemanding or 'doss' course. This is why I claim that
social anthropology has had an anomalous relationship to the twentieth century universities. In its open-ended anarchy may lie the seeds of an adaptation
to the world lying beyond state capitalism.

Dracklé's paper, the only one considered in this section from outside
Britain, reminds us that teaching and learning anthropology can draw on a
counter-cultural discourse which flourished in the 1960s and 1970s and has its
roots in a longer tradition of co-operative socialism and anarchism. Her
emphasis on an egalitarian alternative to hierarchy is well-taken. What
remains is to place such a call within some sort of historical analysis. Why
now? Mascarenhas-Keyes, drawing on more than a decade's experience, some
of it spent working with Wright, addresses what has been seen by many,
including elements of the national bureaucracy, as an increasingly critical
problem. Far from being over-adapted to state capitalism, social anthropology is seen as being insufficiently geared to its labour markets, being too
academic, élitist and withdrawn from the real world. In addressing what is
needed to make anthropology suitable training for professional practice, she
has been forced to develop innovative teaching methods. Wright's own paper
is based on an engagement with British social anthropology's need to escape
from its former ivory tower that is second to none. The word 'reflection'
comes up a lot these days, since most academics feel that they no longer have
any time for it. Here Wright makes a persuasive case for social anthropologists to study themselves and their working environment in order to develop
reflexive teaching and learning practices.

The last two papers considered here truly provide battlefront reports from
the crisis of the universities. Landres and Hough give some indication of the
sort of pressures being placed on university teachers by the British government,
resulting, among other things, in a drive to make courses more 'transparent' and
'accountable', that is, more visible as a mountain of paperwork. Their approach,
based on an appeal to the fieldwork tradition, conforms to the classical canons
of social anthropology. It describes and analyses the behaviour of collectivities,
reported at first hand, but mostly devoid of reference to individual experience
or to personalities. Coleman and Simpson's account of teaching social anthropology in Stockton/Durham, however, makes a sharper break with traditional
methods. They have been trying to develop courses aimed largely at a local,
working-class and mature student body, quite unlike the students for social
anthropology in its post-war élitist heyday, who were mobile, middle-class and
adolescent with, until recently, good prospects of jobs similar to those of their
parents. Their approach is striking for its emphasis on getting students to use
anthropology to reflect on their own lives. The authors are aware that this may
be construed as amateur psychology, journalism or worse, but they stick to
their guns and the results are, to my mind, impressive. The next section, deal-

ing with various innovations in university teaching methods, takes up this theme of individual subjectivity.

A Copernican Revolution in Anthropology?[2]

Copernicus solved the problem of the movement of the heavenly bodies by having the spectator revolve while they were at rest, instead of them revolve around the spectator. Kant extended this achievement for physics into metaphysics. In his preface to the second edition of *The Critique of Pure Reason* (Kant 1998), he writes, 'Hitherto it has been assumed that all our knowledge must conform to objects... (but what) if we suppose that objects must conform to our knowledge?'[3] In order to understand the world, we must begin not with the empirical existence of objects, but with the reasoning embedded in our experience itself and in each of the judgments we have made.[4] Which is to say that the world is inside each of us as much as it is out there. Our task is to bring them together as individuals who share things in common with the rest of humanity.

The nineteenth and twentieth centuries, in identifying society with the nation-state, constitute a counter-revolution against Kant's Copernican revolution launched by Hegel, whose *Philosophy of Right* (1967) contains the programmes of all three founding fathers of modern social theory rolled into one.[5] This counter-revolution was only truly consummated after the First World War. The result was a separation of the personal from the impersonal, the subject from the object, humanism from science. This is the split which the decline of state capitalism in the face of the digital revolution is allowing us to reverse; and the nine papers considered in this section provide ample evidence of how teachers of anthropology are responding to the challenge. A good portion of them address the possibilities inherent in the new technologies of the digital revolution as it unfolds: de Theije and Brouwer, Engelbrecht and Husmann, Pink, and Zeitlyn. The rest, however, are concerned with exposing individuals and groups to new contexts of experience and performance: Bouquet (museums), Edgar (imagework), Ramnarine (world music), Russell (study tours) and Tescari (drama); and this is where Kantian subjectivity is especially relevant.

One of the principal arguments of my recent book, *Money in an Unequal World* (Hart 2001)[6] is that the cheapening of the cost of information transfers as a result of the digital revolution makes it possible for much more information about individuals to enter into transactions at distance that were until recently largely impersonal. This repersonalisation of the economy has its counterpart in many aspects of contemporary social life, not just in the forms of money and exchange. It involves a new idea of the person, one which is based on digital abstractions as much as on the emergence of more concrete forms of individuality. The customised interactions that most academics now have with amazon.com and similar suppliers of books reflects this trend, at the same time personal and remote. Clearly one consequence of the use of new technologies in teaching is that learning can now be much more individualised; and this in itself poses a threat to the traditions of the academic guilds. Here is one source of a renewed emphasis on subjectivity.

At the same time, the last two decades has seen a revival of interest in objects. As Bouquet points out, museums are enjoying a renaissance, spurred on in no small part by use of the new information technologies. The history and sociology of science has borrowed extensively from social anthropology's ethnographic methods; and with this has come a focus, in the work of Latour and Callon (e.g., Latour 1993), on objects as well as the practices of ordinary actors and their networks. The work of ethno-archaeologists has fed into social anthropology as a greater prominence given these days to material culture (Miller 1998). Films and television are becoming indispensable to teaching at all levels of the educational system; and with this development of audio-visual techniques comes a much more sophisticated scrutiny of the role of the different senses in communication. All of this adds up to a radical revision of conventional attitudes to subject-object relations, grounds indeed for us to reconsider the positivist dogmas on which so much of modern university disciplines are based, including social anthropology's paradigm of scientific ethnography (Grimshaw and Hart 1995).

It has long been obvious to me that learning anthropology would be impossible if we were not, each of us, human beings in the first place. A further development reflected in these papers is an increased focus on performance (music, drama, etc.) and with it on the human agency of individuals and groups. Anthropologists who once could rely on public ignorance as support for their exotic tales must now cope with mass travel; and, as Russell shows, they are organising tours of their own. We have to consider seriously what our expertise can offer that is not delivered more effectively through novels and films, journalism or tourism. We live in a time of mass communications and mobility where both the rhetoric and the reality of markets encourage individuals to choose the means of their enlightenment. It would be surprising if trends in the teaching of anthropology did not reflect all this. Perhaps the most surprising of all the innovative papers on show in this volume is Edgar's probing of the relationship between the conscious and unconscious minds through exercises in visual imagination – I can just imagine the reaction of Disgusted (Cheltenham) to that. But it is so refreshing to see today's anthropologists pushing back the boundaries of anthropological education in this way.

It is only a decade since the end of the Cold War and the social consequences of this event are just beginning to filter through. One feature of the post-war universities has been the rise to a position of dominance of research as a means of evaluating the status of institutions and their individual members. This was led by state and corporate funding of armaments-related research in the period of the Cold War. The social sciences, without the same funding or prestige, followed suit. Social anthropology was no different. Teaching was marginalised to the point of professional insignificance. The papers of this volume show that some anthropologists are interested in teaching again, not just as a way of improving the service they give to their students, but as part of their own intellectual development. I would suggest that the trend is already moving against corporate funding of large academic research enterprises; and that the universities are entering a period in which they will attract a new public, interested in self-learning or die. The humanities in general and anthropology in particular are well-placed to take advantage of such a trend. All is not lost – but our methods will have to change significantly and Kant's Copernican revolution is one beacon lighting the way.

Notes

1. Verena Stolcke: personal communication.
2. I have begun to air my views on possible developments for anthropology in *Anthropology Today* (Hart 2000) and several earlier journalistic efforts, as well as in collaboration with Anna Grimshaw (Grimshaw and Hart 1993, 1995).
3. See Cassirer (1981: 148–49 and *passim*) for an accessible introduction to Kant.
4. I have explored the issue of judgement in relation to critique in Hart (in press).
5. Marx, Durkheim and Weber; see Giddens 1971.
6. This was first published in London as *The Memory Bank*. See also *www.thememorybank.co.uk*.

References

Cassirer, E. 1981. *Kant's Life and Thought*. New Haven: Yale University Press.

Evans-Pritchard, E. 1951. *Social Anthropology*. London: Cohen & West.

Giddens, A. 1971. *Capitalism and Modern Social Theory*. Cambridge: Cambridge University Press.

Grimshaw, A. and Hart, K. 1993. *Anthropology and the Crisis of the Intellectuals*. (Prickly Pear Pamphlet No. 1). Charlottesville: Prickly Pear Pamphlets.

Grimshaw, A. and Hart, K. 1995. 'The Rise and Fall of Scientific Ethnography', in *The Future of Anthropology*, eds A. Ahmed and C. Shore (eds.) London: Athlone Press.

Hart, K. 1998. 'The Politics of Anthropology: Conditions for Thought and Practice (Report on the EASA Conference, Frankfurt)', *Anthropology Today* 14(6): 20–2.

Hart, K. 2000. 'Reflections on a visit to New York', *Anthropology Today* 16(4): 1–3.

Hart, K. 2001. *Money in an Unequal World*. New York and London: Texere.

Hart, K. (in press). 'Cultural Critique in Anthropology', in *International Encyclopaedia of the Social and Behavioral Sciences* (new edition). Oxford: Elsevier.

Hegel, G. 1967. *The Philosophy of Right*. Oxford: Oxford University Press.

Kant, I. 1978. *Anthropology from a Pragmatic Point of View*. Carbondale: Southern Illinois University Press.

Kant, I. 1998. *The Critique of Pure Reason*. Cambridge: Cambridge University Press.

Latour, B. 1993. *We Have Never Been Modern*. Hertfordshire: Harvester Wheatsheaf.

Miller, D. (ed.) 1998. *Material Cultures: Why Some Things Matter*. London: UCL Press.

Radcliffe-Brown, A. 1952. *Structure and Function in Primitive Societies*. London: Oxford University Press.

Notes on the Contributors

Mary Bouquet (Ph.D. Cambridge) lectures at University College Utrecht. Her research and publications include work on the history and practice of anthropology (*Reclaiming English Kinship*, Manchester: Manchester University Press, 1993; *Sans og Samling*, Oslo: Scandinavian University Press, 1996; *Academic Anthropology and the Museum*, Oxford: Berghahn, 2001), kinship and visual representation ('Family Trees and Their Affinities...' *Journal of the Royal Anthropological Institute*, 1996) and family photography ('The family photographic condition' *Visual Anthropology Review*, 2000). Since 1986 she has co-operated in making exhibitions in Portugal, The Netherlands and Norway.

Lenie Brouwer received her Ph.D. from the Vrije University Amsterdam and is currently working as a Lecturer in Ethnic Studies in the Department of Cultural Anthropology at the Vrije University Amsterdam. She conducted research on Turkish families and Turkish and Moroccan runaway girls in the Netherlands (see article in *Muslim European Youth*, edited by S. Vertovec and A. Rogers (Ashgate 1998). She was recently involved in a cyber-anthropology project, studying Muslim migrants and their use of the Internet, in which she presented some papers at international conferences.

Simon Coleman is Reader in Anthropology at the University of Durham. His work focuses on religion, travel and the construction of place. Recent books include *The Globalisation of Charismatic Christianity* (Cambridge 2000), *The Tourism: between Place and Performance* (edited with M. Crang, Berghahn, 2002) and *Pilgrim Voices: Narrative and Authorship in Christian Pilgrimage* (edited with J. Elsner, Berghahn, 2003). With Bob Simpson he has compiled *Discovering Anthropology: A Resource Guide for Teachers and Students* (1998, Royal Anthropological Institute).

Dorle Dracklé is a Professor of Social Anthropology and Intercultural Studies at the University of Bremen, Germany. Fieldwork in Portugal on élites, culture, economy and the European Union. Interests in media, science and technology studies, economy, politics and policy. Recent publications include: *The Rhetorics of Crisis: On the Cultural Poetics of Politics, Bureaucracy and Virtual Economy in Southern Portugal* (2003), *Images of Death* (ed., 2001, with CD-ROM); and various articles, among others on media anthropology, multicultural media, life course, and suicide.

Iain R. Edgar lectures in the Department of Anthropology at Durham University, U.K., and lectures on the Health and Human Sciences Degrees at Queen's College Stockton. He completed his Ph.D. in Sociology and Social Anthropology at the University of Keele, U.K., in 1995. In his study of meaning-making in dreamwork groups in the U.K., published in *Dreamwork, Anthropology and the Caring Professions: A Cultural Approach to Dreamwork* Avebury 1995, he introduced the use of several experiential groupwork methods as research methods, including imagework. He is currently writing a book, *Guide to Imagework: Imagination-based Research Methods* (Routledge: *forthcoming*) on using imagework as a research methodology.

Beate Engelbrecht was born 1952, and studies in anthropology, sociology and economics. Doctor's degree 1985. Career: Assistant at the Anthropological Institute of the University of Basel/Switzerland 1972–74, 1978–79, 1981–83 and 1985. Assistant at the Museum for Anthropology in Basel 1975–78 and 1982. Reader and deputy chairman of the publishing house, Edition día (at that time in Wuppertal and Köln, Germany) 1985–88. Collaborator at the Museum for Anthropology in Zurich, Switzerland 1986 (preparation of an exhibition). Since 1985 official in charge of Anthropology at the Institute for the Scientific Film (Institut für den Wissenschaftlichen Film [IWF] in Göttingen/Germany.

Keith Hart is the author of *Money in an Unequal World* (Texere 2001). He is an anthropologist who introduced to economics the concept of the informal economy. He has taught at several universities, especially Cambridge; has written about Africa; and has worked occasionally as a journalist, consultant and gambler. He is now a Senior Research Fellow in the Arkleton Centre, University of Aberdeen and lives in Paris.

Karen Latricia Hough gained a BA (First Class Honours) in History and Sociology at the University of Lancaster 1993–96. As a member of Christ Church College in Oxford for the past four years, she obtained both a Master's in Social Anthropology (1998) and an M.Phil. (1999) in Social Anthropology from the Department of Social and Cultural Anthropology in Oxford. She is currently embarking upon D.Phil. research that focuses upon a comparative political and cultural explication of Albanian migration to Italy and the United Kingdom.

Rolf Husmann was born in 1950, and received his academic education between 1970 and 1984 at Göttingen University, and the School of Oriental and African

Studies London. In 1984 he obtained his Ph.D. from Göttingen University with a thesis on the history of the Nuba, Sudan. His special fields of interest are Visual Anthropology and the Anthropology of Sport. Periods of fieldwork were spent in the Sudan, on Malta, Samoa and the Cook Islands, mostly in connection with the production of ethnographic films. Among his films are *Nuba Wrestling*, *Destination Samoa* on Pacific migration and identity and the portrait *Firth on Firth*. He is currently a producer of ethnographic films at the Institut für den Wissenschaftlichen Film [IWF], Knowledge and Media, Göttingen. In addition he also teaches at times at Göttingen, Mainz and Malta University.

László Kürti received his doctorate from the University of Massachusetts in 1989. He taught at the American University, in Washington DC, and at the Eotvos Loránd University in Budapest. His expertise is political anthropology, transnationalism, inter-ethnic relations, gender, visual anthropology and youth culture. His articles have been published in *Anthropology Today, East European Societies* and *Politics, Social Anthropology, Ethnos*, and *Current Anthropology*. He co-edited: *Ethnicity, Religion and Nationhood* (Akadémia, 1998), and *Beyond Borders* (Westview, 1997); and wrote *The Remote Borderland: Transylvania in the Hungarian Imagination* (State University of New York [SUNY], 2001). Currently, he is the Chair of the Department of Political Science, University of Miskolc, Hungary, and Secretary of the European Association of Social Anthropologists.

J. Shawn Landres (MA, C.Phil.,University of California, Santa Barbara; M. St., University of Oxford) is Finkelstein Fellow and Lecturer in Jewish & Western Civilization at the University of Judaism in Los Angeles, California. He is the co-editor of *Personal Knowledge and Beyond: Reshaping the Ethnography of Religion* (New York University Press, 2002). He has been a faculty member at the Institute of Social and Cultural Studies, Matej Bel University Banská Bystrica, Slovakia. Prior to that he was a Keith Murray Senior Scholar in Lincoln College, Oxford. He is the co-editor of *Personal Knowledge and Beyond: Reshaping the Ethnography of Religion* (New York University Press, 2002). He has published several articles on Generation X and religion, as well as sociological and anthropological studies in ritual, identity, and civil society in East-Central Europe and the U.S. He has done fieldwork in the Slovak Republic and the United States and currently is completing dissertations in religious studies and social anthropology.

Stella Mascarenhas-Keyes has an MA in Higher and Professional Education 1999, (Institute of Education, London University) and a Ph.D. in Social Anthropology (1987, School of Oriental and African Studies, London University). She has taught anthropology at undergraduate and postgraduate levels, run a variety of training courses, and undertaken applied anthropological and educational research. She has directed applied anthropology courses for postgraduate students under the auspices of the Group for Anthropology in Policy and Practice. She is the principal author of 1995 *Report on the Teaching and Learning of Social Anthropology in the U.K.*, and contributed to and compiled *Professional Practice in Anthropology: A Curriculum Resource Manual for University Teachers (1997)*. She is currently employed as a Senior Researcher in the Higher Education Division of the Department for Education and Skills, England.

David Mills is writing a political history of social anthropology. He is also Anthropology Co-ordinator of the Centre for learning and teaching Sociology, Anthropology and Politics (C-SAP) based at the University of Birmingham, part of the learning and teaching support network. C-SAP aims to research, promote and share developments in learning and teaching in the three disciplines in the U. K. (www.c-sap.bham.ac.uk)

Sarah Pink is Lecturer in Sociology at Loughborough University. She has a BA and Ph.D. in Social Anthropology from the University of Kent, and an MA in Visual Anthropology from the University of Manchester. Her research has been in Spain, Guinea Bissau and England, focusing mainly on visual and material culture, gender and performance in public contexts and events and the home, always using visual images and technologies as part of research and representation. Her printed publications include *Women and Bullfighting: Gender, Sex and the Consumption of Tradition* (Berg 1997), *Doing Visual Ethnography: Images, Media and Representation in Research* (Sage 2001) and *Materialising Genders: Resituating Gender Identities at Home* (Berg, forthcoming). She has also published her work using CD-ROM, Internet and video including *The Bullfighter's Braid* (1998), *Interweaving Lives* (1998) and *Gender at Home* (2000).

Tina K. Ramnarine is a violinist and Lecturer in Ethnomusicology and Social Anthropology at Royal Holloway University of London. She has undertaken field research in Scandinavia, the Caribbean, U.K., U.S.A. and Canada, exploring folk musics, popular Caribbean musics, Celtic revivals and the politics of musical expression. She is author of *Creating Their Own Space: The Development of an Indian-Caribbean Musical Tradition* (University of West Indies Press, 2001) and *Ilmatar's Inspirations: Nationalism, Globalisation, and the Changing Soundscapes of Finnish Folk Music* (University of Chicago Press, 2003).

Andrew Russell is a Senior lecturer in the Department of Anthropology at the University of Durham, where he teaches on the Human Sciences, and Health and Human Sciences degrees at its Stockton campus (Queen's). His doctoral research was conducted in East Nepal, and he has subsequently conducted further fieldwork in Nepal and north-east India. He is currently involved in a number of health-related projects in the north-east of England, as well as a project funded by the European Union on responsible tourism in European wetlands. He is editor (with Iain Edgar) of *The Anthropology of Welfare*

(1998), and (with Elisa Sobo and Mary Thompson) of *Contraception Across Cultures: Technologies, Choices, Constraints* (2000).

Bob Simpson is a senior lecturer in anthropology at the University of Durham. He has research interests in Sri Lanka where he has carried out doctoral research into healing rituals and the transmission of ritual knowledge. He has also carried out research into various aspects of divorce and separation in the U.K. and has written widely on this *topic* (*Changing Families: An Ethnographic Approach to Divorce and Separation*, Berg, 1998). More recently he has carried out research into kinship and the new reproductive and genetic technologies in the U.K. and Sri Lanka. He has a long-standing interest in the teaching of anthropology. Along with Simon Coleman he compiled and edited *Discovering Anthropology: A Resource Guide*.

Alex Strating has studied anthropology at the University of Leyden and obtained his Ph.D. at the University of Amsterdam, where at present he has a permanent position in the Department of Sociology and Anthropology. His research mainly concerns the anthropology of Europe, focusing on the relation between culture and economics. He is currently administrative director of the anthropology programme and has for more than ten years been managing co-ordinator of the ERASMUS/SOCRATES exchange programmes. Among his recent publications: *Les gens des fleurs restent, les diplômés partent; Parente, famille et négoce des fleurs dans une communauté néerlandaise, Terrain* (2001) 36, pp. 85–97.

Giuliano Tescari is Lecturer in Cultural Anthropology at the University of Turin, Italy. During the last two decades he has done extensive field research in Mexico among the Huichol Indians of the Sierra Madre. His main fields of research are ritual symbolism, shamanism, oral tradition and the anthropology of performance. In close co-operation with the Huichol native Leocadio López Carrillo he published *Vámos a Tûríkyé. Sciamanismo e storia sacra wirrárika* (2000) about Huichol myths and shamanism.

Marjo de Theije received her Ph.D. from Utrecht University, and is currently working as a lecturer in the Department of Cultural Anthropology at the Vrije Universiteit Amsterdam. In 2001 she was visiting professor at the Federal University of Pernambuco, in Recife, Brazil. She has done research in Brazil on the religious brotherhoods in Minas Gerais and on pilgrimage, base communities and charismatic prayer groups in Pernambuco. Her publications include *Tudo o que é de Deus é bom. Uma antropologia do catolicismo liberacionista em Garanhuns, Brasil* (Recife: Massangano, 2002), as well as articles in the edited volumes *More Than Opium. An Anthropological Approach to Latin American and Caribbean Pentecostal Praxis* (Lanham, Md., and London: The Scarecrow Press, 1998) and *Latin American Religion in Motion* (New York and London: Routledge, 1999).

Susan Wright (D.Phil. in Social Anthropology, Oxford) is professor of educational anthropology at the Danish University of Education, Copenhagen. Her recent publications have been on the reform of higher education, and especially the introduction of 'audit culture' in the U.K. Now she is researching university reform in Denmark. She is interested in local interactions with large processes of political transformation, whether neo-liberal governance in Britain or, earlier, modernisation and revolution in Iran. She ran the educational development programme of the National Network for Teaching and Learning Anthropology (1994–99) and established and directed C-SAP, the Centre for Learning and Teaching in Sociology, Anthropology and Politics (2002–2003). Her publications (with Chris Shore) include *Anthropology of Policy: Critical Perspectives on Governance and Power* (EASA Series), London: Routledge, 1997; 'Audit culture and anthropology', *Journal of the Royal Anthropological Institute* 1999, 7(4): 759–63; and 'Coercive accountability: the rise of audit culture in higher education', in M. Strathern (ed.) *Audit cultures: Anthropological Studies in Accountability, Ethics and the Academy* (EASA Series), London: Routledge, 2000.

David Zeitlyn is a Senior Lecturer in Social Anthropology, Deputy Director of the Centre for Social Anthropology and Computing, Department of Anthropology, University of Kent at Canterbury. Co-Director of the Experience Rich Anthropology Project and active in the use and development of anthropological archives. Field research concentrates on a Mambila village in Cameroon concerning religion socio-linguistics and demography. Other research involves the use/non-use of bibliographic databases in U.K. University Libraries.

General Index

Index of Names